Staff Acknowledgments

We would like to thank:

Pam Weston, Vice President, Publishing, for setting the quality standards for production integrity and managing the publication to completion.

Diane Goldschmidt, Associate Editor, for post-production quality assurance.

Anne Winthrop Esposito, Senior Editor, for coordination of revisions.

Christine Saul, Senior Graphic Artist, for cover design.

The *High School* TUTOR®

PRE-CALCULUS

Staff of Research & Education Association

Research & Education Association
Visit our website at
www.rea.com

Research & Education Association
61 Ethel Road West
Piscataway, New Jersey 08854
E-mail: info@rea.com

**THE HIGH SCHOOL TUTOR®
FOR PRE-CALCULUS**

Published 2009

Copyright © 2006, 2001, 1999, 1997, 1993 by Research & Education Association, Inc. All rights reserved. No part of this book may be reproduced in any form without permission of the publisher.

Printed in the United States of America

Library of Congress Control Number 2006902907

ISBN-13: 978-0-87891-910-9
ISBN-10: 0-87891-910-4

THE HIGH SCHOOL TUTOR® and REA® are registered trademarks of Research & Education Association, Inc.

REA's High School Tutor Series®
Designed with You in Mind

REA's High School Tutor® series gives you everything you need to excel in your high school classes, especially on midterms, finals, and even pop quizzes.

Think of this book as access to your own private tutor. Here, right at your fingertips, in a handy Q & A format, is a great companion to your textbook. You'll also find that the High School Tutor® lends greater depth to classroom lectures. You've heard all about the theorems, the timelines, the big ideas, and the key principles; this book equips you to break it all down into bite-size chunks.

To obtain maximum benefit from the book, students should familiarize themselves with the tips below.

Larry Kling
High School Tutor Program Director

How to Use This Book

Pre-Calculus students will find this book to be an invaluable supplement to their textbooks. The book is divided into 42 chapters, each dealing with a separate topic. The information is presented in question-and-answer format to match the format of the tests and quizzes teachers are likely to use. By reviewing the questions and the provided answers, students can prepare themselves for actual test situations.

How to Grasp a Topic Fully

1.   Refer to your class text and read the section pertaining to the topic. You should become acquainted with the themes discussed there.

2.   Locate the topic you are looking for by referring to the Table of Contents in the front of this book.

To learn and understand a topic thoroughly and retain its contents, it will generally be necessary for you to review the problems several times. Repeated review is essential to gain experience in recognizing the themes that are most relevant and selecting the best solution techniques.

How to Find a Question Type

To locate one or more questions related to particular subject matter, refer to the index. The numbers in the index refer to *question* numbers, not to page numbers. This arrangement is intended to facilitate finding a question rapidly, since two or more questions may appear on a page.

If a particular type of question cannot be found readily, it is recommended that you refer to the Table of Contents in the front pages and then turn to the chapter that is applicable to the question being sought.

In preparing for an exam, it is useful to find the topics to be covered on the exam in the Table of Contents, and then review the questions under those topics several times. This should equip you with what might be needed for the exam.

Contents

SECTION 1 - ALGEBRA

1   NUMBERS AND NOTATIONS 1

2   DEFINITIONS AND NOTATIONS OF SETS AND
    SET OPERATIONS 7

3   FUNDAMENTAL ALGEBRAIC LAWS AND OPERATIONS
    WITH NUMBERS 11

4   FUNDAMENTAL ALGEBRAIC LAWS AND OPERATIONS
    WITH ALGEBRAIC EXPRESSIONS 17

5   FACTORING 24

6   EXPONENT, RADICAL, AND POWER 30

7   RATIOS, PROPORTIONS, AND VARIATIONS 37

8   FUNCTIONS 42

9   LINEAR FUNCTIONS 49

10 SYSTEMS OF LINEAR EQUATIONS 58

11 QUADRATIC EQUATIONS AND SYSTEMS OF EQUATIONS
INVOLVING QUADRATICS 67

12 EQUATIONS OF DEGREE GREATER THAN TWO 84

13 INTERVALS AND INEQUALITIES 92

14 PROGRESSIONS, SEQUENCES, AND SERIES 104

SECTION 2 - TRIGONOMETRY

15 LOGARITHMS AND EXPONENTIALS 124

16 ANGLES AND ARCS 136

17 TRIGONOMETRIC FUNCTIONS 143

18 TABLES AND LOGARITHMS
OF TRIGONOMETRIC FUNCTIONS 150

19 TRIGONOMETRIC IDENTITIES AND FORMULAS 154

20 SOLVING TRIANGLES 166

21 INVERSE TRIGONOMETRIC FUNCTIONS 171

22 TRIGONOMETRIC EQUATIONS 177

23 HYPERBOLIC AND INVERSE HYPERBOLIC FUNCTIONS 183

SECTION 3 - GRAPHING

24   PROJECTIONS, MIDPOINTS, AND THE DISTANCE
      FORMULA..187

25   STRAIGHT LINES AND FAMILIES OF STRAIGHT LINES 197

26   CIRCLES, PARABOLAS, ELLIPSES, AND HYPERBOLAS........206

27   TRANSFORMATION OF COORDINATES..................................225

28   POLAR COORDINATES AND PARAMETRIC EQUATIONS........231

29   FUNCTION 236

30   LINEAR FUNCTIONS AND SYSTEMS OF LINEAR
      FUNCTIONS..247

31   QUADRATIC EQUATIONS AND
      SYSTEMS OF QUADRATIC EQUATIONS..................................254

32   EQUATIONS OF DEGREE GREATER THAN TWO.....................264

33   INEQUALITIES..266

34   LOGARITHMS, EXPONENTIALS, AND EXPONENTS................271

35   TRIGONOMETRIC, INVERSE TRIGONOMETRIC,
      AND HYPERBOLIC FUNCTIONS 275

36   CIRCLES, PARABOLAS, ELLIPSES, AND HYPERBOLAS........285

37   POLAR COORDINATES AND PARAMETRIC EQUATIONS........296

SECTION 4 - CALCULUS

38   LIMITS... 304

39   CONTINUITY.. 307

40   DELTA (Δ) FUNCTION AND DERIVATIVE 310

41   APPLICATIONS OF THE DERIVATIVE 317

42   THE INTEGRAL 321

      INDEX... 325

SECTION 1

ALGEBRA

CHAPTER 1

NUMBERS AND NOTATIONS

Given these two number lines, explain how the space between the points (numbers) on each line differs.

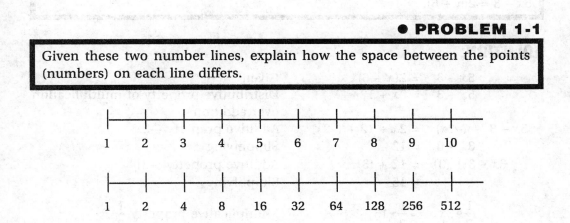

SOLUTION:

The spacing between any two points on line 1 represents an equal difference. The numbers on this line are spaced in an arithmetic progression. (For more on progression see Chapter 14.) The spacing on line 2 is based on a geometric progression. The space between any two points represents a progressively larger difference as one moves from left to right on the number line.

1

Is it possible to establish a one–to–one correspondence between the set of real numbers and the points on a number line?

SOLUTION:

It is not possible since there are an infinity of real numbers. However, by the Number Line Postulate, one must assume that such a correspondence exists. The Number Line Postulate is also known as the axiom of continuity.

Use the field properties to derive the equation $x = 5$ from the equation $5x - 3 = 2(x + 6)$.

SOLUTION:

$5x - 3$	$= 2(x + 6)$	Given
$5x - 3$	$= 2x + 12$	Distributive property of multiplication over addition
$5x - 3 + (-2x)$	$= 2x + 12 + (-2x)$	Additive property $(-2x)$
$3x - 3$	$= 12$	Simplifying
$3x - 3 + (3)$	$= 12 + (3)$	Additive property $(+3)$
$3x$	$= 15$	Simplifying
$\frac{1}{3} \cdot 3x$	$= \frac{1}{3} \cdot 15$	Multiplicative property $\frac{1}{3}$
x	$= 5$	Simplifying

We could also derive $5x - 3 = 2(x + 6)$ from $x = 5$ by reversing the steps in the solution. Let us see if 5 will make the equation $5x - 3 = 2 (x + 6)$ true.

$$5(5) - 3 \overset{?}{=} 2(5 + 6)$$
$$22 = 22$$

Two equations are equivalent if and only if they have the same solution set. Since $5x - 3 = 2(x + 6)$ and $x = 5$ have the same solution set, $\{5\}$, the two equations are equivalent.

(a)   Is zero a natural number?
       Is zero an integer?
       Is zero a positive number or a negative number?
       Is zero an odd number or an even number?

(b)   Give three examples of each of the following:
       (1) Integers
       (2) Rational numbers
       (3) Irrational numbers
       (4) Natural numbers
       (5) Prime numbers
       (6) Complex numbers

(c)   What is a real number?

SOLUTION:

(a) Zero is not a natural number. The natural numbers begin with 1 and continue up through positive infinity, i.e., 1, 2, 3, 4, 5, 6, 7, ... Zero is an integer. Zero divides the positive integers from the negative integers on a number line. An example of a set of integers is ..., –5, –4, –3, –2, –1, 0, 1, 2, 3, 4, 5, ... Zero is an even number as 2, 4, 6, and 8. Zero is neither a positive number nor a negative number.

  (b) (1) An integer is a whole number (not a fraction or a decimal) which can be either positive or negative. Examples of integers are 1, 5, and –9.

      (2) Rational numbers are those numbers which can be represented as

$\dfrac{p}{q}$ where p and q are integers, and $q \neq 0$.

Examples of rational numbers are $\dfrac{8}{5}$, $\dfrac{8}{12}$, and $-\dfrac{4}{3}$.

      (3) Irrational numbers are those numbers which are not rational and cannot be represented as $\dfrac{p}{q}$. Examples of irrational numbers are

$-\sqrt{2}, \pi$, and $\sqrt[5]{-3}$.

      (4) Examples of natural numbers are 2, 7, and 9.

      (5) A prime number is a number which is divisible by only ±1, and plus or minus itself. Examples of prime numbers are 2, 3, and 13.

      (6) A complex number is a number of the form $a + bi$, where a and b

are real numbers and $i = \sqrt{-1}$. The real part of a complex number is a, and the imaginary part of a complex number is bi. Examples of complex numbers are $6 + \sqrt{3}i$, $4.5 - 2i$, and $-9 + 16i$.

(c) The real numbers consist of all positive and negative rational and irrational numbers, and zero.

● **PROBLEM 1-5**

Classify each of the following numbers into as many different sets as possible. Example: real, integer, rational ...

(a) 0   (d) $\dfrac{1}{2}$

(b) 9   (e) $\dfrac{2}{3}$

(c) $\sqrt{6}$ (f) 1.5

SOLUTION:

(a) Zero is a real number and an integer.
(b) 9 is real, rational, natural number, and an integer.
(c) $\sqrt{6}$ is an irrational, real number.
(d) $\dfrac{1}{2}$ is a rational, real number.
(e) $\dfrac{2}{3}$ is a rational, real number.
(f) 1.5 is a rational, real number, and a decimal.

● **PROBLEM 1-6**

Find the absolute value for each of the following:

(a) 0   (c) $-\pi$

(b) 4   (d) a, where a is a real number

4

SOLUTION:

The absolute value of a number is represented by 2 vertical lines around the number, and is equal to the given number, regardless of sign.

(a) $|0| = 0$

(b) $|4| = 4$

(c) $|-\pi| = \pi$

(d) for $a > 0$ $|a| = a$

      for $a = 0$ $|a| = 0$

      for $a < 0$ $|a| = -a$,

i.e. $|a| = \begin{cases} a \text{ if } a > 0 \\ 0 \text{ if } a = 0 \\ -a \text{ if } a < 0 \end{cases}$

● **PROBLEM 1-7**

Write $\dfrac{2}{7}$ as a repeating decimal.

SOLUTION:

To write a fraction as a repeating decimal, divide the numerator by the denominator, until a pattern of repeated digits appears.

$2 \div 7 = .285714285714...$

Identify the entire portion of the decimal which is repeated. The repeating decimal can then be written in the shortened form:

$\dfrac{2}{7} = .\overline{285714}$

● **PROBLEM 1-8**

Find the common fraction form of the repeating decimal 0.4242....

5

SOLUTION:

Let x represent the repeating decimal.

$$x = 0.4242...$$

multiplying by 100 $\qquad\qquad 100x = 42.42...$

subtracting x from $100x$ $\qquad \underline{\quad x = 0.42...\quad}$

$$99x = 42 \qquad\qquad (1)$$

Divide both sides of equation (1) by 99.

$$\frac{99x}{99} = \frac{42}{99}$$

$$x = \frac{42}{99} = \frac{14}{33}$$

The repeating decimal of this example had 2 digits that repeated. The first step in the solution was to multiply both sides of the original equation by the 2nd power of 10 or 10^2 or 100. If there were 3 digits that repeated, the first step in the solution would be to multiply both sides of the original equation by the 3rd power of 10 or 10^3 or 1,000.

● **PROBLEM 1-9**

Use scientific notation to express each number.

(a) 4,375   (b) 186,000   (c) 0.00012   (d) 4,005

SOLUTION:

A number expressed in scientific notation is written as a product of a number between 1 and 10 and a power of 10. The number between 1 and 10 is obtained by moving the decimal point of the number (actual or implied) the required number of digits. The power of 10, for a number greater than 1, is positive and is one less than the number of digits before the decimal point in the original number. The power of 10, for a number less than 1, is negative and one more than the number of zeros immediately following the decimal point in the original number. Hence,

(a) $4,375 = 4.375 \times 10^3$ (c) $0.00012 = 1.2 \times 10^{-4}$

(b) $186,000 = 1.86 \times 10^5$ (d) $4,005 = 4.005 \times 10^3$

6

CHAPTER 2

DEFINITIONS AND NOTATIONS OF SETS AND SET OPERATIONS

List all the subsets of $C = \{1, 2\}$.

SOLUTION:

$\{1\}$, $\{2\}$, $\{1,2\}$, ø, where ø is the empty set. Each set listed in the solution contains at least one element of the set C. The set $\{2, 1\}$ is identical to $\{1, 2\}$ and therefore is not listed. ø is included in the solution because ø is a subset of every set.

Given the set $S = \{1, 2, 3, 4, 5, 6\}$, find a partition of S.

SOLUTION:

A partition of a set S is a subdivision of the set into subsets that are disjoint and exhaustive, i.e., every element of S must belong to one and only one of the subsets. Each subset in the partition is also called a cell.

Therefore, $(S_1, S_2, ..., S_n)$ is a partition of S if

(a) $S_i \cap S_j = \emptyset$ (where ø is the empty set) for all $i \neq j$ (the cells are disjoint),

7

and

(b) $S_1 \cup S_2 \cup S_3 \cup \ldots \cup S_n = S$ (the cells are exhaustive).

Hence, one of the partitions of S is

{ {1, 2, 3},{ +4},{ +5, 6} }. The partition { {1}, {2}, {3}, {4}, {5}, {6} } is a partition into unit sets.

● **PROBLEM 2-3**

$U = \{1, 2, 3, 4, 5, 6, 7, 8, 9, 10\}$, $P = \{2, 4, 6, 8, 10\}$, $Q = \{1, 2, 3, 4, 5\}$,

find (a) $\overline{P}$ and (b) $\overline{Q}$.

SOLUTION:

$\overline{P}$ and $\overline{Q}$ are the complements of P and Q, respectively.

That is, $\overline{P}$ is the set of all elements in the universal set, U, that are not elements of P, and $\overline{Q}$ is the set of elements in U that are not in Q, Therefore,

(a) $\overline{P} = \{1, 3, 5, 7, 9\}$; (b) $\overline{Q} = \{6, 7, 8, 9, 10\}$.

● **PROBLEM 2-4**

Show that the complement of the complement of a set is the set itself.

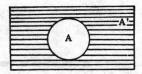

SOLUTION:

The complement of set A is given by A'. Therefore, the complement of the complement of a set is given by $(A')'$. This set, $(A')'$, must be shown to be the set A; that is, that $(A')' = A$. In the figure, the complement of the set A, or A', is the set of all points not in set A; that is, all points in the rectangle that are not

8

in the circle. This is the shaded area in the figure. Therefore, this shaded area is A'. The complement of this set, or $(A')'$, is the set of all points of the rectangle that are not in the shaded area; that is, all points in the circle, which is the set A. Therefore, the set $(A')'$ is the same as set A; that is $(A')' = A$.

● **PROBLEM 2-5**

State the laws of set operations.

SOLUTION:

If S is an algebra of sets and if A, B, C, ... , ø, U,... are elements of S, then the following hold for $\cap$, $\cup$, and '.

IDENTITY LAWS
1a. $A \cup \text{ø} = A$ 1b. $A \cap \text{ø} = \text{ø}$
2a. $A \cup U = U$ 2b. $A \cap U = A$

IDEMPOTENT LAWS
3a. $A \cup A = A$ 3b. $A \cap A = A$

COMPLEMENT LAWS

4a. $A \cup A' = U$ 4b. $A \cap A' = \text{ø}$

5a. $(A')' = A$ 5b. $\text{ø}' = U; U' = \text{ø}$

COMMUTATIVE LAWS
6a. $A \cup B = B \cup A$ 6b. $A \cap B = B \cap A$

ASSOCIATIVE LAWS
7a. $(A \cup B) \cup C = A \cup (B \cup C)$
7b. $(A \cap B) \cap C = A \cap (B \cap C)$

DISTRIBUTIVE LAWS
8a. $A \cup (B \cap C) = (A \cup B) \cap (A \cup C)$
8b. $A \cap (B \cup C) = (A \cap B) \cup (A \cap C)$

DE MORGAN'S LAWS
9a. $(A \cup B)' = A' \cap B'$ 9b. $(A \cap B)' = A' \cup B'$

If $A = \{2, 3, 5, 7\}$ and $B = \{1, -2, 3, 4, -5, \sqrt{6}\}$, find (a) $A \cup B$ and (b) $A \cap B$.

SOLUTION:

(a) $A \cup B$ is the set of all elements in A or in B or in both A and B, with no element included twice in the union set.

$A \cup B = \{1, 2, -2, 3, 4, 5, -5, \sqrt{6}, 7\}$

(b) $A \cap B$ is the set of all elements in both A and B.

$A \cap B = \{3\}$

Sometimes two sets have no elements in common. Let $S = \{3, 4, 7\}$ and $T = \{2, -4, 6\}$. What is the intersection of S and T? In this case $S \cap T$ has no elements. Hence $S \cap T = \emptyset$, the empty set. In that case, the sets are said to be disjoint.

The set of all elements entering a discussion is called the universal set, U. When the universal set is not given, we assume it to be the set of real numbers. The set of all elements in the universal set that are not elements of A is called the complement of A, written $\overline{A}'$.

Find $A - B$ and $A - (A \cap B)$ for

$A = \{1, 2, 3, 4\}$ and

$B = \{2, 4, 6, 8, 10\}$.

SOLUTION:

The relative complement of subsets A and B of the universal set U is defined as the set

$A - B = \{x, |x \in A \text{ and } x \notin B\}$. Note that it is not assumed that $B \subseteq A$.

Hence, $A - B = \{1, 3\}$.

To find $A - (A \cap B)$, first find $A \cap B$. The set $A \cap B$ is a set of elements that are common to both A and B, so $A \cap B = \{2, 4\}$.

Therefore, $A - (A \cap B) = \{1, 3\}$.

CHAPTER 3

FUNDAMENTAL ALGEBRAIC LAWS AND OPERATIONS WITH NUMBERS

Evaluate $2 - \{5 + (2 - 3) + [2 - (3 - 4)]\}$.

SOLUTION:

When working with a group of nested parentheses, we evaluate the inner-most parenthesis first.

Thus, $2 - \{5 + (2 - 3) + [2 - (3 - 4)]\}$

$= 2 - \{5 + (2 - 3) + [2 - (-1)]\}$

$= 2 - \{5 + (-1) + [2 + 1]\}$

$= 2 - \{5 + (-1) + 3\}$

$= 2 - \{4 + 3\}$

$= 2 - 7$

$= -5$

Simplify $4[-2(3 + 9) \div 3] + 5$.

11

SOLUTION:

To simplify means to find the simplest expression. We perform the operations within the innermost grouping symbols first. That is $3 + 9 = 12$.

Thus, $4[-2(3 + 9) \div 3] + 5 = 4[-2(12) \div 3] + 5$

Next we simplify within the brackets:

$$= 4\ [-24 \div 3] + 5$$
$$= 4 \cdot (-8) + 5$$

We now perform the multiplication, since multiplication is done before addition:

$$= -32 + 5$$
$$= -27$$

Hence, $4\ [-2(3 + 9) \div 3] + 5 = -27$.

● PROBLEM 3-3

Calculate the value of

$$5 - \left[6 \cdot \left[1.5 \cdot 10\% + \left(-0.25 + 4\frac{3}{10}\right) \div \frac{4}{8}\right] - \frac{3}{9} \cdot 6 \div |-6.7 + 3| \right.$$

$$\left. + 4 \div \left(1 + \frac{1}{2 + \frac{1}{4}}\right)\right]$$

to the fifth decimal place.

SOLUTION:

The rule for solving this type of problem is to work from the innermost parenthesis out. The order of operations are multiplication and division, then subtraction and addition.

The first step in this problem is to change everything to decimals.

$5 - [6 \cdot [1.5 \cdot 0.1 +(-0.25 + 4.3) \div 0.5] - 0.33 \cdot 6 + |-6.7 + 3| + 4 \div (1.44444)]$

The second step is to reduce the parentheses.

$5 - [6 \cdot [1.5 \cdot 0.1 + (4.05) \div 0.5] - 2 \div 3.7 + 4 \div (1.44444)]$

$= 5 - [6 \cdot [0.15 + 8.1] - 0.540541 + 2.769231]$

12

$= 5 - [6 \cdot (8.25) - 0.540541 + 2.769231]$

$= 5 - [49.5 + 2.228690]$

$= 5 - 51.72869$

$= -46.72869$

Calculate the value of each of the following expressions:

(a) $\left\| 2-5 \right| + 6 - 14 \right|$

(b) $\left| -5 \right| \cdot \left| 4 \right| + \dfrac{\left| -12 \right|}{4}$

(c) $1.6\% + 18\% + 12\left(26 - (1-3) \div \left| -2 \right| \right)$

(d) $\dfrac{1}{6} \cdot 1.25 - \left(12.5 + 4\dfrac{1}{2} \right) \div 50\%$

SOLUTION:

Before solving this problem, one must remember the order of operations: parenthesis, multiplication and division, addition and subtraction.

(a) $\left\| -3 \right| + 6 - 14 \right| = \left| 3 + 6 - 14 \right| = \left| 9 - 14 \right| = \left| -5 \right| = 5$

(b) $(5 \cdot 4) + \dfrac{12}{4} = 20 + 3 = 23$

(c) $0.016 + 0.18 + 12(26 - (-2) \div 2)$
$0.016 + 0.18 + 12(26 - (-1))$
$0.196 + 12(27) = 0.196 + 324 = 324.196$

(d) $\dfrac{1.25}{6} - \left(12.5 + \dfrac{9}{2} \right) \div 0.5 = \dfrac{1.25}{6} - \left(\dfrac{34}{2} \right)\left(\dfrac{2}{1} \right)$

$\dfrac{1.25}{6} - 34 = \dfrac{1.25}{6} - \dfrac{204}{6} = -33.792$

Simplify the following expression: $1 - \dfrac{1}{2 - \dfrac{1}{3}}$.

SOLUTION:

In order to combine the denominator, $2 - \dfrac{1}{3}$, we must convert 2 into thirds.

$2 = 2 \bullet 1 = 2 \bullet \dfrac{3}{3} = \dfrac{6}{3}$. Thus

$$1 - \dfrac{1}{2 - \dfrac{1}{3}} = 1 - \dfrac{1}{\dfrac{6}{3} - \dfrac{1}{3}} = 1 - \dfrac{1}{\dfrac{5}{3}}$$

Since division by a fraction is equivalent to multiplication by that fraction's reciprocal

$$1 - \dfrac{1}{\dfrac{5}{3}} = 1 - (1)\left(\dfrac{3}{5}\right) = 1 - \dfrac{3}{5} = \dfrac{5}{5} - \dfrac{3}{5} = \dfrac{2}{5}$$

Therefore, $1 - \dfrac{1}{2 - \dfrac{1}{3}} = \dfrac{2}{5}$.

Simplify $\dfrac{\dfrac{2}{3} + \dfrac{1}{2}}{\dfrac{3}{4} - \dfrac{1}{3}}$.

SOLUTION:

A first method is to just add the terms in the numerator and denominator.

Since 6 is the least common denominator of the numerator, $\left(\dfrac{2}{3} + \dfrac{1}{2}\right)$, we con-

vert $\dfrac{2}{3}$ and $\dfrac{1}{2}$ into sixths:

$\dfrac{2}{3} = \dfrac{2}{3} \cdot 1 = \dfrac{2}{3} \cdot \dfrac{2}{2} = \dfrac{4}{6}$ and $\dfrac{1}{2} = \dfrac{1}{2} \cdot 1 = \dfrac{1}{2} \cdot \dfrac{3}{3} = \dfrac{3}{6}$. Therefore $\dfrac{2}{3} + \dfrac{1}{2} = \dfrac{4}{6} + \dfrac{3}{6} = \dfrac{7}{6}$.

Since 12 is the least common denominator of the denominator, $\left(\dfrac{3}{4} - \dfrac{1}{3}\right)$, we convert $\dfrac{3}{4}$ and $\dfrac{1}{3}$ into twelfths:

$\dfrac{3}{4} = \dfrac{3}{4} \cdot 1 = \dfrac{3}{4} \cdot \dfrac{3}{3} = \dfrac{9}{12}$ and $\dfrac{1}{3} = \dfrac{1}{3} \cdot 1 = \dfrac{1}{3} \cdot \dfrac{4}{4} = \dfrac{4}{12}$. Therefore $\dfrac{3}{4} - \dfrac{1}{3} = \dfrac{9}{12} - \dfrac{4}{12} = \dfrac{5}{12}$.

Thus, $\dfrac{\dfrac{2}{3} + \dfrac{1}{2}}{\dfrac{3}{4} - \dfrac{1}{3}} = \dfrac{\dfrac{7}{6}}{\dfrac{5}{12}}$

Division by a fraction is equivalent to multiplication by the reciprocal; hence, $\dfrac{\dfrac{7}{6}}{\dfrac{5}{12}} = \dfrac{7}{6} \cdot \dfrac{12}{5}$

Cancelling 6 from the numerator and denominator:

$$= \dfrac{7}{1} \cdot \dfrac{2}{5} = \dfrac{14}{5}$$

A second method is to multiply both the numerator and the denominator by the least common denominator of the entire fraction. Since we have already seen that LCD of the numerator is 6 and the LCD of the denominator is 12, and 12 is divisible by 6, we use 12 as the LCD of the entire fraction. Thus,

$$\dfrac{\dfrac{2}{3} + \dfrac{1}{2}}{\dfrac{3}{4} - \dfrac{1}{3}} = \dfrac{12\left(\dfrac{2}{3} + \dfrac{1}{2}\right)}{12\left(\dfrac{3}{4} - \dfrac{1}{3}\right)}$$

Distribute: $= \dfrac{12\left(\dfrac{2}{3}\right) + 12\left(\dfrac{1}{2}\right)}{12\left(\dfrac{3}{4}\right) - 12\left(\dfrac{1}{3}\right)}$

$$= \dfrac{4 \cdot 2 + 6}{3 \cdot 3 - 4} = \dfrac{8 + 6}{9 - 4} = \dfrac{14}{5}$$

Evaluate $p = \dfrac{(a-b)(ab+c)}{(cb-2a)}$ when $a = 2$, $b = -\dfrac{1}{2}$, and $c = -3$.

SOLUTION:

Inserting the given values of a, b, and c

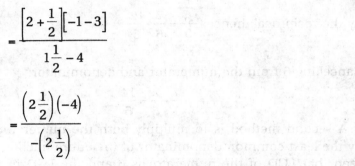

$$p = \frac{\left[2 - \left(-\dfrac{1}{2}\right)\right]\left[(2)\left(-\dfrac{1}{2}\right) + (-3)\right]}{\left[(-3)\left(-\dfrac{1}{2}\right) - 2(2)\right]}$$

$$= \frac{\left[2 + \dfrac{1}{2}\right][-1-3]}{1\dfrac{1}{2} - 4}$$

$$= \frac{\left(2\dfrac{1}{2}\right)(-4)}{-\left(2\dfrac{1}{2}\right)}$$

The $2\dfrac{1}{2}$ in the numerator cancels the $2\dfrac{1}{2}$ in the denominator.

$$p = \frac{-4}{-1}.$$

CHAPTER 4

FUNDAMENTAL ALGEBRAIC LAWS AND OPERATIONS WITH ALGEBRAIC EXPRESSIONS

● PROBLEM 4-1

Simplify $x = a + 2[b - (c - a + 3b)]$.

SOLUTION:

When working with several groupings, we perform the operations in the innermost parenthesis first, and work outward. Thus, we first subtract $(c - a + 3b)$ from b:

$x = a + 2[b - (c - a + 3b)]$ $\quad = a + 2(b - c + a - 3b)$

Combining terms, $\quad = a + 2(-c + a - 2b)$

distributing the 2, $\quad = a - 2c + 2a - 4b$

combining terms, $\quad = 3a - 2c - 4b$

To check that $a + 2[b - (c - a + 3b)]$ is equivalent to $3a - 2c - 4b$, replace a, b, and c by any values. Letting $a = 1$, $b = 2$, $c = 3$, the original form $a + 2[b - (c - a + 3b)]$ $= 1 + 2[2 - (3 - 1 + 3 \cdot 2)]$

$\qquad = 1 + 2[2 - (3 - 1 + 6)]$

$\qquad = 1 + 2[2 - 8]$

$\qquad = 1 + 2(-6)$

$\qquad = 1 + (-12)$

$\qquad = -11$

The final form, $3a - 2c - 4b = 3(1) - 2(3) - 4(2) = 3 - 6 - 8 = -11$. Thus, both forms yield the same result.

Solve for x when $|5 - 3x| = -2$.

SOLUTION:

This problem has no solution. The absolute value can never be negative, therefore we need not proceed further.

Solve for x when $|2x - 1| = |4x + 3|$.

SOLUTION:

Replacing the absolute symbols with equations that can be handled algebraically according to the conditions implied by the given equation, we have:

$$2x - 1 = 4x + 3$$

or

$$2x - 1 = -(4x + 3).$$

Solving the first equation, we have $x = -2$; solving the second, we obtain

$$x = -\frac{1}{3},$$

thus giving us two solutions to the original equation. (We could also write: $-(2x - 1) = -(4x + 3)$, but this is equivalent to the first of the equations above.)

Combine into a single fraction in lowest terms.

(a) $\dfrac{6(a+1)}{a+8} - \dfrac{3(a-4)}{a+8} - \dfrac{2(a+5)}{a+8}$

(b) $\dfrac{7x-3y+6}{x+y} - \dfrac{2(x-4y+3)}{x+y}$

(c) $\dfrac{5x+2}{x-6} - \dfrac{3(x+4)}{x-6} - \dfrac{x-7}{x-6}$

SOLUTION:

Noting $\dfrac{a}{x}+\dfrac{b}{x}+\dfrac{c}{x}=\dfrac{a+b+c}{x}$ (where a, b, c are any real numbers and x any non-zero real number), we proceed to evaluate these expressions:

(a) $\dfrac{6(a+1)}{a+8}-\dfrac{3(a-4)}{a+8}-\dfrac{2(a+5)}{a+8}=\dfrac{6(a+1)-3(a-4)-2(a+5)}{a+8}$

Distributing,

$$\dfrac{6a+6-3a+12-2a-10}{a+8}=\dfrac{6a-3a-2a+6+12-10}{a+8}=\dfrac{a+8}{a+8}=1$$

(b) $\dfrac{7x-3y+6}{x+y}-\dfrac{2(x-4y+3)}{x+y}=\dfrac{7x-3y+6-2(x-4y+3)}{x+y}$

Distributing,

$$=\dfrac{7x-3y+6-2x+8y-6}{x+y}=\dfrac{7x-2x-3y+8y+6-6}{x+y}=\dfrac{5x+5y}{x+y}=\dfrac{5(x+y)}{x+y}=5$$

(c) $\dfrac{5x+2}{x-6}-\dfrac{3(x+4)}{x-6}-\dfrac{x-7}{x-6}=\dfrac{5x+2-3(x+4)-(x-7)}{x-6}$

Distributing,

$$\dfrac{5x+2-3x-12-x+7}{x-6}=\dfrac{5x-3x-x+2-12+7}{x-6}=\dfrac{x-3}{x-6}$$

● **PROBLEM 4-5**

Simplify $\dfrac{\dfrac{1}{x-1}-\dfrac{1}{x-2}}{\dfrac{1}{x-2}-\dfrac{1}{x-3}}$.

SOLUTION:

Simplify the expression in the numerator by using the addition rule:

$$\dfrac{a}{b}+\dfrac{c}{d}=\dfrac{ad+bc}{bd}$$

Notice bd is the least common denominator, LCD.

We obtain $\dfrac{x-2-(x-1)}{(x-1)(x-2)} = \dfrac{-1}{(x-1)(x-2)}$ in the numerator.

Repeat this procedure for the expression in the denominator.

$$\frac{x-3-(x-2)}{(x-2)(x-3)} = \frac{-1}{(x-2)(x-3)}$$

We now have $\dfrac{\dfrac{-1}{(x-1)(x-2)}}{\dfrac{-1}{(x-2)(x-3)}}$, which is simplified by inverting the fraction in

the denominator and multiplying it by the numerator and cancelling like terms.

$$\frac{-1}{(x-1)(x-2)} \bullet \frac{(x-2)(x-3)}{-1} = \frac{x-3}{x-1}$$

(a) If $x = \dfrac{c-ab}{a-b}$, find the value of the expression $a(x + b)$.

(b) Also, if $x = \dfrac{c-ab}{a-b}$, find the value of the expression $bx + c$.

SOLUTION:

(a) Substituting $x = \dfrac{c-ab}{a-b}$ for x in the expression $a(x + b)$,

$$a(x+b) = a\left(\frac{c-ab}{a-b} + b\right) \tag{1}$$

Obtaining a common denominator of $a - b$ for the two terms in parenthesis; equation (1) becomes:

$$a(x+b) = a\left[\frac{c-ab}{a-b} + \frac{(a-b)b}{a-b}\right]$$

Distributing the numerator of the second term in brackets:

$$a(x + b) = a\left[\frac{c - ab}{a - b} + \frac{ab - b^2}{a - b}\right] = a\left[\frac{c - ab + ab - b^2}{a - b}\right]$$

$$= a\left[\frac{c - b^2}{a - b}\right]$$

$$a(x + b) = \frac{a(c - b^2)}{a - b}$$

(b) Substituting $x = \dfrac{c - ab}{a - b}$ for x in the expression $bx + c$,

$$bx + c = b\left(\frac{c - ab}{a - b}\right) + c$$

$$= \frac{b(c - ab)}{a - b} + c \tag{2}$$

Obtaining a common denominator of $a - b$ for the two terms on the right side of equation (2):

$$bx + c = \frac{b(c - ab)}{a - b} + \frac{(a - b)c}{a - b}$$

Distributing the numerator of each term on the right side:

$$bx + c = \frac{bc - ab^2}{a - b} + \frac{ac - bc}{a - b}$$

$$= \frac{bc - ab^2 + ac - bc}{a - b} = \frac{-ab^2 + ac}{a - b}$$

$$= \frac{ac - ab^2}{a - b}$$

Factoring out the common factor of a from the numerator of the right side:

$$bx + c = \frac{a(c - b^2)}{a - b}$$

● PROBLEM 4-7

Multiply $(4x - 5)(6x - 7)$.

SOLUTION:

We can apply the FOIL method. The letters indicate the order in which the

21

terms are to be multiplied.

F = first terms
O = outer terms
I = inner terms
L = last terms

Thus,

$$(4x - 5)(6x - 7) = (4x)(6x) + (4x)(-7) + (-5)(6x) + (-5)(-7)$$
$$= 24x^2 - 28x - 30x + 35 = 24x^2 - 58x + 35$$

Another way to multiply algebraic expressions is to apply the distributive law of multiplication with respect to addition. If a, b, and c are real numbers, then $a(b + c) = ab + ac$. In this case let $a = (4x - 5)$ and $b + c = 6x - 7$.

$$(4x - 5)(6x - 7) = (4x - 5)(6x) + (4x - 5)(-7)$$

Then, apply the law again.

$$(4x - 5)(6x - 7) = (4x)(6x) - (5)(6x) + (4x)(-7) + (-5)(-7)$$
$$(4x - 5)(6x - 7) = 24x^2 - 30x - 28x + 35$$

Add like terms.

$$(4x - 5)(6x - 7) = 24x^2 - 58x + 35.$$

● **PROBLEM 4-8**

Find the product of $(2x^2 - 3xy + y^2)(2x - y)$.

SOLUTION:

Multiplication of polynomials can be carried out very much the same way we multiply numbers. One polynomial is written under the other, and then multiplied term by term. Like terms in the product are arranged in columns and added.

$$
\begin{array}{r}
2x^2 - 3xy + y^2 \\
2x - y \\
\hline
4x^3 - 6x^2y + 2xy^2 \\
-2x^2y + 3xy^2 - y^3 \\
\hline
4x^3 - 8x^2y + 5xy^2 - y^3
\end{array}
$$

We are applying the Distributive Law in the following way:

$$\left(2x^2 - 3xy + y^2\right)\left(2x - y\right) = \left(2x^2 - 3xy + y^2\right)2x + \left(2x^2 - 3xy + y^2\right)\left(-y\right)$$

$$\left(2x^2 - 3xy + y^2\right)\left(2x - y\right) = 4x^3 - 6x^2y + 2xy^2 + \left(-2x^2y\right) + 3xy^2 - y^3$$

$$\left(2x^2 - 3xy + y^2\right)\left(2x - y\right) = 4x^3 - 8x^2y + 5xy^2 - y^3$$

22

Divide $(37 + 8x^3 - 4x)$ by $(2x + 3)$.

SOLUTION:

Arrange both polynomials in descending powers of the variable. The first polynomial becomes: $8x^3 - 4x + 37$. The second polynomial stays the same: $2x + 3$. The problem is: $2x + 3 \overline{\smash{\big)}\, 8x^3 - 4x + 37}$. In the dividend, $8x^3 - 4x + 37$, all powers of x must be included. The only missing power of x is x^2. To include this power of x, a coefficient of 0 is used; that is, $0x^2$. This term, $0x^2$, can be added to the dividend without changing the dividend because $0x^2 = 0$ (anything multiplied by 0 is 0).

Now to accomplish the division we proceed as follows: divide the fist term of the divisor into the first term of the dividend. Multiply the quotient from this division by each term of the divisor and subtract the products of each term from the dividend. We then obtain a new dividend. Use this dividend, and again divide by the first term of the divisor, and repeat all steps again until we obtain a remainder which is a degree lower than that of the divisor or zero. Following this procedure we obtain:

$$
\begin{array}{r}
4x^2 - 6x + 7 \\
2x + 3 \overline{\smash{\big)}\, 8x^3 - 4x + 37} \\
\underline{8x^3 + 12x^2 } \\
-12x^2 - 4x + 37 \\
\underline{-12x^2 - 18x } \\
14x + 37 \\
\underline{14x + 21} \\
16
\end{array}
$$

The degree of a polynomial is the highest power of the variable in the polynomial.

The degree of the divisor is 1. The number 16 can be written as $16x^0$ where $x^0 = 1$. Therefore, the number 16 has degree 0. When the degree of the divisor is greater than the degree of the dividend, we stop dividing.

Since the degree of the divisor in this problem is 1 and the degree of the dividend (16) is 0, the degree of the divisor is greater than the degree of the dividend. Therefore, dividing is stopped and the remainder is 16. Therefore, the quotient is $4x^2 - 6x + 7$ and the remainder is 16.

In order to verify this, multiply the quotient, $4x^2 - 6x + 7$, by the divisor, $2x + 3$, and then add 16. These two operations should total up to the dividend $8x^3 - 4x + 37$. Thus,

$(4x^2 - 6x + 7)(2x + 3) + 16 =$

$8x^3 - 12x^2 + 14x + 12x^2 - 18x + 21 + 16 = 8x^3 - 4x + 37,$

which is the desired result.

CHAPTER 5

FACTORING

● **PROBLEM 5-1**

Factor.   (a) $4a^2b - 2ab$

(b) $9ab^2c^3 - 6a^2c + 12ac$

(c) $ac + bc + ad + bd$

SOLUTION:

Find the highest common factor of each polynomial.

(a) $4a^2b = 2 \cdot 2 \cdot a \cdot a \cdot b$
       $2ab = 2 \cdot a \cdot b$

The highest common factor of the two terms is therefore $2ab$. Hence,

$4a^2b - 2ab = 2ab(2a - 1)$

(b) $9ab^2c^3 = 3 \cdot 3 \cdot a \cdot b \cdot b \cdot c \cdot c \cdot c$
       $6a^2c = 3 \cdot 2 \cdot a \cdot a \cdot c$
       $12ac = 3 \cdot 2 \cdot 2 \cdot a \cdot c$

The highest common factor of the three terms is $3ac$. Then,

$9ab^2c^3 - 6a^2c + 12ac = 3ac(3b^2c^2 - 2a + 4)$

(c) An expression may sometimes be factored by grouping terms having a common factor and thus getting new terms containing a common factor. The type form for this case is $ac + bc + ad + bd$, because the terms ac and bc have the common factor c, and ad and bd have the common factor d. Then,

$ac + bc + ad + bd = c(a + b) + d(a + b)$

Factoring out $(a + b)$,

$$= (a + b)(c + d).$$

Factor the following polynomials:

(a) $15ac + 6bc - 10ad - 4bd$

(b) $3a^2c + 3a^2d^2 + 2b^2c + 2b^2d^2$

SOLUTION:

(a) Group terms which have a common factor. Here, they are already grouped. Then factor.

$$15ac + 6bc - 10ad - 4bd = 3c(5a + 2b) - 2d(5a + 2b)$$

Factoring out $(5a + 2b)$

$$3c(5a + 2b) - 2d(5a + 2b) = (5a + 2b)(3c - 2d)$$

(b) Apply the same method as in (a)

$$3a^2c + 3a^2d^2 + 2b^2c + 2b^2d^2 = 3a^2(c + d^2) + 2b^2(c + d^2)$$
$$= (c + d^2)(3a^2 + 2b^2)$$

Hence, $(x + 2y)(x - 2y)$

Simplify $(x + 2y)(x - 2y)(x^2 + 4y^2)$.

SOLUTION:

Here we use the factoring formula $a^2 - b^2 = (a - b)(a + b)$ to rewrite the product $(x + 2y)(x - 2y)$:

$$(x + 2y)(x - 2y) = (x)^2 - (2y)^2 \text{ difference of two squares}$$
$$= x^2 - 4y^2$$

Hence, $(x + 2y)(x - 2y)(x^2 + 4y^2) = (x^2 - 4y^2)(x^2 + 4y^2)$ (1)

Now, again use the factoring formula given above to rewrite the right side of equation (1) in which $x^2 = a$ and $4y^2 = b$.

Hence, $(x^2 - 4y^2)(x^2 + 4y^2) = (x^2)^2 - (4y^2)^2$
$$= x^4 - 4^2y^4 \text{ since } (a^x)^y = a^{x \cdot y}$$
$$= x^4 - 16y^4$$

Hence, equation (1) becomes:

$$(x + 2y)(x - 2y)(x^2 + 4y^2) = x^4 - 16y^4$$

Factor $(x + y)^3 + z^3$.

SOLUTION:

The given expression is the sum of two cubes. The formula for the sum of two cubes can be used to factor the given expression. This formula is

$$a^3 + b^3 = (a + b)(a^2 - ab + b^2).$$

Using this formula and replacing a with $x + y$ and b with z:

$$(x + y)^3 + z^3 = [(x + y) + z][(x + y)^2 - (x + y)z + z^2]$$

Factor $a^4 - b^4$.

SOLUTION:

Note that $a^4 = \left(a^2\right)^2$ and $b^4 = \left(b^2\right)^2$; thus $a^4 - b^4 = \left(a^2\right)^2 - \left(b^2\right)^2$, the difference of two squares. Thus, we apply the formula for the difference of two squares,

$$x^2 - y^2 = (x + y)(x - y),$$

replacing x by a^2 and y by b^2 to obtain

$$a^4 - b^4 = \left(a^2\right)^2 - \left(b^2\right)^2 = \left(a^2 + b^2\right)\left(a^2 - b^2\right).$$

Since $a^2 - b^2$ is also the difference of two squares, we once again apply the above formula to obtain

$$a^2 - b^2 = (a + b)(a - b).$$

Therefore, $a^4 - b^4 = \left(a^2 + b^2\right)(a + b)(a - b).$

Find the LCM of $(x - 1)^2$, $(1 - x)^3$, and $1 - x^3$.

SOLUTION:

Factor each polynomial completely. Notice in the factoring of the second and the third polynomials that -1 may be factored from the expressions first so that the terms of highest degree in the factors will have positive coefficients.

$$(x-1)^2 = (x-1)^2$$

$$(1-x)^3 = \left[-1(x-1)\right]^3 = (-1)^3(x-1)^3 = -(x-1)^3$$

$$1-x^3 = (-1)(x^3-1) = -(x-1)(x^2+x+1)$$

($x^3 - 1$ is the difference of two cubes.)

Each of the factors of these expressions appears in the product known as the LCM. Each factor is raised to the highest power to which it appears in any one of the expressions. Therefore, the

$$\text{LCM} = (x-1)^3(x^2+x+1)$$

Combine $\dfrac{3x+y}{x^2-y^2} - \dfrac{2y}{x(x-y)} - \dfrac{1}{x+y}$ into a single fraction.

SOLUTION:

Fractions which have unlike denominators must be transformed into fractions with the same denominator before they may be combined. This identical denominator is the least common denominator (LCD), the least common multiple of the denominators of the fractions to be added. In the process of transforming the fractions to a common denominator we make use of the fact that the numerator and denominator of a fraction may be multiplied by the same non-zero number without changing the value of the fraction. In our case the denominators are $x^2 - y^2 = (x+y)(x-y)$, $x(x-y)$, and $x + y$. Therefore, the LCD is $x(x+y)(x-y)$, and we proceed as follows:

$$\frac{3x+y}{x^2-y^2} - \frac{2y}{x(x-y)} - \frac{1}{x+y} = \frac{3x+y}{(x+y)(x-y)} - \frac{2y}{x(x-y)} - \frac{1}{x+y}$$

$$= \frac{x(3x+y)}{x(x+y)(x-y)} - \frac{(x+y)2y}{(x+y)(x)(x-y)} - \frac{x(x-y)}{x(x-y)(x+y)}$$

$$= \frac{3x^2+xy}{x(x+y)(x-y)} - \frac{2xy+2y^2}{x(x+y)(x-y)} - \frac{x^2-xy}{x(x+y)(x-y)}$$

$$= \frac{3x^2+xy-(2xy+2y^2)-(x^2-xy)}{x(x+y)(x-y)}$$

$$= \frac{3x^2+xy-2xy-2y^2-x^2+xy}{x(x+y)(x-y)}$$

$$= \frac{3x^2-x^2+xy+xy-2xy-2y^2}{x(x+y)(x-y)}$$

$$= \frac{2x^2-2y^2}{x(x+y)(x-y)}$$

$$= \frac{2(x^2-y^2)}{x(x+y)(x-y)}$$

$$= \frac{2\cancel{(x+y)}\cancel{(x-y)}}{x\cancel{(x+y)}\cancel{(x-y)}}$$

$$= \frac{2}{x}$$

Reduce $\dfrac{x^2-5x+4}{x^2-7x+12}$ to lowest terms.

SOLUTION:

Factor the expressions in both the numerator and denominator and cancel like terms.

$$\frac{x^2-5x+4}{x^2-7x+12} = \frac{(x-1)(x-4)}{(x-3)(x-4)}$$

$$= \frac{x-1}{x-3}$$

The numerator and the denominator were both divided by $x-4$.

Perform the indicated operation, $\dfrac{x^3 - y^3}{x^2 - 5x + 6} \cdot \dfrac{x^2 - 4}{x^2 - 2xy + y^2}$

SOLUTION:

We factor numerators and denominators to enable us to cancel terms.

$$x^3 - y^3$$

is the difference of two cubes. Thus, we factor it applying the formula for the difference of two cubes,

$$a^3 - b^3 = (a - b)(a^2 + ab + b^2),$$

replacing a by x and b by y. Thus,

$$x^3 - y^3 = (x - y)(x^2 + xy + y^2)$$

$x^2 - 5x + 6$ is factored as $(x - 2)(x - 3)$.

$$x^2 - 4 = x^2 - 2^2,$$

the difference of two squares. Applying the formula for the difference of two squares,

$$a^2 - b^2 = (a + b)(a - b),$$

and replacing a by x and b by 2 we obtain

$$x^2 - 4 = (x + 2)(x - 2)$$
$$x^2 - 2xy + y^2 = (x - y)(x - y)$$

Thus,

$$\frac{x^3 - y^3}{x^2 - 5x + 6} \cdot \frac{x^2 - 4}{x^2 - 2xy + y^2} = \frac{(x - y)(x^2 + xy + y^2)}{(x - 2)(x - 3)} \cdot \frac{(x + 2)(x - 2)}{(x - y)(x - y)}$$

$$= \frac{(x^2 + xy + y^2)\cancel{(x - y)}\cancel{(x - 2)}(x + 2)}{(x - 3)\cancel{(x - 2)}\cancel{(x - y)}(x - y)}$$

$$= \frac{(x^2 + xy + y^2)(x + 2)}{(x - 3)(x - y)}$$

CHAPTER 6

EXPONENT, RADICAL, AND POWER

Simplify the following expressions:

$$\text{(a) } -3^{-2}$$
$$\text{(b) } (-3)^{-2}$$
$$\text{(c) } \frac{-3}{4^{-1}}$$

SOLUTION:

(a) Here the exponent applies only to 3.

Since $x^{-y} = \dfrac{1}{x^y}, -3^{-2} = -\left(3^{-2}\right) = -\dfrac{1}{3^2} = -\dfrac{1}{9}$.

(b) In this case the exponent applies to the negative base. Thus,

$$-\left(3\right)^{-2} = \frac{1}{(-3)^2} = \frac{1}{(-3)(-3)} = \frac{1}{9}.$$

(c) $\dfrac{-3}{4^{-1}} = \dfrac{-3}{\left(\dfrac{1}{4}\right)^1} = \dfrac{-3}{\dfrac{1^1}{4^1}} = \dfrac{-3}{\dfrac{1}{4}}.$

Division by a fraction is equivalent to multiplication by that fraction's reciprocal. Thus,

$$\frac{-3}{\frac{1}{4}} = -3 \cdot \frac{4}{1} = -12, \text{ and } \frac{-3}{4^{-1}} = -12.$$

Evaluate the following:

(a) $8\left(-\frac{1}{4}\right)^0$ (b) $6^0 + (-6)^0$ (c) $-7(-3)^0$ (d) 9^{-1} (e) 7^{-2}

SOLUTION:

Note $x^0 = 1$ and $x^{-a} = \frac{1}{x^a}$ for all non–zero real numbers x,

(a) $8\left(-\frac{1}{4}\right)^0 = 8(1) = 8$

(b) $6^0 + (-6)^0 = 1 + 1 = 2$

(c) $-7(-3)^0 = -7(1) = -7$

(d) $9^{-1} = \frac{1}{9^1} = \frac{1}{9}$

(e) $7^{-2} = \frac{1}{7^2} = \frac{1}{49}$

Use the theorems on exponents to perform the indicated operations.

(a) $5x^5 \cdot 2x^2$ (b) $\left(x^4\right)^6$ (c) $\frac{8y^8}{2y^2}$ (d) $\left(\frac{x^3}{x^6}\right)\left(\frac{7}{x}\right)^2$

SOLUTION:

Noting the following properties of exponents:

we proceed to evaluate these expressions.

(1) $a^b \cdot a^c = a^{b+c}$ (2) $\left(a^b\right)^c = a^{b \cdot c}$ (3) $\dfrac{a^b}{a^c} = a^{b-c}$ (4) $\left(\dfrac{a}{b}\right)^c = \dfrac{a^c}{b^c}$

we proceed to evaluate these expressions.

(a) $5x^5 \cdot 2x^2 = 5 \cdot 2 \cdot x^5 x^2 = 10 \cdot x^5 \cdot x^2 = 10x^{5+2} = 10x^7$

(b) $\left(x^4\right)^6 = x^{4 \cdot 6} = x^{24}$

(c) $\dfrac{8y^8}{2y^2} = \dfrac{8}{2} \cdot \dfrac{y^8}{y^2} = 4 \cdot y^{8-2} = 4y^6$

(d) $\left(\dfrac{x^3}{x^6}\right)\left(\dfrac{7}{x}\right)^2 = \left(\dfrac{x^3}{x^6}\right)\left(\dfrac{7^2}{x^2}\right) = \dfrac{x^3 \cdot 49}{x^6 \cdot x^2} = \dfrac{49x^3}{x^{6+2}} = \dfrac{49x^3}{x^8} = \dfrac{49x^3}{x^{5+3}}$

$$= \dfrac{49x^3}{x^5 \cdot x^3} = \dfrac{49}{x^5}$$

● **PROBLEM 6-4**

Perform the indicated operations.

$$(7 \cdot 10^5)^3 \cdot (3 \cdot 10^{-3})^4.$$

SOLUTION:

Since $(ab)^x = a^x b^x$, $(7 \cdot 10^5)^3 \cdot (3 \cdot 10^{-3})^4 = (7)^3 (10^5)^3 \cdot (3)^4 (10^{-3})^4$. Recall that $(a^x)^y = a^{xy}$. Thus,

$$= (7^3)(10^{5 \cdot 3}) \cdot (3^4)(10^{-3 \cdot 4})$$
$$= (7^3)(10^{15}) \cdot (3^4)(10^{-12})$$
$$= (7^3)(3^4)(10^{15})(10^{-12})$$

Since $a^x \cdot a^y = a^{x+y}$, $= (7^3)(3^4)(10^{15+(-12)})$
$$= 7^3 3^4 10^3$$

● **PROBLEM 6-5**

Evaluate the following expressions.

(a) $\dfrac{-12x^{10}y^9z^5}{3x^2y^3z^6}$ (b) $\dfrac{-16x^{16}y^6z^4}{-4x^4y^2z^7}$

32

SOLUTION:

Noting (1) $\dfrac{abcd}{efgh} = \dfrac{a}{e} \cdot \dfrac{b}{f} \cdot \dfrac{c}{g} \cdot \dfrac{d}{h}$, (2) $a^{-b} = \dfrac{1}{a^b}$, and (3) $\dfrac{a^b}{a^c} = a^{b-c}$ for all non-zero real values of a, e, f, g, and h, we proceed to evaluate these expressions:

(a) $\dfrac{-12x^{10}y^9z^5}{3x^2y^3z^6} = \dfrac{-12}{3} \cdot \dfrac{x^{10}}{x^2} \cdot \dfrac{y^9}{y^3} \cdot \dfrac{z^5}{z^6} = -4 \cdot x^{10-2} \cdot y^{9-3} \cdot z^{5-6}$

$$= -4x^8y^6z^{-1} = \dfrac{-4x^8y^6}{z^1}$$

Thus, $\dfrac{-12x^{10}y^9z^5}{3x^2y^3z^6} = \dfrac{-4x^8y^6}{z}$

(b) $\dfrac{-16x^{16}y^6z^4}{-4x^4y^2z^7} = \dfrac{-16}{-4} \cdot \dfrac{x^{16}}{x^4} \cdot \dfrac{y^6}{y^2} \cdot \dfrac{z^4}{z^7}$

$$= 4x^{16-4} \cdot y^{6-2} \cdot z^{4-7} = 4x^{12}y^4z^{-3} = \dfrac{4x^{12}y^4}{z^3}$$

● PROBLEM 6-6

Use the properties of exponents to perform the indicated operations in

$$\left(2^3 x^4 5^2 y^7\right)^5$$

SOLUTION:

Since the product of several numbers raised to the same exponent equals the product of each number raised to that exponent (i.e., $(abcd)^x = a^x b^x c^x d^x$), we obtain

$$\left(2^3 x^4 5^2 y^7\right)^5 = \left(2^3\right)^5 \left(x^4\right)^5 \left(5^2\right)^5 \left(y^7\right)^5$$

Recall that $\left(x^a\right)^b = x^{a \cdot b}$; thus,

$$\left(2^3 x^4 5^2 y^7\right)^5 = \left(2^3\right)^5 \left(x^4\right)^5 \left(5^2\right)^5 \left(y^7\right)^5$$

$$= \left(2^{3 \cdot 5}\right)\left(x^{4 \cdot 5}\right)\left(5^{2 \cdot 5}\right)\left(y^{7 \cdot 5}\right)$$

$$= 2^{15} x^{20} 5^{10} y^{35}$$

Write the expression $(x + y^{-1})^{-1}$ without using negative exponents.

SOLUTION:

Since $x^{-a} = \dfrac{1}{x^a}$, $y^{-1} = \dfrac{1}{y^1} = \dfrac{1}{y}$

$$\left(x + y^{-1}\right)^{-1} = \left(x + \frac{1}{y}\right)^{-1}$$

$$= \frac{1}{x + \dfrac{1}{y}}$$

Multiply numerator and denominator by y in order to eliminate the fraction in the denominator.

$$\frac{y(1)}{y\left(x + \dfrac{1}{y}\right)} = \frac{y}{yx + \dfrac{y}{y}} = \frac{y}{yx + 1}$$

Thus, $\left(x + y^{-1}\right)^{-1} = \dfrac{y}{yx + 1}$

Rewrite the value of each of the following terms in exponential form.

(a) $\dfrac{0.000000074}{1200000}$ (b) $0.000080 \div 0.000043$

SOLUTION:

(a) $\dfrac{7.4 \cdot 10^{-8}}{1.2 \cdot 10^{6}} = \dfrac{7.4}{1.2} \cdot 10^{-14} = 6.167 \cdot 10^{-14}$

(b) $\dfrac{8.0 \cdot 10^{-5}}{4.3 \cdot 10^{-5}} = \dfrac{8.0}{4.3} = 1.860$

Express $\left(5^{\frac{1}{2}} + 9^{\frac{1}{8}}\right) \div \left(5^{\frac{1}{2}} - 9^{\frac{1}{8}}\right)$

as an equivalent fraction with a rational denominator.

SOLUTION:

The given expression can be rewritten as

$$\frac{5^{\frac{1}{2}} + 9^{\frac{1}{8}}}{5^{\frac{1}{2}} - 9^{\frac{1}{8}}},$$

and since

$$9^{\frac{1}{8}} = \left(3^2\right)^{\frac{1}{8}} = 3^{\frac{1}{4}}$$

we write:

$$\frac{5^{\frac{1}{2}} + 3^{\frac{1}{4}}}{5^{\frac{1}{2}} - 3^{\frac{1}{4}}}$$

To rationalize the denominator, put $5^{\frac{1}{2}} = x$, $3^{\frac{1}{4}} = y$; then, since

$$x^4 - y^4 = \left(5^{\frac{1}{2}}\right)^4 - \left(3^{\frac{1}{4}}\right)^4 = 5^2 - 3 = 25 - 3 = 22,$$

which is rational, we can write

$$x^4 - y^4 = \left(x - y\right)\left(x^3 + x^2 y + xy^2 + y^3\right)$$

and the factor which rationalizes $x - y$, or $5^{\frac{1}{2}} - 3^{\frac{1}{4}}$ is $x^3 + x^2 y + xy^2 + y^3$ and substituting for x and y:

$$\left(5^{\frac{1}{2}}\right)^3 + \left(5^{\frac{1}{2}}\right)^2 \cdot 3^{\frac{1}{4}} + 5^{\frac{1}{2}} \cdot \left(3^{\frac{1}{4}}\right)^2 + \left(3^{\frac{1}{4}}\right)^3$$

$$= 5^{\frac{3}{2}} + 5^{\frac{2}{2}} \cdot 3^{\frac{1}{4}} + 5^{\frac{1}{2}} \cdot 3^{\frac{2}{4}} + 3^{\frac{3}{4}};$$

and the rational denominator is $x^4 - y^4 = 5^{\frac{4}{2}} - 3^{\frac{4}{4}} = 5^2 - 3 = 22$. Now, since

$$x^4 - y^4 = (x-y)(x^3 + x^2 y + xy^2 + y^3), \text{ then } (x-y) = \frac{x^4 - y^4}{x^3 + x^2 y + xy^2 + y^3},$$

and substituting: $5^{\frac{1}{2}} - 3^{\frac{1}{4}} = \dfrac{22}{5^{\frac{3}{2}} + 5^{\frac{2}{2}} \cdot 3^{\frac{1}{4}} + 5^{\frac{1}{2}} \cdot 3^{\frac{2}{4}} + 3^{\frac{3}{4}}}$

Therefore, the given expression

$$= \frac{5^{\frac{1}{2}} + 3^{\frac{1}{4}}}{\dfrac{22}{5^{\frac{3}{2}} + 5^{\frac{2}{2}} \cdot 3^{\frac{1}{4}} + 5^{\frac{1}{2}} \cdot 3^{\frac{2}{4}} + 3^{\frac{3}{4}}}}$$

$$= \frac{\left(5^{\frac{1}{2}} + 3^{\frac{1}{4}}\right)\left(5^{\frac{3}{2}} + \left(5^{\frac{2}{2}} \cdot 3^{\frac{1}{4}}\right) + \left(5^{\frac{1}{2}} \cdot 3^{\frac{2}{4}}\right) + 3^{\frac{3}{4}}\right)}{22}$$

$$= \frac{5^{\frac{4}{2}} + 5^{\frac{3}{2}} \cdot 3^{\frac{1}{4}} + 5^{\frac{3}{2}} \cdot 3^{\frac{1}{4}} + 5^{\frac{2}{2}} \cdot 3^{\frac{2}{4}} + 5^{\frac{2}{2}} \cdot 3^{\frac{2}{4}} + 5^{\frac{1}{2}} \cdot 3^{\frac{3}{4}} + 5^{\frac{1}{2}} \cdot 3^{\frac{3}{4}} + 3^{\frac{4}{4}}}{22}$$

$$= \frac{5^{\frac{4}{2}} + \left(2 \cdot 5^{\frac{3}{2}} \cdot 3^{\frac{1}{4}}\right) + \left(2 \cdot 5^{\frac{2}{2}} \cdot 3^{\frac{2}{4}}\right) + \left(2 \cdot 5^{\frac{1}{2}} \cdot 3^{\frac{3}{4}}\right) + 3^{\frac{4}{4}}}{22}$$

$$= \frac{5^2 + 2\left(5^{\frac{3}{2}} \cdot 3^{\frac{1}{4}} + 5^{\frac{2}{2}} \cdot 3^{\frac{2}{4}} + 5^{\frac{1}{2}} \cdot 3^{\frac{3}{4}}\right) + 3}{22}$$

$$= \frac{28 + 2\left(5^{\frac{3}{2}} \cdot 3^{\frac{1}{4}} + 5^{\frac{2}{2}} \cdot 3^{\frac{2}{4}} + 5^{\frac{1}{2}} \cdot 3^{\frac{3}{4}}\right)}{22}$$

$$= \frac{14 + 5^{\frac{3}{2}} \cdot 3^{\frac{1}{4}} + 5 \cdot 3^{\frac{1}{2}} + 5^{\frac{1}{2}} \cdot 3^{\frac{3}{4}}}{11}$$

CHAPTER 7

RATIOS, PROPORTIONS, AND VARIATIONS

● **PROBLEM 7-1**

On a map, $\frac{3}{16}$ inch represents 10 miles. What would be the length of a line on the map which represents 96 miles?

SOLUTION:

The lengths of line segments on the map are proportional to the actual distances on the earth. If L represents the length of the line segment on the map corresponding to a distance of 96 miles, then

$$\frac{\frac{3}{16} \text{ inches}}{L \text{ inches}} = \frac{10 \text{ miles}}{96 \text{ miles}}$$

by cross multiplying $\frac{3}{16}(96) = 10L$

$$L = \frac{(3)(96)}{(16)(10)} = \frac{3(6)}{10}$$

$$L = \frac{18}{10}$$

$$L = 1\frac{4}{5} \text{ inches.}$$

Find the ratios of $x : y : z$ from the equations $7x = 4y + 8z$, and $3z = 12x + 11y$.

SOLUTION:

By transposition we have
$$7x - 4y - 8z = 0$$
$$12x + 11y - 3z = 0$$

To obtain the ratio of $x : y$ we convert the given system into an equation in terms of just x and y. z may be eliminated as follows: multiply each term of the first equation by 3, and each term of the second equation by 8, and then subtract the second equation from the first. We thus obtain:

$$21x - 12y - 24z = 0$$
$$-(96x + 88y - 24z = 0)$$
$$\overline{-75x - 100y \qquad = 0}$$

Dividing each term of the last equation by 25, we obtain
$$-3x - 4y = 0 \text{ or}$$
$$-3x = 4y$$

Dividing both sides of this equation by 4 and by –3, we have the proportion:
$$\frac{x}{4} = \frac{y}{-3}$$

We are now interested in obtaining the ratio of $y : z$. To do this we convert the given system of equations into an equation in terms of just y and z, by eliminating x as follows: multiply each term of the first equation by 12, and each term of the second equation by 7, and then subtract the second equation from the first. We thus obtain:

$$84x - 48y - 96z = 0$$
$$-(84x + 77y - 21z = 0)$$
$$\overline{-125y - 75z = 0}$$

Dividing each term of the last equation by 25 we obtain:
$$-5y - 3z = 0 \text{ or}$$
$$-3z = 5y$$

Dividing both sides of this equation by 5 and by –3, we have the proportion:
$$\frac{z}{5} = \frac{y}{-3}$$

From this result and our previous result, we obtain: $\frac{x}{4} = \frac{y}{-3} = \frac{z}{5}$ as the desired ratios.

If $(2ma + 6mb + 3nc + 9nd)(2ma - 6mb - 3nc + 9nd) = (2ma - 6mb + 3nc - 9nd)(2ma + 6mb - 3nc - 9nd)$, prove that a, b, c, and d are proportionals.

SOLUTION:

Dividing both sides of the given equation by $(2ma - 6mb - 3nc + 9nd)$, and then by $(2ma - 6mb + 3nc - 9nd)$ we have

$$\frac{2ma + 6mb + 3nc + 9nd}{2ma - 6mb + 3nc - 9nd} = \frac{2ma + 6mb - 3nc - 9nd}{2ma - 6mb - 3nc + 9nd}.$$

Since the above two ratios are of the form $\frac{a}{b} = \frac{c}{d}$, we can use the Law of

Proportions which states that $\frac{a + b}{a - b} = \frac{c + d}{c - d}$.

Doing this we obtain,

$$\frac{2ma + 6mb + 3nc + 9nd + \left(2ma - 6mb + 3nc - 9nd\right)}{2ma + 6mb + 3nc + 9nd - \left(2ma - 6mb + 3nc - 9nd\right)} =$$

$$\frac{2ma + 6mb - 3nc - 9nd + \left(2ma - 6mb - 3nc + 9nd\right)}{2ma + 6mb - 3nc - 9nd - \left(2ma - 6mb - 3nc + 9nd\right)}$$

or, $\dfrac{4ma + 6nc}{12mb + 18nd} = \dfrac{4ma - 6nc}{12mb - 18nd}$; and factoring gives us

$$\frac{2\left(2ma + 3nc\right)}{2\left(6mb + 9nd\right)} = \frac{2\left(2ma - 3nc\right)}{2\left(6mb - 9nd\right)} \quad \text{or} \quad \frac{2ma + 3nc}{6mb + 9nd} = \frac{2ma - 3nc}{6mb - 9nd}.$$

Now, since $\frac{a}{b} = \frac{c}{d}$ can be alternately written as $\frac{a}{c} = \frac{b}{d}$, we write:

$$\frac{2ma + 3nc}{2ma - 3nc} = \frac{6mb + 9nd}{6mb - 9nd}.$$

Now, rewriting this last proportion as,

$$\frac{2ma + 3nc + \left(2ma - 3nc\right)}{2ma + 3nc - \left(2ma - 3nc\right)} = \frac{6mb + 9nd + \left(6mb - 9nd\right)}{6mb + 9nd - \left(6mb - 9nd\right)}$$

we obtain:

$$\frac{4ma}{6nc} = \frac{12mb}{18nd}.$$

Again, using the fact that $\frac{a}{b} = \frac{c}{d}$ can be rewritten as $\frac{a}{c} = \frac{b}{d}$, we write:

$$\frac{4ma}{12mb} = \frac{6nc}{18nd} \text{ or } \frac{a}{3b} = \frac{c}{3d}.$$

Thus, $\frac{a}{b} = \frac{c}{d}$ or $a : b = c : d$.

● PROBLEM 7-4

If y varies inversely as the cube of x, and $y = 7$ when $x = 2$, express y as a function of x.

SOLUTION:

The relationship "y varies inversely with respect to x" is expressed as $y = \frac{k}{x}$.

The inverse variation is now with respect to the cube of x, x^3, and we have

$$y = \frac{k}{x^3}.$$

Since $y = 7$ and $x = 2$ must satisfy this relation, we replace x and y by these

values, $7 = \frac{k}{2^3} = \frac{k}{8}$, and we find $k = 7 \cdot 8 = 56$. Substitution of this value of k in

the general relation gives $y = \frac{56}{x^3}$, which expresses y as a function of x. We may

now, in addition, find the value of y corresponding to any value of x. If we have the added requirement to find the value of y when $x = 1.2$, $x = 1.2$ would be substituted in the function so that for $x = 1.2$, we have

$$y = \frac{56}{(1.2)^3} = \frac{56}{1.728} = 32.41.$$

Other expressions in use are "is proportional to" for "varies directly," and "is inversely proportional to" for "varies inversely."

● PROBLEM 7-5

The weight W of an object above the earth varies inversely as the square of the distance d from the center of the earth. If a man weighs 180 pounds on the surface of the earth, what would his weight be at an altitude of 1,000 miles? Assume the radius of the earth to be 4,000 miles.

SOLUTION:

W varies inversely with d^2; therefore, $W = \dfrac{k}{d^2}$ where k is the proportionality

constant. Similarly, $W_1 = \dfrac{k}{d_1^2}, W_2 = \dfrac{k}{d_2^2}$ and, solving these two equations for k,

$W_1 d_1^2 = k$ and $W_2 d_2^2 = k$. Hence, $k = W_1 d_1^2 = W_2 d_2^2$ or

$$\frac{W_1 d_1^2}{W_2} = \frac{W_2 d_2^2}{W_2}$$

$$\frac{W_1 d_1^2}{W_2} = d_2^2$$

$$\frac{W_1 d_1^2}{W_2 d_1^2} = \frac{d_2^2}{d_1^2}$$

$$\frac{W_1}{W_2} = \frac{d_2^2}{d_1^2} \qquad (1)$$

Letting d_1 = radius of the earth, 4000, then d_2 = 4000 + 1000 = 5000. Substituting the given values in equation (1):

$$\frac{180}{W_2} = \frac{5000^2}{4000^2} = \frac{(5 \times 1000)^2}{(4 \times 1000)^2} = \frac{5^2 \times 1000^2}{4^2 \times 1000^2}$$

$$= \frac{5^2}{4^2}$$

$$= \frac{25}{16}$$

$$\frac{180}{W_2} = \frac{25}{16}$$

$$W_2 \left(\frac{180}{W_2}\right) = W_2 \left(\frac{25}{16}\right)$$

$$180 = \frac{25}{16} W_2$$

$$\frac{16}{25} \overset{36}{(180)} = \frac{16}{25}\left(\frac{25}{16} W_2\right)$$
$$\underset{5}{}$$

$$\frac{576}{5} = W_2$$

$115\dfrac{1}{5}$ pounds = W_2 or 115.2 pounds = W_2.

CHAPTER 8

FUNCTIONS

Describe the domain and range of the function $f = (x,y) | y = \sqrt{9 - x^2}$ if x and y are real numbers.

SOLUTION:

In determining the domain we are interested in the values of x which yield a real value for y. Since the square root of a negative number is not a real number, the domain is restricted to those values of x which make the radicand positive or zero. Therefore, x^2 cannot exceed 9 which means that x cannot exceed 3 or be less than –3. A convenient way to express this is to write $-3 \le x \le 3$, which is read "x is greater than or equal to –3 and less than or equal to 3." This is the domain of the function. The range is the set of values that y can assume. To determine the range of the function we note that the largest value of y occurs when $x = 0$. Then $y = \sqrt{9 - 0} = 3$. Likewise, the smallest value of y occurs when $x = 3$ or $x = -3$. Then $y = \sqrt{9 - 9} = 0$. Since this is an inclusive interval of the real axis, the range of y is $0 \le y \le 3$.

If $g(x) = x^2 - 2x + 1$, find the given element in the range.

  (a) $g(-2)$ (b) $g(0)$ (c) $g(a + 1)$ (d) $g(a - 1)$

SOLUTION:

  (a) To find $g(-2)$, substitute -2 for x in the given equation.

$$g(x) = g(-2)$$
$$= (-2)^2 - 2(-2) + 1$$
$$= 4 + 4 + 1$$
$$= 8 + 1$$
$$= 9$$

Hence, $g(-2) = 9$.

  (b) To find $g(0)$, substitute 0 for x in the given equation.

$$g(x) = g(0)$$
$$= (0)^2 - 2(0) + 1$$
$$= 0 - 0 + 1$$
$$= 1$$

Hence, $g(0) = 1$.

  (c) To find $g(a + 1)$, substitute $a + 1$ for x in the given equation.

$$g(x) = g(a + 1)$$
$$= (a + 1)^2 - 2(a + 1) + 1$$
$$= (a^2 + 2a + 1) - 2a - 2 + 1$$
$$= a^2 + 2a + 1 - 2a - 2 + 1$$
$$= a^2 + 1 - 2 + 1$$
$$= a^2 + 0$$
$$= a^2$$

Hence, $g(a + 1) = a^2$.

  (d) To find $g(a - 1)$, substitute $a - 1$ for x in the given equation.

$$g(x) = g(a - 1)$$
$$= (a - 1)^2 - 2(a - 1) + 1$$
$$= (a^2 - 2a + 1) - 2a + 2 + 1$$
$$= a^2 - 2a + 1 - 2a + 2 + 1$$
$$= a^2 - 4a + 4$$

Hence, $g(a - 1) = a^2 - 4a + 4$

If $f(x) = 3x + 4$ and $D = \{x| -1 \le x \le 3\}$, find the range of $f(x)$.

We first prove that the value of $3x + 4$ increases when x increases. If $X > x$, then we may multiply both sides of the inequality by a positive number to obtain an equivalent inequality. Thus, $3X > 3x$. We may also add a number to both sides of the inequality to obtain an equivalent inequality. Thus,

$$3X + 4 > 3x + 4.$$

Hence, if x belongs to D, the function value $f(x) = 3x + 4$ is least when $x = -1$ and greatest when $x = 3$. Consequently, since $f(-1) = -3 + 4 = 1$ and $f(3) = 9 + 4 = 13$, the range is all y from 1 to 13; that is,

$$R = \{y|\ 1 \leq y \leq 13\}.$$

● **PROBLEM 8-4**

Find the domain D and the range R of the function $\left(x, \dfrac{x}{|x|}\right)$.

SOLUTION:

Note that the y–value of any coordinate pair (x, y) is $\dfrac{x}{|x|}$. We can replace x in the formula $\dfrac{x}{|x|}$ with any number except 0, since the denominator, $|x|$, cannot equal 0, (i.e., $|x| \neq 0$) which is equivalent to $x \neq 0$. This is because division by 0 is undefined. Therefore, the domain D is the set of all real numbers except 0. If x is negative, i.e., $x < 0$, then $|x| = -x$ by definition. Hence, if x is negative, then $\dfrac{x}{|x|} = \dfrac{x}{-x} = -1$. If x is positive, i.e., $x > 0$, then $|x| = x$ by definition. Hence, if x is positive, then $\dfrac{x}{|x|} = \dfrac{x}{x} = 1$. (The case where $x = 0$ has already been found to be undefined.) Thus, there are only two numbers, –1 and 1, in the range R of the function; that is, R = {–1, 1}.

If D = {x | x is an integer and –2 ≤ x ≤ 1}, find the function
{(x, f(x)) | f(x) = x³ – 3 and x belongs to D}.

SOLUTION:

D = {–2, –1, 0, 1}. Substituting these values of x in the equation $f(x) = x^3 - 3$, we find the corresponding $f(x)$ values. Thus,

$f(-2) = (-2)^3 - 3 = -8 - 3 = -11$

$f(-1) = (-1)^3 - 3 = -1 - 3 = -4$

$f(0) = 0^3 - 3 = 0 - 3 = -3$ and

$f(1) = 1^3 - 3 = 1 - 3 = -2$.

Hence, $f = \{(x, f(x)) \mid f(x) = x^3 - 3$ and x belongs to D$\}$

$= \{(-2, -11), (-1, -4), (0, -3), (1, -2)\}$

What are the degrees of the following equations?

(a) $x + 3$ (b) $x^4 + 3x^2 + 7$ (c) $2x + 4x^3 + 3 + 7x^8$ (d) 7

SOLUTION:

The degree of an equation is the value of the highest power in the equation.
(a) 1   (b) 4   (c) 8   (d) 0

Determine the degrees of the following equations in each of the indicated unknowns.

$x^2 + xy + z^4x^4 + 14 = 0$ $x; y; z; x$ and $y; x$ and $z; y$ and z.

SOLUTION:

$x : 4$	x and $y : = 2$
$y : 1$	x and $z : = 8$
$z : 4$	y and $z : = 0$

45

Find the zeros of $f(x) = 2x^2 + 4x + 8$.

SOLUTION:

A zero of a function $f(x)$ is that value of x for which $f(x) = 0$.
Hence, to find the zeros of the given function, set $f(x) = 0$ and solve for x.

$$f(x) = 2x^2 + 4x + 8 = 0$$
$$x^2 + 2x + 4 = 0$$

$$x = \frac{-b \pm \sqrt{b^2 - 4ac}}{2a}$$

$$= \frac{-2 \pm \sqrt{4 - 4 \cdot 1 \cdot 4}}{2 \cdot 1}$$

$$= \frac{-2 \pm \sqrt{-12}}{2} = -1 \pm i\sqrt{3}$$

Therefore, the zeros of $f(x)$ are $-1 + i\sqrt{3}$ and $-1 - i\sqrt{3}$.

Find the zeros of the function $\dfrac{2x+7}{5} + \dfrac{3x-5}{4} + \dfrac{33}{10}$.

SOLUTION:

Let the function $f(x)$ be equal to $\dfrac{2x+7}{5} + \dfrac{3x-5}{4} + \dfrac{33}{10}$.

A number, a, is a zero of a function $f(x)$ if $f(a) = 0$. A zero of $f(x)$ is a root of the equation $f(x) = 0$. Thus, the zeros of the function are the roots of the equation

$$\frac{2x+7}{5} + \frac{3x-5}{4} + \frac{33}{10} = 0.$$

The least common denominator, LCD, of the denominators of 5, 4, and 10 is 20. This is a fractional equation which can be solved by multiplying both members of the equation by the LCD.

$$20\left(\frac{2x+7}{5} + \frac{3x-5}{4} + \frac{33}{10}\right) = (20)(0)$$

$$4(2x + 7) + 5(3x - 5) + (2 \cdot 33) = 0.$$

Distributing,

$$8x + 28 + 15x - 25 + 66 = 0$$
$$23x + 69 = 0$$
$$23x = -69$$
$$x = -3$$

Hence, $x = -3$ is the zero of the given function.

● **PROBLEM 8-10**

Let f be the linear function that is defined by the equation $f(x) = 3x + 2$. Find the equation that defines the inverse function f^{-1}.

SOLUTION:

To find the inverse function f^{-1}, the given equation must be solved for x in terms of y. Let $x = f^{-1}(y)$.

Solving the given equation for x:

$$y = 3x + 2, \text{ where } y = f(x).$$

Subtract 2 from both sides of this equation:

$$y - 2 = 3x + 2 - 2$$
$$y - 2 = 3x$$

Divide both sides of this equation by 3:

$$\frac{y - 2}{3} = \frac{3x}{3}$$

$$\frac{y - 2}{3} = x \text{ or}$$

$$x = \frac{y}{3} - \frac{2}{3}$$

Hence, the inverse function f^{-1} is given by:

$$x = f^{-1}(y) = \frac{y}{3} - \frac{2}{3} \text{ or}$$

$$x = f^{-1}(y) = \frac{1}{3}y - \frac{2}{3}$$

Of course, the letter that we use to denote a number in the domain of the inverse function is of no importance whatsoever, so this last equation can be rewritten

$$f^{-1}(u) = \frac{1}{3}u - \frac{2}{3}, \text{ or } f^{-1}(s) = \frac{1}{3}s - \frac{2}{3}$$

and it will still define the same function f^{-1}.

47

Show that the inverse of the function $y = x^2 + 4x - 5$ is not a function.

SOLUTION:

Given the function f such that no two of its ordered pairs have the same second element, the inverse function f^{-1} is the set of ordered pairs obtained from f by interchanging in each ordered pair the first and second elements. Thus, the inverse of the function

$$y = x^2 + 4x - 5 \text{ is } x = y^2 + 4y - 5.$$

The given function has more than one first component corresponding to a given second component. For example, if $y = 0$, then $x = -5$ or 1. If the elements $(-5, 0)$ and $(1, 0)$ are reversed, we have $(0, -5)$ and $(0, 1)$ as elements of the inverse. Since the first component 0 has more than one second component, the inverse is not a function (a function can have only one y value corresponding to each x value).

Let $f: R \to R$ and $g: R \to R$ be two functions, given by $f(x) = 2x + 5$ and $g(x) = 4x^2$, respectively for all x in R, where R is the set of real numbers. Find expressions for the compositions $(f \circ g)(x)$ and $(g \circ f)(x)$.

SOLUTION:

Consider functions $f: A \to B$ and $g: B \to C$ — that is where the co-domain of f is the domain of g. Then the function $g \circ f$ is defined as $g \circ f: A \to C$, where $(g \circ f)(x) = g(f(x))$ for all x in A, and it is called the coposition of f and g.

In another notation,

$g \circ f = \{(x, z) \text{ A} \cdot \text{C} \mid \text{for all } y \in B \text{ such that } (x, y) \in f \text{ and } (y, z) \in g\}$.

Therefore,

$$\begin{aligned}
(f \circ g)(x) &= f(g(x)) \\
&= f(4x^2) \\
&= 2[4x^2] + 5 \\
&= 8x^2 + 5 \text{ and}
\end{aligned}$$

$$\begin{aligned}
(g \circ f)(x) &= g(f(x)) \\
&= g(2x+5) \\
&= 4[2x + 5]^2 \\
&= 4(4x^2 + 20x + 25) \\
&= 16x^2 + 80x + 100
\end{aligned}$$

It's seen from the results that $f \circ g \neq g \circ f$. This is true in general, i.e., functional compositions are not commutative operations.

CHAPTER 9

LINEAR FUNCTIONS

● **PROBLEM 9-1**

Answer the following questions:
(a) What is a linear function?

(b) Give an example of a linear function and an example of a non-linear function.

(c) Give an example of a function of three variables.

SOLUTION:

(a) A straight line is formed by the graph of $y = ax + b$, where a and b are constants. Hence, $f(x) = ax + b$ is called a linear function.

(b) Linear function: $\qquad y = 6x + \dfrac{3}{2}$

Non-linear function: $\qquad y = 2x^2 + 3$

(c) $y = 3x^2 + 2y + z$

● **PROBLEM 9-2**

Solve the equation $\dfrac{3}{4}x + \dfrac{7}{8} + 1 = 0$.

SOLUTION:

There are several ways to proceed. First we observe that $\frac{3}{4}x + \frac{7}{8} + 1 = 0$ is

equivalent to $\frac{3}{4}x + \frac{7}{8} + \frac{8}{8} = 0$, where we have converted 1 into $\frac{8}{8}$. Now, combining fractions we obtain:

$$\frac{3}{4}x + \frac{15}{8} = 0.$$

Subtract $\frac{15}{8}$ from both sides:

$$\frac{3}{4}x = \frac{-15}{8}$$

Multiply both sides by $\frac{4}{3}$:

$$\left(\frac{4}{3}\right)\frac{3}{4}x = \left(\frac{4}{3}\right)\left(\frac{-15}{8}\right)$$

Cancel like terms in the numerator and denominator:

$$x = \frac{-5}{2}$$

A second method is to multiply both sides of the equation by the least common denominator, 8:

$$8\left(\frac{3}{4}x + \frac{7}{8} + 1\right) = 8(0)$$

Distribute. $\quad 8\left(\frac{3}{4}\right)x + 8\left(\frac{7}{8}\right) + 8 \bullet 1 = 0$

$$(2 \bullet 3)x + 7 + 8 = 0$$

$$6x + 15 = 0$$

Subtract 15 from both sides:

$$6x = -15$$

Divide both sides by 6:

$$x = \frac{-15}{6}$$

Cancel 3 from the numerator and denominator:

$$x = \frac{-5}{2}$$

Solve the equation $2(x + 3) = (3x + 5) - (x - 5)$.

SOLUTION:

We transform the given equation to an equivalent equation where we can easily recognize the solution set.

$$2(x + 3) = (3x + 5) - (x - 5)$$

Distribute. $2x + 6 = 3x + 5 - x + 5$

Combine terms. $2x + 6 = 2x + 10$

Subtract $2x$ from both sides. $6 = 10$

Since $6 = 10$ is not a true statement, there is no real number which will make the original equation true. The equation is inconsistent and the solution set is ø, the empty set.

Solve each equation (find the solution set), and check each solution.

(a) $4(6x + 5) - 3(x - 5) = 0$

(b) $8 + 3x = -4(x - 2)$

SOLUTION:

(a) $4(6x + 5) - 3(x - 5) = 0$

Distribute. $24x + 20 - 3x + 15 = 0$

Combine like terms. $21x + 35 = 0$

Add (-35) to both sides. $21x = -35$

Divide both sides by 21. $x = \dfrac{-35}{21} = \dfrac{-5}{3}$

Therefore, the solution set to this equation is $\left\{ \dfrac{-5}{3} \right\}$.

Check: Replace x by $\dfrac{-5}{3}$ in the equation.

$$4(6x + 5) - 3(x - 5) = 0$$

$$4\left[6\left(\frac{-5}{3}\right) + 5\right] - 3\left[\frac{-5}{3} - 5\right] = 0$$

$$4\left(-\frac{30}{3}+5\right)-3\left(\frac{-5}{3}-\frac{15}{3}\right)=0$$

$$4\left(-10+5\right)-3\left(\frac{-20}{3}\right)=0$$

$$4\left(-5\right)+20=0$$

$$-20+20=0$$

$$0=0$$

(b) $8 + 3x = -4\ (x - 2)$

Distribute. $8 + 3x = -4x + 8$

Add $4x$ to both sides. $8 + 7x = 8.$

$$7x = 0$$

$$x = 0$$

Therefore, the solution to this equation is $\{0\}$

● **PROBLEM 9-5**

Solve $A = \dfrac{h}{2}\left(b+B\right)$ for h.

SOLUTION:

Since the given equation is to be solved for h, obtain h on one side of the equation. Multiply both sides of the equation $A = \dfrac{h}{2}\left(b+B\right)$ by 2. Then, we have:

$$2\left(A\right)=2\left(\frac{h}{2}\left(b+B\right)\right)$$

Therefore: $2\left(A\right)=\dfrac{2h}{2}\left(b+B\right)$

$$2A = h(b+B) \tag{1}$$

Since it is desired to obtain h on one side of the equation, divide both sides of equation (1) by $(b + B)$.

$$\frac{2A}{\left(b+B\right)}=\frac{h\left(b+B\right)}{\left(b+B\right)}$$

Therefore: $\dfrac{2A}{\left(b+B\right)}=h$

Thus, the given equation, $A = \dfrac{h}{2}(b + B)$, is solved for h.

This is the form of the formula used to determine values of h for a set of trapezoids, if the area and lengths of the bases are known.

● **PROBLEM 9-6**

Find the solutions of the equation $\dfrac{4x - 7}{x - 2} = 3 + \dfrac{1}{x - 2}$.

SOLUTION:

Assume that there is a number x such that $\dfrac{4x - 7}{x - 2} = 3 + \dfrac{1}{x - 2}$.

In order to eliminate the fractions, multiply both sides of the equation by $x - 2$ to obtain

$$(x - 2)\frac{4x - 7}{x - 2} = \left(3 + \frac{1}{x - 2}\right)(x - 2)$$

Thus,
$$4x - 7 = 3(x - 2) + \frac{x - 2}{x - 2}$$
$$4x - 7 = 3(x - 2) + 1$$
$$4x - 7 = 3x - 6 + 1$$
$$4x - 7 = 3x - 5$$

Add $(-3x)$ to both sides. $4x - 7 + (-3x) = -5$
$$x - 7 = -5$$

Add 7 to both sides. $x = -5 + 7$
and hence $x = 2$.

We have shown that if x is a solution of the equation $\dfrac{4x - 7}{x - 2} = 3 + \dfrac{1}{x - 2}$, then $x = 2$. But if we substitute $x = 2$ in the right-hand member of the equation we

obtain $3 + \dfrac{1}{0}$

and we know that we cannot divide by zero. Hence, 2 is not a solution.

Before we analyze the process which led to the conclusion that 2 was a possible solution to our equation, let us see exactly why our equation has no solution. To do this, we note that

$$3 + \frac{1}{x - 2} = 3 \cdot \frac{x - 2}{x - 2} + \frac{1}{x - 2} = \frac{3(x - 2) + 1}{x - 2} = \frac{3x - 6 + 1}{x - 2} = \frac{3x - 5}{x - 2}$$

53

and hence, that the original equation is equivalent to

$$\frac{4x-7}{x-2} = \frac{3x-5}{x-2}$$

Now we know that two fractions, $\frac{a}{b}$ and $\frac{c}{d}$, are equal if and only if $ad = bc$. Thus (1) holds, providing that $x \neq 2$, if and only if

$$(x-2)(4x-7) = (x-2)(3x-5) \qquad (2)$$

holds. But, since $x \neq 2$, $x - 2 \neq 0$, and we can divide both sides of (2) by $x - 2$ and have

$$4x - 7 = 3x - 5$$

which gives $x = 2$, a contradiction. In other words, the only possible solution is a number which we knew in advance could not be a solution, and hence there are no solutions to our given equation.

Solve the equation $\dfrac{5}{x-1} + \dfrac{1}{4-3x} = \dfrac{3}{6x-8}$.

SOLUTION:

By factoring out a common factor of –2 from the denominator of the term on the right side of the given equation, the given equation becomes:

$$\frac{5}{x-1} + \frac{1}{4-3x} = \frac{3}{-2(-3x+4)} = \frac{3}{-2(4-3x)} = \frac{3}{2(4-3x)}$$

Hence,

$$\frac{5}{x-1} + \frac{1}{4-3x} = -\frac{3}{2(4-3x)}$$

Adding $\dfrac{3}{2(4-3x)}$ to both sides of this equation:

$$\frac{5}{x-1} + \frac{1}{4-3x} + \frac{3}{2(4-3x)} = 0. \qquad (1)$$

Now, in order to combine the fractions, the least common denominator (LCD) must be found. The LCD is found in the following way: list all the different factors of the denominators of the fractions. The exponent to be used for each factor in the LCD is the greatest value of the exponent for each factor in any denominator. Therefore, the LCD of the given fractions is:

$$2^1(x-1)^1 (4 - 3x)^1 = 2(x - 1)(4 - 3x)$$

Hence, equation (1) becomes:

$$\frac{(2)(4-3x)(5)}{(2)(4-3x)(x-1)}+\frac{(2)(x-1)(1)}{(2)(x-1)(4-3x)}+\frac{(x-1)(3)}{(x-1)(2)(4-3x)}=0 \qquad (2)$$

Simplifying equation (2):

$$\frac{10(4-3x)+2(x-1)+3(x-1)}{2(x-1)(4-3x)}=0$$

$$\frac{40-30x+2x-2+3x-3}{2(x-1)(4-3x)}=0$$

$$\frac{-25x+35}{2(x-1)(4-3x)}=0$$

Multiplying both sides of this equation by $2(x-1)(4-3x)$:

$$2\overline{(x-1)(4-3x)}\frac{-25x+35}{2(x-1)(4-3x)}=2(x-1)(4-3x)(0)$$

$$-25x+35=0$$

Adding $25x$ to both sides of this equation:

$$-25x+35+25x=0+25x$$

$$35=25x$$

Dividing both sides of this equation by 25:

$$\frac{35}{25}=\frac{25x}{25}$$

$$\frac{7}{5}=x$$

Therefore, the solution set to the equation $\dfrac{5}{x-1}+\dfrac{1}{4-3x}=\dfrac{3}{6x-8}$ is $\left\{\dfrac{7}{5}\right\}$.

● PROBLEM 9-8

Solve $\sqrt{4x+5}+2\sqrt{x-3}=17$.

SOLUTION:

Transpose: $\qquad\qquad \sqrt{4x+5}-17=-2\sqrt{x-3}$

Square: $\qquad 4x+5-34\sqrt{4x+5}+289=4(x-3)$

$$4x+5-34\sqrt{4x+5}+289 = 4x-12$$

Transpose: $\qquad -34\sqrt{4x+5} = 4x-12-4x-5-289$

Simplify: $\qquad -34\sqrt{4x+5} = -306$

$$\sqrt{4x+5} = 9$$

Square: $\qquad 4x+5 = 81$

Solve for x: $\qquad x = 19$

Check: $\qquad \sqrt{4(19)+5}+2\sqrt{(19)-3} \overset{?}{=} 17$

$$\sqrt{81}+2\sqrt{16} \overset{?}{=} 17$$

$$9+2(4) \overset{?}{=} 17$$

$$17 = 17$$

Sol: $x = 19$.

● **PROBLEM 9-9**

Solve the equation $\dfrac{\sqrt{x+1}+\sqrt{x-1}}{\sqrt{x+1}-\sqrt{x-1}} = \dfrac{4x-1}{2}$.

SOLUTION:

We can use the following law to rewrite the given proportion:

If $\dfrac{a}{b} = \dfrac{c}{d}$, then $\dfrac{a+b}{a-b} = \dfrac{c+d}{c-d}$.

Applying this law we have:

$$\frac{\sqrt{x+1}+\sqrt{x-1}+\left(\sqrt{x+1}-\sqrt{x-1}\right)}{\sqrt{x+1}+\sqrt{x-1}+\left(\sqrt{x+1}-\sqrt{x-1}\right)} = \frac{4x-1+(2)}{4x-1-(2)} \text{ or,}$$

$$\frac{2\sqrt{x+1}}{2\sqrt{x-1}} = \frac{4x+1}{4x-3}.$$

Eliminating $\dfrac{2}{2}$ we have $\dfrac{\sqrt{x+1}}{\sqrt{x-1}} = \dfrac{4x+1}{4x-3}$.

Squaring both sides of the equation gives us,

$$\left(\frac{\sqrt{x+1}}{\sqrt{x-1}}\right)^2 = \left(\frac{4x+1}{4x-3}\right)^2 \text{ or } \frac{\left(\sqrt{x+1}\right)^2}{\left(\sqrt{x-1}\right)^2} = \frac{(4x+1)^2}{(4x-3)^2}.$$

Finding the above squares we obtain

$$\frac{x+1}{x-1} = \frac{16x^2+8x+1}{16x^2-24x+9}.$$

We can again rewrite this new proportion as

$$\frac{x+1+(x-1)}{x+1-(x-1)} = \frac{16x^2+8x+1+\left(16x^2-24x+9\right)}{16x^2+8x+1-\left(16x^2-24x+9\right)} \text{ or}$$

$$\frac{2x}{2} = \frac{32x^2-16x+10}{32x-8};$$

therefore, $x = \dfrac{32x^2-16x+10}{32x-8} = \dfrac{2\left(16x^2-8x+5\right)}{2\left(16x-4\right)}$; thus, $x = \dfrac{16x^2-8x+5}{16x-4}$; and

multiplying both sides of this equation by $(16x - 4)$ we have,
$x(16x - 4) = 16x^2 - 8x + 5$ or $16x^2 - 4x = 16x^2 - 8x + 5$.

Now, combining similar terms we obtain
$16x^2 - 16x^2 - 4x + 8x = 5$ or $4x = 5$.

Therefore, $x = \dfrac{5}{4}$.

CHAPTER 10

SYSTEMS OF LINEAR EQUATIONS

● **PROBLEM 10-1**

Solve for x and y.

$$x + 2y = 8 \qquad (1)$$
$$3x + 4y = 20 \qquad (2)$$

SOLUTION:

Solve equation (1) for x in terms of y:

$$x = 8 - 2y \qquad (3)$$

Substitute $(8 - 2y)$ for x in (2):

$$3(8 - 2y) + 4y = 20 \qquad (4)$$

Solve (4) for y as follows:

Distribute. $\qquad 24 - 6y + 4y = 20$

Combine like terms and then subtract 24 from both sides:

$$24 - 2y = 20$$
$$24 - 24 - 2y = 20 - 24$$
$$-2y = -4 \qquad \text{Divide both sides by } -2:$$
$$y = 2$$

Substitute 2 for y in equation (1).

$$x + 2(2) = 8$$
$$x = 4$$

Thus, our solution is $x = 4$, $y = 2$.

Check: Substitute $x = 4$, $y = 2$ in equations (1) and (2):

$$4 + 2(2) = 8$$
$$8 = 8$$

$$3(4) + 4(2) = 20$$
$$20 = 20$$

● PROBLEM 10-2

Solve the equations $2x + 3y = 6$ and $y = -(2x/3) + 2$ simultaneously.

SOLUTION:

We have two equations in two unknowns,

$$2x + 3y = 6 \qquad\qquad (1)$$
$$y = -(2x/3) + 2 \qquad\qquad (2)$$

There are several methods of solution for this problem. Since equation (2) already gives us an expression for y, we use the method of substitution. Substituting $-(2x/3) + 2$ for y in the first equation:

$$2x + 3\left(-\frac{2x}{3} + 2\right) = 6$$

Distributing,
$$2x - 2x + 6 = 6$$
$$6 = 6$$

Apparently we have gotten nowhere! The result $6 = 6$ is true, but indicates no solution. Actually, our work shows that no matter what real number x is, if y is determined by the second equation, then the first equation will always be satisfied.

The reason for this peculiarity may be seen if we take a closer look at the equation $y = -(2x/3) + 2$. It is equivalent to $3y = -2x + 6$, or $2x + 3y = 6$.

In other words, the two equations are equivalent. Any pair of values of x and y which satisfies one satisfies the other.

It is hardly necessary to verify that in this case the graphs of the given equations are identical lines, and that there are an infinite number of simultaneous solutions for these equations

● PROBLEM 10-3

Solve algebraically:
$$\begin{cases} 4x + 2y = -1 & (1) \\ 5x - 3y = 7 & (2) \end{cases}$$

SOLUTION:

We arbitrarily choose to eliminate x first.

Multiply (1) by 5: $20x + 10y = -5$ (3)

Multiply (2) by 4: $20x - 12y = 28$ (4)

Subtract (3) – (4): $22y = -33$ (5)

Divide (5) by 22: $$y = -\frac{33}{22} = -\frac{3}{2}$$

To find x, substitute $y = -\dfrac{3}{2}$ in either of the original equations. If we use Equation (1), we obtain

$$4x + 2\,(-3/2) = -1$$
$$4x - 3 = -1$$
$$4x = 2, \quad x = \frac{1}{2}.$$

The solution $\left(\dfrac{1}{2}, -\dfrac{3}{2}\right)$ should be checked in both equations of the given system.

Replacing $\left(\dfrac{1}{2}, -\dfrac{3}{2}\right)$ in Equation (1):

$$4x + 2y = -1$$
$$4\left(\frac{1}{2}\right) + 2\left(-\frac{3}{2}\right) = -1$$
$$\frac{4}{2} - 3 = -1$$
$$2 - 3 = -1$$
$$-1 = -1$$

Replacing $\left(\dfrac{1}{2}, -\dfrac{3}{2}\right)$ in Equation (2):

$$5x - 3y = 7$$
$$5\left(\frac{1}{2}\right) - 3\left(-\frac{3}{2}\right) = 7$$
$$\frac{5}{2} + \frac{9}{2} = 7$$
$$\frac{14}{2} = 7$$
$$7 = 7$$

(Instead of eliminating x from the two given equations, we could have eliminated y by multiplying Equation (1) by 3, multiplying Equation (2) by 2, and then adding the two derived equations.)

● PROBLEM 10-4

Solve the system of equations,

$$2x - y - 4z = 3 \tag{1}$$
$$-x + 3y + z = -10 \tag{2}$$
$$3x + 2y - 2z = -2 \tag{3}$$

SOLUTION:

To solve a system of three equations in three unknowns, we first reduce it to a system of two equations in two unknowns, a process which can often be done many ways. Although various other algebraic manipulations may be used to arrive at the same result, we will employ the following method: Multiplying equation (1) by (–1) we obtain,

$$-2x + y + 4z = -3 \tag{4}$$

Adding equations (4), (2), and (3) we obtain,

$$
\begin{aligned}
-2x + \ \ y + 4z &= -3 \\
-x + 3y + \ \ z &= -10 \\
\underline{3x + 2y - 2z} &= \underline{-2} \\
6y + 3z &= -15
\end{aligned}
\tag{5}
$$

Multiplying equation (2) by 3 we obtain,

$$-3x + 9y + 3z = -30 \tag{6}$$

Adding equations (6) and (3) we obtain,

$$
\begin{aligned}
-3x + 9y + 3z &= -30 \\
\underline{3x + 2y - 2z} &= \underline{-2} \\
11y + \ \ z &= -32
\end{aligned}
\tag{7}
$$

Multiplying equation (7) by (–3) we obtain,

$$-33y - 3z = 96 \tag{8}$$

Adding equations (8) and (5) we obtain,

$$
\begin{aligned}
-33y - 3z &= 96 \\
\underline{6y + 3z} &= \underline{-15} \\
-27y \quad\ \ &= 81 \\
y \quad\ \ &= -3
\end{aligned}
$$

Solving for z, we replace, y by (–3) in equation (5).

$$
\begin{aligned}
6y + 3z &= -15 \\
6(-3) + 3z &= -15 \\
-18 + 3z &= -15 \\
3z &= 3 \\
z &= 1
\end{aligned}
$$

Solving for x, we replace y by (-3) and z by 1 in equation (1).

$$2x - y - 4z = 3$$
$$2x - (-3) - 4(1) = 3$$
$$2x + 3 - 4 = 3$$
$$2x - 1 = 3$$
$$2x = 4$$
$$x = 2$$

Thus, the solution to this system is $x = 2$, $y = -3$, and $z = 1$.

Check: Replace x, y, and z by 2, -3, and 1 in each equation.

$$2x - y - 4z = 3 \qquad (1)$$
$$2(2) - (-3) - 4(1) = 3$$
$$4 + 3 - 4 = 3$$
$$3 = 3$$

$$-x + 3y + z = -10 \qquad (2)$$
$$-(2) + 3(-3) + 1 = -10$$
$$-2 - 9 + 1 = -10$$
$$-10 = -10$$

$$3x + 2y - 2z = -2 \qquad (3)$$
$$3(2) + 2(-3) - 2(1) = -2$$
$$6 - 6 - 2 = -2$$
$$-2 = -2$$

● **PROBLEM 10-5**

Find the solution set for the system:
$$3x + 4y - z = -2$$
$$2x - 3y + z = 4$$
$$x - 6y + 2z = 5$$

SOLUTION:

Adding the first and second equations, we obtain another equation without a term involving z:

$$3x + 4y - z = -2$$
$$\underline{2x - 3y + z = 4}$$
$$5x + y = 2$$

Similarly, after multiplying through by -2 in the second equation, we can use this new equation and the third one to obtain another equation without a term involving z:

$$-4x + 6y - 2z = -8$$
$$\underline{x - 6y + 2z = 5}$$
$$-3x = -3$$

62

Our problem has been somewhat simplified in that not only have we obtained an equation without a term involving z, but we have obtained one without a y term.

The solution set of $-3x = -3$ is $\{1\}$. Upon substituting this into the equation, $5x + y = 2$, we find that $y = -3$. Finally, upon substituting these values for x and y in either of the three equations of the system, we can obtain a value for z. If we use the first equation, $3x + 4y - z = -2$, we find that $z = -7$. Hence, the solution set for this system is $\{(1, -3, -7)\}$.

● **PROBLEM 10-6**

Two airfields A and B are 400 miles apart, and B is due east of A. A plane flew from A to B in 2 hours and then returned to A in $2\frac{1}{2}$ hours. If the wind blew with a constant velocity from the west during the entire trip, find the speed of the plane in still air and the speed of the wind.

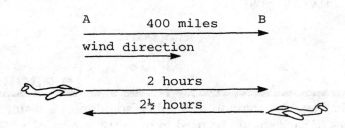

SOLUTION:

The essential point in solving this problem is that the wind helps the plane in flying from A to B and hinders it in flying from B to A. We therefore have the basis for two equations that involve the speed of the plane, the speed of the wind, and the time for each trip.

We let x = speed of plane in still air, in miles per hour

            y = speed of wind, in miles per hour

Then, since the wind blew constantly from the west,

    $x + y$ = speed of plane from A to B (wind helping)

    $x - y$ = speed of plane from B to A (wind hindering)

The distance traveled each way was 400 miles, and so we have the following equations based on the formula distance/rate = time.

$$\frac{400}{x + y} = 2 = \text{time required for eastward trip} \tag{1}$$

$$\frac{400}{x-y} = 2\frac{1}{2} = \text{time required for westward trip} \qquad (2)$$

We solve these equations simultaneously for x and y.

multiplying (1) by $x + y$	$400 = 2x + 2y$	(3)
multiplying (2) by $2(x - y)$	$800 = 5x - 5y$	(4)
multiplying (3) by 5	$2,000 = 10x + 10y$	(5)
multiplying (4) by 2	$1,600 = 10x - 10y$	(6)
adding equations (5) and (6)	$3,600 = 20x$	
solving for x	$180 = x$	
replacing x by 180 in (3)	$400 = 360 + 2y$	
	$2y = 40$	
	$y = 20$	

Therefore the solution set of equations (1) and (2) is {(180, 20)}, and it follows that the speed of the plane in still air is 180 miles per hour and the speed of the wind is 20 miles per hour.

Check:

$$\frac{400}{180+20} = \frac{400}{200} = 2 \qquad \text{from (1)}$$

$$\frac{400}{180-20} = \frac{400}{160} = \frac{5}{2} = 2\frac{1}{2} \qquad \text{from (2)}$$

● PROBLEM 10-7

A chemist has an 18% solution and a 45% solution of a disinfectant. How many ounces of each should be used to make 12 ounces of a 36% solution?

SOLUTION:

Let x = number of ounces from the 18% solution and
   y = number of ounces from the 45% solution

$$x + y = 12 \qquad (1)$$
$$.18x + .45y = .36 (12) = 4.32 \qquad (2)$$

Note that .18 of the first solution is pure disinfectant and that .45 of the second solution is pure disinfectant. When the proper quantities are drawn from each mixture the result is 12 ounces of mixture which is .36 pure disinfectant, i.e., the resulting mixture contains 4.32 ounces of pure disinfectant. When the equations are solved, it is found that $x = 4$ and $y = 8$.

Find two numbers such that twice the first added to the second equals 19, and three times the first is 21 more than the second.

SOLUTION:

Let x = the first number and y = the second number. The equations are

$2x + y = 19$ (twice the first added to the second equals 19)

$3x = y + 21$ (three times the first is 21 more than the second)

To solve this system

$$2x + y = 19$$
$$3x = y + 21$$

Obtain all the variables on one side of the equations.

$$2x + y = 19 \tag{1}$$
$$3x - y = 21 \tag{2}$$

Add (2) to (1)

$$2x + y = 19 \tag{1}$$
$$\underline{3x - y = 21} \tag{2}$$
$$5x \quad = 40 \tag{3}$$

Divide by 5 to obtain x.

$$x = 8$$

Substitute $x = 8$ into (1) or (2).

$$2x + y = 19 \tag{1}$$
$$2(8) + y = 19$$
$$16 + y = 19$$
$$y = 3$$

The solution of this system is

$x = 8$, the first number

$y = 3$, the second number

To check the solution, show that the two numbers satisfy the conditions of the problem.

Twice the first number is $2(8) = 16$. Add this result to the second is $16 + 3 = 19$. Thus, $19 = 19$. Then three times the first number is $3(8) = 24$ which is 21 more than 3. That is, $24 = 21 + 3$; $24 = 24$.

A man invested $7,800, part at 6% and part at 4%. If the income of the 4% investment exceeded the investment at 6% by $92, how much was invested at each rate?

SOLUTION:

Let x = Amount invested at 4%

And y = Amount invested at 6%

$x + y = 7,800$ (1)

$.04x = .06y + 92$ (2)

When the equations are solved it is found that x = \$5,600, i.e., the amount invested at 4%, and y = \$2,200, i.e., the amount invested at 6%.

CHAPTER 11

QUADRATIC EQUATIONS AND SYSTEMS OF EQUATIONS INVOLVING QUADRATICS

● PROBLEM 11-1

Solve the equation $(3x - 7)(x + 2) = 0$.

SOLUTION:

When a given product of two numbers that are equal to zero, $ab = 0$, either a must equal zero or b must equal zero (or both equal zero). So if $(3x - 7)(x + 2) = 0$, then $(3x - 7) = 0$ or $(x + 2) = 0$.

$3x - 7 = 0$	$x + 2 = 0$
Add 7 to both sides.	Subtract 2 from both sides.
$3x = 7$	
Divide both sides by 3.	
$x = \dfrac{7}{3}$	$x = -2$

Hence, $x = \dfrac{7}{3}$ or $x = -2$, and our solution set is $\left\{\dfrac{7}{3}, -2\right\}$.

● PROBLEM 11-2

Solve the equation $x^2 + 8x + 15 = 0$.

SOLUTION:

Since $(x + a)(x + b) = x^2 + bx + ax + ab = x^2 + (a + b) x + ab$, we may factor the given equation, $0 = x^2 + 8x + 15$, replacing $a + b$ by 8 and ab by 15.

Thus,

$$a + b = 8, \text{ and}$$
$$ab = 15$$

We want the two numbers a and b whose sum is 8 and whose product is 15. We check all pairs of numbers whose product is 15:

(a) $1 \cdot 15 = 15$; thus $a = 1$, $b = 15$ and $ab = 15$.

   $1 + 15 = 16$; therefore, we reject these values because $a + b \neq 8$.

(b) $3 \cdot 5 = 15$; thus $a = 3$, $b = 5$, and $ab = 15$.

   $3 + 5 = 8$. Therefore, $a + b = 8$, and we accept these values.

Hence, $x^2 + 8x + 15 = 0$ is equivalent to

$$0 = x^2 + (3 + 5)x + 3 \cdot 5 = (x + 3)(x + 5)$$

Hence, $x + 5 = 0$ or $x + 3 = 0$, since the product of these two numbers is zero, one of the numbers must be zero. Hence, $x = -5$, or $x = -3$, and the solution set is $x = \{-5, -3\}$.

The student should note that $x = -5$ or $x = -3$. We are certainly not making the statement, that $x = -5$, and $x = -3$. Also, the student should check that both these numbers do actually satisfy the given equations and hence are solutions.

Check: Replacing x by (-5) in the original equation:

$$x^2 + 8x + 15 = 0$$
$$(-5)^2 + 8(-5) + 15 = 0$$
$$25 - 40 + 15 = 0$$
$$-15 + 15 = 0$$
$$0 = 0$$

Replacing x by (-3) in the original equation:

$$x^2 + 8x + 15 = 0$$
$$(-3)^2 + 8(-3) + 15 = 0$$
$$9 - 24 + 15 = 0$$
$$-15 + 15 = 0$$
$$0 = 0$$

● **PROBLEM 11-3**

Solve $\dfrac{x+1}{x^2-5x+6} + \dfrac{x+2}{x^2-7x+12} = \dfrac{6}{x^2-6x+8}$.

SOLUTION:

Factor the denominator of each fraction to obtain

$$\frac{x+1}{(x-2)(x-3)} + \frac{x+2}{(x-3)(x-4)} = \frac{6}{(x-2)(x-4)}$$

Obtain the least common denominator, LCD, by multiplying the denominators of each fraction together and using the highest power of each factor only once, that is,

$$(x-2)(x-3)(x-3)(x-4)(x-2)(x-4)$$

LCD = $\quad (x-2)(x-3)(x-4)$

Multiply both sides of the equation by the LCD to remove all fractions and obtain,

$$(x-2)(x-3)(x-4)\left(\frac{x+1}{(x-2)(x-3)} + \frac{x+2}{(x-3)(x-4)}\right)$$

$$= \left(\frac{6}{(x-2)(x-4)}\right)(x-2)(x-3)(x-4)$$

$$(x+1)(x-4) + (x+2)(x-2) = 6(x-3)$$
$$(x+1)(x-4) + (x+2)(x-2) = 6x - 18$$
$$(x^2 - 3x - 4) + (x^2 - 4) = 6x - 18$$
$$2x^2 - 3x - 8 = 6x - 18$$
$$2x^2 - 9x + 10 = 0$$
$$(2x - 5)(x - 2) = 0$$

$$
\begin{array}{c|c}
2x - 5 = 0 & x - 2 = 0 \\
2x = 5 & x = 2 \\
x = \dfrac{5}{2} &
\end{array}
$$

Substituting $x = 2$ into the original equation shows that $x = 2$ is an extraneous root, since it is not an admissible value for the original equation. (It makes two of the denominators, $(x-2)(x-3)$ and $(x-2)(x-4)$, equal to zero.) $x = \frac{5}{2}$ is an admissible value of x for the original equation and is a solution if it will satisfy the original equation.

Check: $x = \dfrac{5}{2}$

$$\frac{\frac{7}{2}}{\left(\frac{1}{2}\right)\left(-\frac{1}{2}\right)} + \frac{\frac{9}{2}}{\left(-\frac{1}{2}\right)\left(-\frac{3}{2}\right)} = \frac{6}{\left(\frac{1}{2}\right)\left(-\frac{3}{2}\right)}$$

69

$$\frac{14}{-1} + \frac{18}{3} = \frac{24}{-3}$$

$$-14 + 6 = -8$$

$$-8 = -8$$

Solve the equation $\sqrt{x^2 - 3x} = 2x - 6$.

SOLUTION:

Remove the radical by squaring both sides of the equation, and obtain,

$$\left(\sqrt{x^2 - 3x}\right)^2 = \left(2x - 6\right)^2 \text{ or}$$

$$x^2 - 3x = 4x^2 - 24x + 36$$

Writing in standard form, move every term to one side of the equation.

$$3x^2 - 21x + 36 = 0$$

Dividing all terms by 3, and factoring,

$$\frac{3x^2}{3} - \frac{21x}{3} + \frac{36}{3} = \frac{0}{3}$$

$$x^2 - 7x + 12 = 0$$

$$(x - 3)(x - 4) = 0$$

The roots are: $x = 3$, $x = 4$.

Check: Substituting $x = 3$ in the original equation

$$\sqrt{9 - 9} = 6 - 6$$

$$0 = 0$$

Substituting $x = 4$ in the original equation

$$\sqrt{4} = 8 - 6$$

$$2 = 2$$

Observe that both $x = 3$ and $x = 4$ satisfy the original equation, and there are no extraneous roots.

Solve the equation $2x^{\frac{2}{5}} + 5x^{\frac{1}{5}} - 3 = 0$.

SOLUTION:

This equation may be solved as a quadratic equation if we let $P(x) = y = x^{\frac{1}{5}}$.

Then $x^{\frac{2}{5}} = y^2$ and, by substituting these expressions in the equation to be solved, we have $2y^2 + 5y - 3 = 0$. We can solve this equation for y by factoring.

$$2y^2 + 5y - 3 = 0$$
$$(2y - 1)(y + 3) = 0$$
$$(2y - 1) = 0 \text{ or } (y + 3) = 0$$

Therefore, $y = \frac{1}{2}$ or $y = -3$

Now recall that $y = x^{\frac{1}{5}}$. Hence, $x^{\frac{1}{5}} = \frac{1}{2}$ or $x^{\frac{1}{5}} = -3$. Hence, by raising both sides of each of these equations to the fifth power, we have $x = \frac{1}{32}$ or $x = -243$. Therefore the solution set is $\{\frac{1}{32}, -243\}$.

Complete the square in both x and y in $x^2 + 2x + y^2 - 3y$.

SOLUTION:

To complete the square in x, take half the coefficient of x and square it. Add and subtract this value from the given expression. Therefore,

$$\left[\frac{1}{2}(2)\right]^2 = [1]^2 = 1, \text{ and } x^2 + 2x + y^2 - 3y = x^2 + 2x + y^2 - 3y + 1 - 1.$$

Commuting,
$$x^2 + 2x + y^2 - 3y = x^2 + 2x + 1 + y^2 - 3y - 1$$
$$= (x+1)^2 + y^2 - 3y - 1. \qquad (1)$$

Now, take half the coefficient of y and square it. Add and subtract this value from equation (1).

$$\left[\frac{1}{2}(-3)\right]^2 = \left[\frac{-3}{2}\right]^2 = \frac{9}{4} \text{ and}$$

$$x^2 + 2x + y^2 - 3y = (x + 1)^2 + y^2 - 3y - 1 + \frac{9}{4} - \frac{9}{4}.$$

Commuting,

$$x^2 + 2x + y^2 - 3y = (x + 1)^2 + y^2 - 3y + \frac{9}{4} - 1 - \frac{9}{4}$$

$$= (x+1)^2 + \left(y - \frac{3}{2}\right)^2 - 1 - \frac{9}{4} = (x+1)^2 + \left(y - \frac{3}{2}\right)^2 - \frac{4}{4} - \frac{9}{4}. \text{ Hence,}$$

$$x^2 + 2x + y^2 - 3y = (x+1)^2 + \left(y - \frac{3}{2}\right)^2 - \frac{13}{4}$$

● PROBLEM 11-7

Solve the equation $4x^2 = 8x - 7$ by means of the quadratic formula.

SOLUTION:

The quadratic formula, $x = \dfrac{-b \pm \sqrt{b^2 - 4ac}}{2a}$, applies to equations of the form $ax^2 + bx + c = 0$. If we add $(-8x + 7)$ to both sides of our given equation we obtain $4x^2 - 8x + 7 = 0$ which is an equation in the form $ax^2 + bx + c = 0$ with $a = 4$, $b = -8$, and $c = 7$. Substituting these values into the quadratic formula we obtain

$$x = \frac{-(-8) \pm \sqrt{(-8)^2 - 4(4)(7)}}{2(4)}$$

$$= \frac{8 \pm \sqrt{64 - 112}}{8}$$

$$= \frac{8 \pm \sqrt{-48}}{8}$$

Since $\sqrt{ab} = \sqrt{a} \cdot \sqrt{b}, \sqrt{-48} = \sqrt{-1 \cdot 48} = \sqrt{-1}\sqrt{48}$. Recall $\sqrt{-1} = i$.

Thus, $\sqrt{-48} = \sqrt{-1}\sqrt{48} = i\sqrt{48}$ and $x = \dfrac{8 \pm i\sqrt{48}}{8}$.

We can further break down this radical by noting

$$\sqrt{48} = \sqrt{16 \cdot 3} = \sqrt{16} \cdot \sqrt{3} = 4\sqrt{3}$$

Thus, $\qquad\qquad x = \dfrac{8 \pm 4i\sqrt{3}}{8}$

$$x = \dfrac{8}{8} \pm \dfrac{4i\sqrt{3}}{8}$$

$$x = 1 \pm \dfrac{i\sqrt{3}}{2}$$

Hence, the solution set is $\left\{ 1 + \dfrac{i\sqrt{3}}{2}, 1 - \dfrac{i\sqrt{3}}{2} \right\}$.

We can verify that these two complex numbers are the roots of the given equation by means of the following check: we replace x by $1 + \dfrac{i\sqrt{3}}{2}$ in the original equation:

$$4\left(1 + \dfrac{i\sqrt{3}}{2}\right)^2 = 8\left(1 + \dfrac{i\sqrt{3}}{2}\right) - 7$$

$$4\left[1 + \dfrac{2i\sqrt{3}}{2} + \left(\dfrac{i\sqrt{3}}{2}\right)^2\right] = 8 + 8\dfrac{i\sqrt{3}}{2} - 7$$

$$4\left[1 + \dfrac{2i\sqrt{3}}{2} + i^2\left(\dfrac{\sqrt{3}}{2}\right)^2\right] = 1 + 4i\sqrt{3}$$

$$4\left[1 + i\sqrt{3} - 1\left(\dfrac{\sqrt{3}}{2}\dfrac{\sqrt{3}}{2}\right)\right] = 1 + 4i\sqrt{3}$$

$$4\left[1 + i\sqrt{3} - \dfrac{3}{4}\right] = 1 + 4i\sqrt{3}$$

$$4 + 4i\sqrt{3} - 3 = 1 + 4i\sqrt{3}$$

$$1 + 4i\sqrt{3} = 1 + 4i\sqrt{3}$$

Now we replace x by $1 - \dfrac{i\sqrt{3}}{2}$ in the original equation:

$$4\left(1 - \frac{i\sqrt{3}}{2}\right)^2 = 8\left(1 - \frac{i\sqrt{3}}{2}\right) - 7$$

$$4\left[1 - \frac{2i\sqrt{3}}{2} + \left(\frac{i\sqrt{3}}{2}\right)^2\right] = 8 - \frac{8i\sqrt{3}}{2} - 7$$

$$4\left[1 - i\sqrt{3} + i^2\left(\frac{\sqrt{3}}{2}\right)^2\right] = 1 - 4i\sqrt{3}$$

$$4\left[1 - i\sqrt{3} - 1\left(\frac{\sqrt{3}}{2}\right)^2\right] = 1 - 4i\sqrt{3}$$

$$4\left[1 - i\sqrt{3} - \frac{3}{4}\right] = 1 - 4i\sqrt{3}$$

$$4 - 4i\sqrt{3} - 3 = 1 - 4i\sqrt{3}$$

$$1 - 4i\sqrt{3} = 1 - 4i\sqrt{3}$$

● PROBLEM 11-8

Show that the roots of the quadratic equation $x^2 - x - 3 = 0$ are

$x_1 = \dfrac{1 + \sqrt{13}}{2}$ and $x_2 = \dfrac{1 - \sqrt{13}}{2}$.

SOLUTION:

We use the quadratic formula derived from the quadratic equation, $ax^2 + bc + c = 0$:

$$x = \frac{-b \pm \sqrt{b^2 - 4ac}}{2a}$$

For $x^2 - x - 3 = 0$, $a = 1$, $b = -1$, and $c = -3$. Replacing these values in the quadratic formula,

$$x = \frac{-(-1) \pm \sqrt{(-1)^2 - 4(1)(-3)}}{2(1)}$$

74

$$x = \frac{1 \pm \sqrt{13}}{2}$$

$$x_1 = \frac{1 + \sqrt{13}}{2} \qquad x_2 = \frac{1 - \sqrt{13}}{2}$$

According to the Factor Theorem: If r is a root of the equation $f(x) = 0$, i.e., if $f(r) = 0$, then $(x - r)$ is a factor of $f(x)$.

x_1 and x_2 are roots of $x^2 - x - 3 = 0$. Thus,

$$\left(x - \frac{1 + \sqrt{13}}{2}\right)\left(x - \frac{1 - \sqrt{13}}{2}\right)$$

are factors, and $x^2 - x - 3 = \left(x - \frac{1 + \sqrt{13}}{2}\right)\left(x - \frac{1 - \sqrt{13}}{2}\right)$

If the equation $x^2 + 2(k + 2)x + 9k = 0$ has equal roots, find k.

SOLUTION:

The given equation is a quadratic equation of the form $ax^2 + bx + c = 0$. In the given equation, $a = 1$, $b = 2(k + 2)$, and $c = 9k$. A quadratic equation has equal roots if the discriminant, $b^2 - 4ac$, is zero.

$$b^2 - 4ac = [2(k + 2)]^2 - 4(1)(9k) = 0$$
$$4(k + 2)^2 - 36k = 0$$
$$4(k + 2)(k + 2) - 36k = 0$$
$$4(k^2 + 4k + 4) - 36k = 0$$

Distributing, $\quad 4k^2 + 16k + 16 - 36k = 0$
$$4k^2 - 20k + 16 = 0$$

Divide both sides of this equation by 4. $\quad \dfrac{4k^2 - 20k + 16}{4} = \dfrac{0}{4}$ or

$$k^2 - 5k + 4 = 0$$

Factoring the left side of this equation into a product of two polynomials:
$$(k - 4)(k - 1) = 0.$$

When the product $ab = 0$, where a and b are any two numbers, either $a = 0$ or $b = 0$. Hence, in the case of this problem, either $k - 4 = 0$ or $k - 1 = 0$. Therefore, $k = 4$ or $k = 1$.

Compute the value of the discriminant and then determine the nature of the roots of each of the following four equations.

(a) $4x^2 - 12x + 9 = 0$ (c) $5x^2 + 2x - 9 = 0$
(b) $3x^2 - 7x - 6 = 0$ (d) $x^2 + 3x + 5 = 0$

SOLUTION:

The discriminant, the term of the quadratic formula which appears under the radical, is $b^2 - 4ac$. It can be used to determine the nature of the roots of equations in the form $ax^2 + bx + c = 0$. Assuming a, b, and c are real numbers, then,

(1) if $b^2 - 4ac > 0$, the roots are real and unequal
(2) if $b^2 - 4ac = 0$, the roots are real and equal
(3) if $b^2 - 4ac < 0$, the roots are imaginary

Assuming a, b, and c are real and rational numbers then,

(1) if $b^2 - 4ac$ is a perfect square $\neq 0$, the roots are real, rational, and unequal,
(2) if $b^2 - 4ac = 0$, the roots are real, rational, and equal,
(3) if $b^2 - 4ac > 0$, but not a perfect square, the roots are real, irrational, and unequal,
(4) if $b^2 - 4ac < 0$, the roots are imaginary.

(a) $4x^2 - 12x + 9 = 0$
Here a, b, and c are rational numbers, $a = 4$, $b = -12$ and $c = 9$.
Therefore, $b^2 - 4ac = (-12)^2 - 4(4)(9) = 144 - 144 = 0$
Since the discriminant is 0, the roots are rational and equal.

(b) $3x^2 - 7x - 6 = 0$
Here a, b, and c are rational numbers, $a = 3$, $b = -7$, and $c = -6$.
Therefore, $b^2 - 4ac = (-7)^2 - 4(3)(-6) = 49 + 72 = 121 = 11^2$
Since the discriminant is a perfect square, the roots are rational and unequal.

(c) $5x^2 + 2x - 9 = 0$
Here a, b, and c are rational numbers, $a = 5$, $b = 2$, and $c = -9$.
Therefore, $b^2 - 4ac = 2^2 - 4(5)(-9) = 4 + 180 = 184$
Since the discriminant is greater than zero, but not a perfect square, the roots are irrational and unequal.

(d) $x^2 + 3x + 5 = 0$
Here a, b, and c are rational numbers, $a = 1$, $b = 3$, and $c = 5$.
Therefore, $b^2 - 4ac = 3^2 - 4(1)(5) = 9 - 20 = -11$
Since the discriminant is negative the roots are imaginary.

Obtain the solution set.

$$x^2 + 4xy - 7x = 12 \qquad (1)$$

$$3x^2 - 4xy + 4x = 15 \qquad (2)$$

SOLUTION:

Since the sum of the xy terms in the left members of equations (1) and (2) is zero, we proceed as follows: add equations (1) and (2).

$$4x^2 - 3x = 27$$
$$4x^2 - 3x - 27 = 0$$

Equations in the form $ax^2 + bx + c = 0$ can be solved using the quadratic formula, $x = \dfrac{-b \pm \sqrt{b^2 - 4ac}}{2a}$. In our case, $a = 4$, $b = -3$, and $c = -27$; thus,

$$x = \frac{-(-3) \pm \sqrt{(-3)^2 - 4(4)(-27)}}{2(4)}$$

$$x = \frac{3 \pm \sqrt{9 + 432}}{8} = \frac{3 \pm \sqrt{441}}{8} = \frac{3 \pm 21}{8}$$

$$x = \frac{3 + 21}{8} = \frac{24}{8} = 3 \text{ or } x = \frac{3 - 21}{8} = \frac{-18}{8} = -\frac{9}{4}$$

Thus, $x = 3, -\dfrac{9}{4}$.

We find the second numbers in the solution pairs as follows: replace x by 3 in equation (1).

$$x^2 + 4xy - 7x = 12$$
$$3^2 + 4(3)y - 7(3) = 12$$
$$9 + 12y - 21 = 12$$
$$12y - 12 = 12$$
$$12y = 24$$
$$y = 2$$

Hence, one simultaneous solution pair is (3, 2). Then, replace x by $-\dfrac{9}{4}$ in equation (1).

$$x^2 + 4xy - 7x = 12$$

$$\left(-\frac{9}{4}\right)^2 + 4\left(-\frac{9}{4}\right)y - 7\left(-\frac{9}{4}\right) = 12$$

$$\frac{81}{16} - 9y + \frac{63}{4} = 12$$

Multiply both sides by 16.

$$81 - 144y + 252 = 192$$
$$-144y + 333 = 192$$
$$-144y = -141$$

$$y = \frac{-141}{-144} = \frac{47}{48}$$

Therefore a second simultaneous solution pair is $\left(-\frac{9}{4}, \frac{47}{48}\right)$, and the simul-

taneous solution set is $\left\{(3, 2), \left(-\frac{9}{4}, \frac{47}{48}\right)\right\}$

Check: Using (3, 2), we have from equation (1):

$$(3)^2 + 4(3)(2) - 7(3) \stackrel{?}{=} 12$$
$$9 + 24 - 21 \stackrel{?}{=} 12$$
$$33 - 21 \stackrel{?}{=} 12$$
$$12 = 12$$

From equation (2):

$$3(3)^2 - 4(3)(2) + 4(3) \stackrel{?}{=} 15$$
$$27 - 24 + 12 \stackrel{?}{=} 15$$
$$3 + 12 \stackrel{?}{=} 15$$
$$15 = 15$$

Using $\left(-\frac{9}{4}, \frac{47}{48}\right)$ we obtain from equation (1):

$$\left(-\frac{9}{4}\right)^2 + 4\left(-\frac{9}{4}\right)\left(\frac{47}{48}\right) - 7\left(-\frac{9}{4}\right) = \frac{81}{16} - \frac{141}{16} + \frac{63}{4} = \frac{81 - 141 + 252}{16} = \frac{192}{16} = 12$$

From equation (2):

$$3\left(-\frac{9}{4}\right)^2 - 4\left(-\frac{9}{4}\right)\left(\frac{47}{48}\right) + 4\left(-\frac{9}{4}\right) = \frac{243}{16} + \frac{141}{16} - 9 = \frac{243 + 141 - 144}{16} = \frac{240}{16} = 15$$

Thus, the two pairs of solutions obtained are valid.

Solve. $x + y + z = 13$ (1)

              $x^2 + y^2 + z^2 = 65$ (2)

              $xy = 10$ (3)

SOLUTION:

We note that the product of two binomials is

$(x + y)^2 = (x + y)(x + y) = x^2 + xy + xy + y^2 = x^2 + 2xy + y^2$

Therefore, if we were just to add (2) and (3) we would be missing an xy term. Thus, multiply (3) by 2.

$$2xy = 20$$

Add this to (2).

$$x^2 + y^2 + z^2 = 65$$
$$+ \quad\quad 2xy = 20$$
$$\overline{x^2 + 2xy + y^2 + z^2 = 85}$$
$$(x + y)^2 + z^2 = 85$$

Put u for $x + y$; then this equation becomes

$$u^2 + z^2 = 85$$

Also from (1), $u + z = 13$

Now to solve this system of one linear equation and one quadratic, we express one of the variables in the linear equation in terms of the other and substitute this result into the quadratic equation.

$$u^2 + z^2 = 85 \quad\quad\quad (4)$$
$$u + z = 13 \quad\quad\quad (5)$$

Solving (5) for z by subtracting u from both sides,

$$z = 13 - u \quad\quad\quad (6)$$

Substituting this expression for z into (4),

$$u^2 + (13 - u)^2 = 85$$
$$u^2 + 169 - 26u + u^2 = 85$$
$$2u^2 - 26u + 169 = 85$$

Subtracting 85 from both sides,

$$2u^2 - 26u + 169 - 85 = 0$$
$$2u^2 - 26u + 84 = 0$$

Dividing by 2, $u^2 - 13u + 42 = 0$

Factor. $(u - 6)(u - 7) = 0$

Whenever the product of two factors is 0, then either one or the other must equal zero. Then, $u - 6 = 0$ or $u - 7 = 0$.

Solve for u, $u = 6$ or $u = 7$.

Substituting these values of u into equation (6) to find the corresponding z values

$$u = 6 \qquad\qquad\qquad u = 7$$

$$(6) \qquad z = 13 - u \qquad (6) \qquad z = 13 - u$$

$$z = 13 - 6 \qquad\qquad z = 13 - 7$$

$$z = 7 \qquad\qquad\qquad z = 6$$

Hence, we obtain $u = 7$ or 6; $z = 6$ or 7. Given that $z = 7$ or $z = 6$, substituting this into equation (1):

$$\text{for } z = 7 \qquad\qquad \text{for } z = 6$$

$$x + y + 7 = 13 \text{ or} \qquad x + y + 6 = 13$$

therefore, $\qquad\quad x + y = 6 \quad$ or $\qquad\quad x + y = 7$

Thus, we have

$$\left.\begin{array}{c} x + y = 7 \\ xy = 10 \end{array}\right\} \quad \text{and} \quad \left.\begin{array}{c} x + y = 6 \\ xy = 10 \end{array}\right\}$$

$$\text{for } z = 6 \qquad\qquad\qquad \text{for } z = 7$$

$$\left.\begin{array}{c} x + y = 7 \\ xy = 10 \end{array}\right\} \quad \text{and} \quad \left.\begin{array}{c} x + y = 6 \\ xy = 10 \end{array}\right\}$$

Solve for y or x. We choose to solve for x.

$$xy = 10$$

$$x = \frac{10}{y} \tag{7}$$

Substituting this expression into $x + y = 7$ or $x + y = 6$:

$$\left(\frac{10}{y}\right) + y = 7 \qquad\qquad \left(\frac{10}{y}\right) + y = 6$$

$$10 + y^2 = 7y \qquad\qquad 10 + y^2 = 6y$$

$$y^2 - 7y + 10 = 0 \qquad\quad y^2 - 6y + 10 = 0 \text{ Solve by the quadratic}$$
$$\text{formula.}$$

$$(y - 5)(y - 2) = 0$$

$$y - 5 = 0, \; y - 2 = 0$$

$$y = 5 \text{ or } y = 2$$

For $z = 6$ and $y = 5$ substituting

into (7) $x = \dfrac{10}{5} = 2$.

For $z = 6$ and $y = 2$ substituting

into (7) $x = \dfrac{10}{2} = 5$

$$y = \frac{-(-6) \pm \sqrt{36 - 4(1)(10)}}{2}$$

$$y = \frac{6 \pm \sqrt{-4}}{2}$$

$$= \frac{6 \pm 2\sqrt{-1}}{2}$$

$$= 3 \pm \sqrt{-1}$$

For $z = 7$ and $y = 3 + \sqrt{-1}$ substitute into (7)

$$x = \frac{10}{3 + \sqrt{-1}}$$

80

$$x = \frac{10}{\left(3 + \sqrt{-1}\right)} \frac{3 - \sqrt{-1}}{3 - \sqrt{-1}}$$

$$= \frac{10}{9 - (-1)}\left(3 - \sqrt{-1}\right)$$

$$= \frac{10}{10}\left(3 - \sqrt{-1}\right)$$

$$= 3 - \sqrt{-1}$$

For $z = 7$ and $y = 3 - \sqrt{-1}$, Substitute into (7)

$$x = \frac{10}{3 - \sqrt{-1}} \frac{\left(3 + \sqrt{-1}\right)}{\left(3 + \sqrt{-1}\right)}$$

$$= \frac{10\left(3 + \sqrt{-1}\right)}{9 - (-1)} = \frac{10}{10}\left(3 + \sqrt{-1}\right)$$

$$= 3 + \sqrt{-1}$$

Hence, the solutions are:

$$\begin{bmatrix} x = 2 \\ y = 5 \\ z = 6 \end{bmatrix} \quad \begin{bmatrix} x = 5 \\ y = 2 \\ z = 6 \end{bmatrix} \quad \begin{bmatrix} x = 3 - \sqrt{-1} \\ y = 3 + \sqrt{-1} \\ z = 7 \end{bmatrix} \quad \begin{bmatrix} x = 3 + \sqrt{-1} \\ y = 3 - \sqrt{-1} \\ z = 7 \end{bmatrix}$$

● **PROBLEM 11-13**

Eliminate x, y, and z from the equations

$y^2 + z^2 = ayz$, $z^2 + x^2 = bzx$, $x^2 + y^2 = cxy$.

SOLUTION:

We wish to isolate a, b, and c on the right side of the three given equations. Dividing, we have:

$$\frac{y^2 + z^2}{yz} = a, \quad \frac{z^2 + x^2}{zx} = b, \quad \frac{x^2 + y^2}{xy} = c.$$

These can be rewritten as $\dfrac{y}{z}+\dfrac{z}{y}=a$, $\dfrac{z}{x}+\dfrac{x}{z}=b$, $\dfrac{x}{y}+\dfrac{y}{x}=c$

Multiplying these three equations together we obtain,

$$\left(\frac{y}{z}+\frac{z}{y}\right)\left(\frac{z}{x}+\frac{x}{z}\right)\left(\frac{x}{y}+\frac{y}{x}\right)=abc$$

$$\left(\frac{y}{z}\bullet\frac{z}{x}+\frac{z}{y}\bullet\frac{z}{x}+\frac{y}{z}\bullet\frac{x}{z}+\frac{z}{y}\bullet\frac{x}{z}\right)\left(\frac{x}{y}+\frac{y}{x}\right)=abc$$

$$\left(\left(\frac{y}{z}\bullet\frac{z}{x}\bullet\frac{x}{y}\right)+\left(\frac{z}{y}\bullet\frac{z}{x}\bullet\frac{x}{y}\right)+\left(\frac{y}{z}\bullet\frac{x}{z}\bullet\frac{x}{y}\right)+\left(\frac{z}{y}\bullet\frac{x}{z}\bullet\frac{x}{y}\right)\right.$$

$$+\left(\frac{y}{z}\bullet\frac{z}{x}\bullet\frac{y}{x}\right)+\left(\frac{z}{y}\bullet\frac{z}{x}\bullet\frac{y}{x}\right)+\left(\frac{y}{z}\bullet\frac{x}{z}\bullet\frac{y}{x}\right)+$$

$$\left.\left(\frac{z}{y}\bullet\frac{x}{z}\bullet\frac{y}{x}\right)\right)=abc$$

Now, simplifying each term by multiplication, and reducing, we have:

$$1+\frac{z^2}{y^2}+\frac{x^2}{z^2}+\frac{x^2}{y^2}+\frac{y^2}{x^2}+\frac{z^2}{x^2}+\frac{y^2}{z^2}+1=abc$$

or

$$2+\frac{y^2}{z^2}+\frac{z^2}{y^2}+\frac{z^2}{x^2}+\frac{x^2}{z^2}+\frac{x^2}{y^2}+\frac{y^2}{x^2}=abc$$

Now, since $\dfrac{y}{z}+\dfrac{z}{y}=a$, then $\left(\dfrac{y}{z}+\dfrac{z}{y}\right)^2=a^2$.

But we can rewrite $\left(\dfrac{y}{z}+\dfrac{z}{y}\right)^2$ as:

$$\left(\frac{y}{z}+\frac{z}{y}\right)^2=\left(\frac{y}{z}+\frac{z}{y}\right)\left(\frac{y}{z}+\frac{z}{y}\right)$$

$$=\frac{y^2}{z^2}+\left(\frac{z}{y}\bullet\frac{y}{z}\right)+\left(\frac{y}{z}\bullet\frac{z}{y}\right)+\frac{z^2}{y^2}$$

$$=\frac{y^2}{z^2}+1+1+\frac{z^2}{y^2}=\frac{y^2}{z^2}+\frac{z^2}{y^2}+2.$$

Similarly, since $\dfrac{z}{x}+\dfrac{x}{z}=b$, and $\dfrac{x}{y}+\dfrac{y}{x}=c$, then $\left(\dfrac{z}{x}+\dfrac{x}{z}\right)^2=b^2$ and

$\left(\dfrac{x}{y}+\dfrac{y}{x}\right)^2=c^2$. But writing these we have:

$$\left(\frac{z}{x}+\frac{x}{z}\right)^2 = \left(\frac{z}{x}+\frac{x}{z}\right)\left(\frac{z}{x}+\frac{x}{z}\right) = \frac{z^2}{x^2}+1+1+\frac{x^2}{z^2} = \frac{z^2}{x^2}+\frac{x^2}{z^2}+2$$

and

$$\left(\frac{x}{y}+\frac{y}{x}\right)^2 = \left(\frac{x}{y}+\frac{y}{x}\right)\left(\frac{x}{y}+\frac{y}{x}\right) = \frac{x^2}{y^2}+1+1+\frac{y^2}{x^2} = \frac{x^2}{y^2}+\frac{y^2}{x^2}+2$$

Thus,

$$\left(\frac{y}{z}+\frac{z}{y}\right)^2 = a^2 = \frac{y^2}{z^2}+\frac{z^2}{y^2}+2$$

$$\left(\frac{z}{x}+\frac{x}{z}\right)^2 = b^2 = \frac{z^2}{x^2}+\frac{x^2}{z^2}+2$$

$$\left(\frac{x}{y}+\frac{y}{x}\right)^2 = c^2 = \frac{x^2}{y^2}+\frac{y^2}{x^2}+2$$

From these three equations we obtain

$$\frac{y^2}{z^2}+\frac{z^2}{y^2} = a^2-2$$

$$\frac{z^2}{x^2}+\frac{x^2}{z^2} = b^2-2$$

$$\frac{x^2}{y^2}+\frac{y^2}{x^2} = c^2-2$$

We can now substitute into the equation.

$$2+\frac{y^2}{z^2}+\frac{z^2}{y^2}+\frac{z^2}{x^2}+\frac{x^2}{z^2}+\frac{x^2}{y^2}+\frac{y^2}{x^2} = abc$$

Doing this we obtain

$$2+\left(a^2-2\right)+\left(b^2-2\right)\left(c^2-2\right) = abc;$$

therefore, $a^2+b^2+c^2-4 = abc$.

CHAPTER 12

EQUATIONS OF DEGREE GREATER THAN TWO

● PROBLEM 12-1

Remove fractional coefficients from the equation $2x^3 - \dfrac{3}{2}x^2 - \dfrac{1}{8}x + \dfrac{3}{16} = 0$.

SOLUTION:

To rewrite this equation without fractional coefficients we must find a common denominator for all the terms of the equation. Observe that a common denominator is 16. Thus,

$$2x^3 - \frac{3}{2}x^2 - \frac{1}{8}x + \frac{3}{16} = 0$$

can be rewritten as $\dfrac{2x^3}{1} - \dfrac{3x^2}{2} - \dfrac{x}{8} + \dfrac{3}{16} = 0$ or $\dfrac{32x^3 - 24x^2 - 2x + 3}{16} = 0.$

Multiplying both sides of the equation by 16 we obtain $32x^3 - 24x^2 - 2x + 3 = 0$. This is the required equation without fractional coefficients.

● PROBLEM 12-2

Find all solutions of the equation $x^3 - 3x^2 - 10x = 0$.

SOLUTION:

Factor out the common factor of x from the terms on the left side of the given equation. Therefore, $x^3 - 3x^2 - 10x = x(x^2 - 3x - 10) = 0$.

Whenever $ab = 0$, where a and b are any two numbers, either $a = 0$ or $b = 0$. Hence, either $x = 0$ or $x^2 - 3x - 10 = 0$. The expression $x^2 - 3x - 10$ factors into $(x - 5)(x + 2)$. Therefore, $(x - 5)(x + 2) = 0$. Applying the above law again:

either $\qquad x - 5 = 0 \qquad$ or $\qquad x + 2 = 0$

$\qquad\qquad\qquad x = 5 \qquad$ or $\qquad x = -2$

Hence, $\qquad x^3 - 3x^2 - 10x = x \qquad (x - 5)(x + 2) = 0$

Either $\qquad x = 0$ or $x = 5$ or $x = -2$

The solution set is $x = \{0, 5, -2\}$.

We have shown that, if there is a number x such that $x^3 - 3x^2 - 10x = 0$, then $x = 0$ or $x = 5$ or $x = -2$. Finally, to see that these three numbers are actually solutions, we substitute each of them in turn in the original equation to see whether or not it satisfies the equation $x^3 - 3x^2 - 10x = 0$.

Check: replace x by 0 in the original equation

$$(0)^3 - 3(0)^2 - 10(0) = 0 - 0 - 0 = 0 \checkmark$$

Replace x by 5 in the original equation

$$(5)^3 - 3(5)^2 - 10(5) = 125 - 3(25) - 50$$
$$= 125 - 75 - 50$$
$$= 50 - 50 = 0 \checkmark$$

Replace x by -2 in the original equation

$$(-2)^3 - 3(-2)^2 - 10(-2) = -8 - 3(4) + 20$$
$$= -8 - 12 + 20$$
$$= -20 + 20 = 0 \checkmark$$

● PROBLEM 12-3

Form the equation whose roots are 2, -3, and $\dfrac{7}{5}$.

SOLUTION:

The roots of the equation are 2, -3, and $\dfrac{7}{5}$.

Hence, $x = 2$, $x = -3$, and $x = \dfrac{7}{5}$. Subtract 2 from both sides of the first equation.

$$x - 2 = 2 - 2 = 0.$$

Add 3 to both sides of the second equation.
$$x + 3 = -3 + 3 = 0$$

Subtract $\frac{7}{5}$ from both sides of the third equation.

$$x - \frac{7}{5} = \frac{7}{5} - \frac{7}{5} = 0$$

Hence, $(x - 2)(x + 3)\left(x - \frac{7}{5}\right) = (0)(0)(0) = 0$ or

$$(x - 2)(x + 3)\left(x - \frac{7}{5}\right) = 0.$$

Multiply both sides of this equation by 5.

$$5(x - 2)(x + 3)\left(x - \frac{7}{5}\right) = 5(0)\ \text{or}$$

$$(x - 2)(x + 3)\,5\left(x - \frac{7}{5}\right) = 0\ \text{or}$$
$$(x - 2)(x + 3)(5x - 7) = 0$$
$$(x^2 + x - 6)(5x - 7) = 0$$
$$5x^3 - 7x^2 + 5x^2 - 7x - 30x + 42 = 0$$
$$5x^3 - 2x^2 - 37x + 42 = 0$$

● PROBLEM 12-4

Solve.
$$4x^3 + 3x^2y + y^3 = 8$$
$$2x^3 - 2x^2y + xy^2 = 1$$

SOLUTION:

Put $y = mx$, and substitute in both equations. Thus,
$$4x^3 + 3x^2(mx) + (mx)^3 = 8$$
$$2x^3 - 2x^2(mx) + x(mx)^2 = 1$$
Factor.
$$x^3(4 + 3m + m^3) = 8 \tag{1}$$
$$x^3(2 - 2m + m^2) = 1 \tag{2}$$
Divide equation (1) by equation (2).

$$\frac{\cancel{x^3}\left(4 + 3m + m^3\right)}{\cancel{x^3}\left(2 - 2m + m^2\right)} = \frac{4 + 3m + m^3}{2 - 2m + m^2} = \frac{8}{1} = 8 \tag{2a}$$

Hence, $\dfrac{4 + 3m + m^3}{2 - 2m + m^2} = 8$ (3)

Multiply both sides of equation (3) by $(2 - 2m + m^2)$.

$$\left(2 - \cancel{2m} + m^2\right)\left(\frac{4 + 3m + m^3}{2 - \cancel{2m} + m^2}\right) = \left(2 - 2m + m^2\right)8$$

$$4 + 3m + m^3 = \left(2 - 2m + m^2\right)8 \qquad (4)$$

Distribute on the right side of equation (4)

$$4 + 3m + m^3 = 16 - 16m + 8m^2 \qquad (5)$$

Subtract $(16 - 16m + 8m^2)$ from both sides of equation (5).

$4 + 3m + m^3 - (16 - 16m + 8m^2) = 16 - 16m + 8m^2 - (16 - 16m + 8m^2)$ $4 + 3m + m^3 - 16 + 16m - 8m^2 = 0$.

Combine like terms.

$$m^3 - 8m^2 + 19m - 12 = 0 \qquad (6)$$

The possible rational roots of equation (6) are all numbers $\pm$ p/q in which the values of p are the positive divisors 1, 2, 3, 4, 6, 12 of the constant term -12 and the values of q are the positive divisors of the leading coefficient 1. Hence, the only value for q is 1. Thus, the possible rational roots of equation (6) are:

$\pm$ 1/1, $\pm$ 2/1, $\pm$ 3/1, $\pm$ 4/1, $\pm$ 6/1, and $\pm$ 12/1

or $\pm$ 1, $\pm$ 2, $\pm$ 3, $\pm$ 4, ±6, and ±12.

Substitution of the values 1, 3, and 4 for m makes equation (6) a true statement. Hence, the roots of m are 1, 3, and 4. Then, $m = 1$, $m = 3$, and $m = 4$. Therefore, $m - 1 = 0$, $m - 3 = 0$, and $m - 4 = 0$. Then,

$$(m -)(m - 3)(m - 4) = (0)(0)(0) = 0 \qquad (7)$$

Also, $(m - 1)(m - 3)(m - 4) = [(m - 1)(m - 3)](m - 4)$

$$= [m^2 - 4m + 3](m - 4)$$

distributing, $= (m^3 - 4m^2 + 3m) - (4m^2 - 16m + 12)$

$$= m^3 - 4m^2 + 3m - 4m^2 + 16m - 12$$

$$(m - 1)(m - 3)(m - 4) = m^3 - 8m^2 + 19m - 12 \qquad (8)$$

From equations (6) and (7):

$m^3 - 8m^2 + 19m - 12 = (m - 1)(m - 3)(m - 4) = 0$

(a) Take $m = 1$, and substitute in either (1) or (2). From (2),

$$x^3(2 - 2(1) + (1)^2) = 1$$

$$x^3(2 - 2 + 1) = 1$$

$$x^3(0 + 1) = 1$$

$$x^3(1) = 1$$

$$x^3 = 1$$

Take the cube root of each side.

$$\sqrt[3]{x^3} = \sqrt[3]{1}$$

$$x = \sqrt[3]{1} = 1$$

Also, $y = mx = 1(1) = 1$.

(b) Take $m = 3$, and substitute in (2); thus,

$$5x^3 = 1$$

$$x^3 = \frac{1}{5}$$

Take the cube root of each side.

$$\sqrt[3]{x^3} = \sqrt[3]{1/5}$$

$$x = \sqrt[3]{1/5}$$

$$y = mx = 3x = 3\sqrt[3]{1/5}.$$

(c) Take $m = 4$; we obtain from (2):

$$10x^3 = 1$$

Then, $x^3 = \frac{1}{10}$. Take the cube root of each side.

$$\sqrt[3]{x^3} = \sqrt[3]{1/10},$$

or

$$x = \sqrt[3]{1/10}$$

and

$$y = mx = 4x = 4\sqrt[3]{1/10}$$

Hence, the complete solution is

$$\begin{array}{lll} x = 1 & x = \sqrt[3]{1/5} & x = \sqrt[3]{1/10} \\ y = 1 & y = 3\sqrt[3]{1/5} & y = 4\sqrt[3]{1/10} \end{array}$$

● PROBLEM 12-5

Solve $x^4 - 2x^2 - 3 = 0$ as a quadratic equation in x^2.

SOLUTION:

We can write the equation as $(x^2)^2 - 2x^2 - 3 = 0$.

Let $x^2 = z$ and we have $z^2 - 2z - 3 = 0$, which is a quadratic equation. We can solve a quadratic equation in the form $ax^2 + bx + c = 0$ using the quadratic formula,

$$x = \frac{-b \pm \sqrt{b^2 - 4ac}}{2a}$$

In our case $a = 1$, $b = -2$, and $c = -3$. Thus,

$$z = \frac{-(-2) \pm \sqrt{(-2)^2 - 4(1)(-3)}}{2(1)}$$

$$= \frac{2 \pm \sqrt{4+12}}{2} = \frac{2 \pm 4}{2} = 1 \pm 2$$

Therefore, $z = 3$ or $z = -1$. Since $z = x^2$, we have $x^2 = 3$ or $x^2 = -1$. If $x^2 = 3$, $x = \pm \sqrt{3}$. If $x^2 = -1$, $x = \pm i$. Hence, the solution set of the original equation is $\{\sqrt{3}, -\sqrt{3}, i, -i\}$.

● PROBLEM 12-6

Find all rational roots of the equation $x^4 - 4x^3 + x^2 - 5x + 4 = 0$.

SOLUTION:

This is a fourth degree equation. We can solve it by synthetic division. Guess at a root by trying to find an x–value which will make the equation equal to zero. $x = 4$ works.

Now write the coefficients of the equation in descending powers of x. Note that if a term is missing, its coefficient is zero. In the corner box, the root 4 is placed. Bring the first coefficient down and multiply it by the root. Place the result below the next coefficient and add. Multiply the result by the root and continue as before.

$$\begin{array}{rrrrr} 1 & -4 & +1 & -5 & +4 \end{array} \qquad \boxed{4}$$
$$\begin{array}{rrrrr} & +4 & 0 & +4 & -4 \\ \hline 1 & 0 & 1 & -1 & 0 \end{array}$$

The last result is zero which indicates $(x - 4)$ is a factor and $x = 4$ is a root. The other results are the coefficients of the third degree expression when $(x - 4)$ is factored.

$$(x - 4)(x^3 + 0x^2 + x - 1) = 0$$
$$(x - 4)(x^3 + x - 1) = 0$$

To find the roots of the third degree equation, call it $g(x)$, we must set it equal to zero.

$$g(x) = x^3 + x - 1 = 0$$

Try to find where the curve of the equation crosses the x–axis which is when $y = 0$.

x	−2	−1	0	1	2
y	−11	−3	−1	1	9

It crosses the x–axis between $x = 0$ and $x = 1$. It is an irrational root.

Since the given equation is a fourth degree equation, it has four roots. All of the real roots, namely the rational number 4, and an irrational number between 0 and 1, have been found. Therefore, the two remaining roots are not real; that is, they are complex numbers.

Solve $\quad x^4 + y^4 = 82$ $\qquad\qquad\qquad\qquad\qquad$ (1)

$\qquad\quad x - y = 2$ $\qquad\qquad\qquad\qquad\qquad\qquad$ (2)

SOLUTION:

Let $x = u + v$ and $y = u - v$. From equation (2)

$$x - y = 2$$
$$u + v - (u - v) = 2$$
$$u + v - u + v = 2$$
$$2v = 2$$
$$v = 1$$

Substitute in equation (1).

$$x^4 + y^4 = 82$$
$$(u + v)^4 + (u - v)^4 = 82$$

Replace v by 1.

$$(u + 1)^4 + (u - 1)^4 = 82 \qquad\qquad\qquad\qquad (3)$$

Now, simplify the left side of equation (3).

$$(u + 1)^2 = (u + 1)(u + 1) = u^2 + 2u + 1$$
$$(u + 1)^3 = (u + 1)(u + 1)^2$$

or $\qquad\qquad (u + 1)^3 = (u + 1)(u^2 + 2u + 1)$

Distribute on the right side of this equation.

$$(u + 1)^3 = (u^3 + 2u^2 + u) + (u^2 + 2u + 1)$$
$$= u^3 + 3u^2 + 3u + 1$$
$$(u + 1)^4 = (u + 1)(u + 1)^3$$

or $\qquad\qquad (u + 1)^4 = (u + 1)(u^3 + 3u^2 + 3u + 1)$

Distribute on the right side of this equation.

$$(u + 1)^4 = (u^4 + 3u^3 + 3u^2 + u) + (u^3 + 3u^2 + 3u + 1)$$
$$(u + 1)^4 = u^4 + 4u^3 + 6u^2 + 4u + 1 \qquad\qquad (4)$$

Also, $\qquad\qquad (u - 1)^2 = (u - 1)(u - 1) = u^2 - 2u + 1$

$$(u - 1)^3 = (u - 1)(u - 1)^2$$

or $\qquad\qquad (u - 1)^3 = (u - 1)(u^2 - 2u + 1)$

Distribute on the right side of this equation.

$$(u - 1)^3 = (u^3 - 2u^2 + u) - (u^2 - 2u + 1)$$
$$= u^3 - 3u^2 + 3u - 1$$
$$(u - 1)^4 = (u - 1)(u - 1)^3$$

or $\qquad\qquad (u - 1)^4 = (u - 1)(u^3 - 3u^2 + 3u - 1)$

Distribute on the right side of this equation.

$$(u - 1)^4 = (u^4 - 3u^3 + 3u^2 - u) - (u^3 - 3u^2 + 3u + 1)$$
$$(u - 1)^4 = u^4 - 4u^3 + 6u^2 - 4u + 1 \qquad\qquad (5)$$

Use equations (4) and (5) to simplify equation (3).

$$(u + 1)^4 + (u - 1)^4 = (u^4 + 4u^3 + 6u^2 + 4u + 1) + (u^4 - 4u^3 + 6u^2 - 4u + 1)$$

$$= u^4 + 4u^3 + 6u^2 + 4u + 1 + u^4 - 4u^3 + 6u^2 - 4u + 1$$
$$= 2u^4 + 12u^2 + 2 = 82$$

Thus, $2u^4 + 12u^2 + 2 = 82$.

Subtract 82 from both sides of this equation.
$$2u^4 + 12u^2 + 2 - 82 = 82 - 82$$
$$2u^4 + 12u^2 - 80 = 0$$

Divide both sides of this equation by 2.
$$\frac{2u^4 + 12u^2 - 80}{2} = \frac{0}{2}, \text{ or}$$
$$u^4 + 6u^2 - 40 = 0$$

Factoring the left side of this equation into a product of two polynomials:
$$(u^2 + 10)(u^2 - 4) = 0$$

Whenever a product $ab = 0$, where a and b are any two numbers, either $a = 0$ or $b = 0$. Hence, either
$$u^2 + 10 = 0 \text{ or } u^2 - 4 = 0$$
$$u^2 = -10 \text{ or } u^2 = 4$$
$$u = \pm\sqrt{-10} \text{ or } u = \pm\sqrt{4} = \pm 2$$

Using the equations relating x and y to u and v in order to solve for x and y:

when $u = \sqrt{-10}$, $x = u + v = \sqrt{-10} + 1 = 1 + \sqrt{-10}$ and
$$y = u - v = \sqrt{-10} - 1 = -1 + \sqrt{-10}$$

when $u = -\sqrt{-10}$, $x = u + v = -\sqrt{-10} + 1 = 1 - \sqrt{-10}$ and
$$y = u - v = -\sqrt{-10} - 1 = -1 - \sqrt{-10}$$

when $u = 2$, $x = u + v = 2 + 1 = 3$ and
$$y = u - v = 2 - 1 = 1$$

when $u = -2$, $x = u + v = -2 + 1 = -1$ and
$$y = u - v = -2 - 1 = -3$$

Thus, the pairs of solutions are:
$$x = 1 + \sqrt{-10}, y = -1 + \sqrt{-10}$$
$$x = 1 - \sqrt{-10}, y = -1 - \sqrt{-10}$$
$$x = 3, y = 1$$
$$x = -1, y = -3$$

CHAPTER 13

INTERVALS AND INEQUALITIES

● PROBLEM 13-1

Rewrite these inequalities, shown on the number lines below, in terms of intervals.

(a)
$$-1 \quad 0$$

(d)
$$-3-2-1\ 0\ 1\ 2\ 3\ 4\ 5$$

(b)
$$-2-1\ 0\ 1\ 2\ 3$$

(e)
$$-2-1\ 0\ 1$$

(c)
$$0\ 1\ 2\ 3\ 4\ 5$$

(f)
$$-1\ 0\ 1\ 2$$

SOLUTION:

(a) $-\infty < x \le -1$, $(-\infty, -1]$ (d) $-3 \le x \le 5$ $[-3, 5]$

(b) $-2 \le x < 3$, $[-2, 3)$ (e) $-2 < x < 1$, $(-2, 1)$

(c) $1 < x \le 5$, $(1, 5]$ (f) $-1 < x < \infty$ $(-1, \infty)$

● PROBLEM 13-2

Solve the compound statement $4x - 5 \ge -6x + 5$.

$$0\ 1$$

$$\{x \mid x \ge 1\} = [1, \infty)$$

92

SOLUTION:

To solve this compound statement we solve for x as follows:

Adding 5 to both sides of the given inequality we have:

$$4x \geq -6x + 10$$

Adding $6x$ to both sides: $10x \geq 10$

Multiplying both sides by $\dfrac{1}{10}$: $x \geq 1$

Therefore, $S = \{x \mid x \geq 1\}$

The region representing this set on the number line is shown in the diagram. You should note that the bracket in the graph includes the point 1.

● **PROBLEM 13-3**

Illustrate one (a) conditional inequality, (b) identity, and (c) inconsistent inequality.

SOLUTION:

(a) A conditional inequality is an inequality whose validity depends on the values of the variables in the sentence. That is, certain values of the variables will make the sentence true, and others will make it false. $3 - y > 3 + y$ is a conditional inequality for the set of real numbers, since it is true for any replacement less than zero and false for all others.

(b) $x + 5 > x + 2$ is an identity for the set of real numbers, since for any real number x, the expression on the left is greater than the expression on the right.

(c) $5y < 2y + y$ is inconsistent for the set of non-negative real numbers. For any x greater than zero the sentence is always false. A sentence is inconsistent if it is always false when its variables assume allowable values.

● **PROBLEM 13-4**

Find the solution set of the inequality $5x - 9 > 2x + 3$.

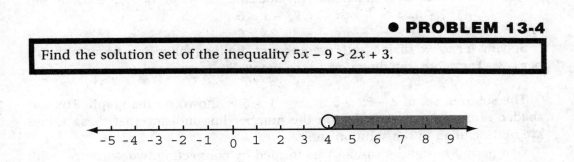

SOLUTION:

To find the solution set of the inequality $5x - 9 > 2x + 3$, we wish to obtain an equivalent inequality in which each term in one member involves x, and each term in the other member is a constant. Thus, if we add $(-2x)$ to both members, only one side of the inequality will have an x term:

$$5x - 9 + (-2x) > 2x + 3 + (-2x)$$
$$5x + (-2x) - 9 > 2x + (-2x) + 3$$
$$3x - 9 > 3$$

Now, adding 9 to both sides of the inequality we obtain,

$$3x - 9 + 9 > 3 + 9$$
$$3x > 12$$

Dividing both sides by 3, we arrive at $x > 4$.

Hence, the solution set is $\{x \mid x > 4\}$, and is pictured in the accompanying figure.

● PROBLEM 13-5

Find the solution set of the following disjunction.

$$2 - 3x > 5 \quad \text{or} \quad 2x - 1 > 5$$

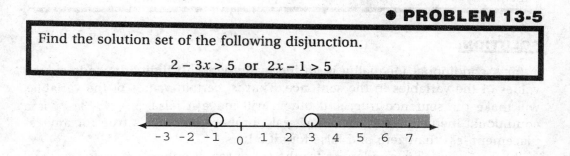

SOLUTION:

A disjunction is a compound sentence using the connective *or*. The union of the solution sets of the two sentences comprising the compound sentence is the solution set of the disjunction. For this problem the solution set is

$$\{x \mid 2 - 3x > 5\} \cup \{x \mid 2x - 1 > 5\}$$

We solve each inequality independently and find the union of their solution set:

$$\begin{array}{ccc} 2 - 3x > 5 & \text{or} & 2x - 1 > 5 \\ -3x > 3 & \text{or} & 2x > 6 \end{array}$$

Solving for x, we divide both members of the inequality by a negative number (-3). Therefore, the direction of the inequality is reversed.

$$x < -1 \quad \text{or} \quad x > 3$$

The solution set of $2 - 3x > 5$ or $2x - 1 > 5$ is shown on the graph. The unshaded circles above -1 and 3 on the number line indicate that these values are not included in the solution set.

Compound sentences can also be formed by connecting two sentences with the word *and*. A compound sentence using the connective *and* is called a con-

94

junction. The solution set of a conjunction is the set of replacements that are common to the solution sets of the sentences making up the conjunction (their intersection). We may write the solution set as:

$$\{x|\ x > a\} \cap \{x|\ x < b\} = \{x|\ a < x < b\}.$$

● PROBLEM 13-6

Find the solution set of the following conjunction.

$$\frac{1}{2}x + 1 > 3 \text{ and } x > 2x - 6$$

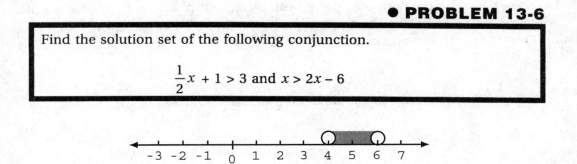

SOLUTION:

The solution set must be such that x satisfies both inequalities simultaneously. The solution set of the conjunction is

$$\{x|\ \frac{1}{2}x + 1 > 3\} \cap \ \{x|\ x > 2x - 6\}$$

$$\frac{1}{2}x + 1 > 3 \text{ and } x > 2x - 6$$

$$\frac{1}{2}x > 2 \text{ and } -x > -6$$

$$x > 4 \text{ and } x < 6$$

(multiplying by negative 1 reverses the inequality).

Note: if $x = 4$ the sentence $\frac{1}{2}x + 1 > 3$ becomes false, i.e.,

$$\frac{1}{2}(4) + 1 = 3 > 3 \qquad \text{false}$$

and if $x = 6$ the sentence $x > 2x - 6$ becomes false also

$$6 > 2(6) - 6 = 6 \qquad \text{false}$$

Therefore, the solution set cannot include these two points, and the values of x which make both sentences true simultaneously are the inequalities x greater than but not equal to 4 and less than but not equal to 6. That is $\{x|\ 4 < x < 6\}$. (See the number line.)

Prove that if $a > b > 0$, then $\dfrac{1}{a} < \dfrac{1}{b}$.

SOLUTION:

Since a and b are both positive (given), ab is positive because the product of two positive numbers is always positive. Now, since $ab > 0$, we may divide both sides $a > b$ by ab to obtain

$$\frac{a}{ab} > \frac{b}{ab}.$$

Cancelling like terms in the numerator and denominator,

$$\frac{1}{b} > \frac{1}{a},$$

which is equivalent to $\dfrac{1}{a} < \dfrac{1}{b}$. To complete the proof, the student should check that the steps are reversible, as follows:

Check $\dfrac{1}{b} > \dfrac{1}{a}$. Multiply both sides of the inequality by the least common denominator obtained by multiplying the two denominators together.

$$\frac{ab}{b} > \frac{ab}{a} = a > b.$$

Solve $\left|\dfrac{x}{3} + 2\right| < 4$

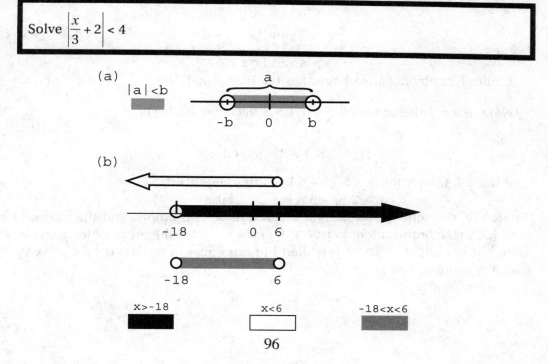

SOLUTION:

Now, if b is a nonnegative real number, then a is a real number for which $|a| < b$ if and only if $-b < a < b$. See number line (a).

We apply this rule to the given problem. Therefore, $\left|\dfrac{x}{3} + 2\right| < 4$ is equivalent to

$-4 < \dfrac{x}{3} + 2 < 4$. In other words, this inequality is satisfied if and only if both

$$\frac{x}{3} + 2 < 4 \text{ and } \frac{x}{3} + 2 > -4$$

are satisfied. By adding -2 to each member of these inequalities, we get

$$\frac{x}{3} < 2 \text{ and } \frac{x}{3} > -6$$

Hence, multiplying by 3 in each case, we note that the original inequality is satisfied by values of x that satisfy both $x < 6$ and $x > -18$. We can observe the solution from diagram (b). Therefore, the solution set is
$$\{x| -18 < x < 6\} \text{ or } \{x|x < 6\} \cap \{x|x > -18\}.$$

● PROBLEM 13-9

What is the largest possible value of $\left|\dfrac{x^2 + 2}{x + 3}\right|$ if x is restricted to the interval $[-4, 4]$?

SOLUTION:

The largest possible value for the expression results when the numerator is largest and the denominator is smallest.

The numerator is largest when the upper limit of $x = 4$ is substituted, as follows:
$$|x^2 + 2| \le |x|^2 + 2 \le 4^2 + 2 = 18.$$

We must now find a smallest value for $x + 3$ if x is in $[-4, 4]$. We see that the expression is not defined for $x = -3$, since then the denominator would be zero, and division by zero is always excluded. Furthermore, if x is a number near -3, the denominator is near zero, the numerator has a value near 11, and the quotient is a "large" number, i.e., it approaches ∞. Hence, in this problem, there is no largest value of the given expression in $[-4, 4]$.

Solve the inequality $x^2 - x - 2 \leq 0$.

SOLUTION:

Factoring the left side of the given inequality,
$$(x - 2)(x + 1) \leq 0.$$
If the product of two numbers is negative, one of the numbers is positive and the other is negative. Hence, there are two cases:

Case 1:　　$x - 2 \geq 0, x + 1 \leq 0$

Solving these two inequalities,
$$x \geq 2, x \leq -1$$
Graph these new inequalities on number line (A).

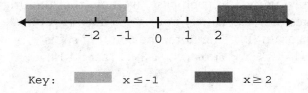

Key:　　⬛ $x \leq -1$　　⬛ $x \geq 2$

Note that there is no value of x which satisfies both inequalities at the same time since these two inequalities do not intersect anywhere on the number line (A).

Thus, $x \leq -1 \cap x \geq 2 = \emptyset$

Case 2:　　$x - 2 \leq 0, x + 1 \geq 0$.

Solving these two inequalities,
$$x \leq 2, x \geq -1$$
Graph these inequalities on number line (B).

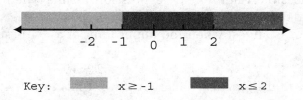

Key:　　⬛ $x \geq -1$　　⬛ $x \leq 2$

The interval of x which satisfies both inequalities at the same time is $-1 \leq x \leq 2$. Note that the two inequalities intersect in this interval on number line (B), that is
$$x \geq -1 \cap x \leq 2 = -1 \leq x \leq 2.$$
Hence, the solution to the inequality $x^2 - x - 2 \leq 0$ is the set:
$$\{x | -1 \leq x \leq 2 \}$$

Solve the inequality.

$$x - 6 > \frac{18 - 15x}{x^2 + 2x - 3}$$

SOLUTION:

We first subtract $\dfrac{18 - 15x}{x^2 + 2x - 3}$ from both sides of the inequality, obtaining

$$x - 6 - \frac{18 - 15x}{x^2 + 2x - 3} > 0.$$

In order to combine terms, we convert $x - 6$ into a fraction with $x^2 + 2x - 3$ as its denominator. Thus,

$$\frac{\left(x^2 + 2x - 3\right)}{\left(x^2 + 2x - 3\right)} \bullet (x - 6) - \frac{18 - 15x}{x^2 + 2x - 3} > 0.$$

Note that since $\dfrac{x^2 + 2x - 3}{x^2 + 2x - 3} = 1$, multiplication of $(x - 6)$ by this fraction does not alter the value of the inequality.

$$\frac{\left(x^2 + 2x - 3\right)(x - 6)}{x^2 + 2x - 3} - \frac{18 - 15x}{x^2 + 2x - 3} > 0$$

$$\frac{x^3 + 2x^2 - 3x - 6x^2 - 12x + 18}{x^2 + 2x - 3} - \frac{18 - 15x}{x^2 + 2x - 3} > 0$$

$$\frac{x^3 - 4x^2 - 15x + 18}{x^2 + 2x - 3} - \frac{18 - 15x}{x^2 + 2x - 3} > 0$$

$$\frac{x^3 - 4x^2 - 15x + 18 - 18 + 15x}{x^2 + 2x - 3} > 0$$

$$\frac{x^3 - 4x^2}{x^2 + 2x - 3} > 0$$

Now we factor the numerator and denominator. Thus,

$$\frac{x^2(x - 4)}{(x - 1)(x + 3)} > 0.$$

We now want all values of x which make $\dfrac{x^2(x - 4)}{(x - 1)(x + 3)}$ greater than zero. If

$(x - 1) = 0$ or $(x + 3) = 0$ this fraction is undefined, thus we must place the restrictions $\quad x - 1 \neq 0 \quad$ and $\quad x + 3 \neq 0$
or $\quad\quad\quad\quad x \neq 1 \quad\quad$ and $\quad x \neq -3$.

Next we must eliminate all values of x which make $\dfrac{x^2(x-4)}{(x-1)(x+3)}$ equal to zero (for we only want it to be greater than zero). The numerator will be zero if $x^2 = 0$ or $x - 4 = 0$, thus $x \neq 0$ and $x \neq 4$. We now have critical values $x = -3$, $x = 0$, $x = 1$, $x = 4$.

We must test values of x in all ranges bordering on these critical values: (a) $x < -3$, (b) $-3 < x < 0$, (c) $0 < x < 1$, (d) $1 < x < 4$, (e) $x > 4$, to find the ranges in which the inequality holds.

(a) To test if the inequality holds for $x < -3$, choose any value of $x < -3$. We will use -4, and replace x by this value in the given inequality.

$$\frac{x^2(x-4)}{(x-1)(x+3)} > 0$$

$$\frac{(-4)^2(-4-4)}{(-4-1)(-4+3)} > 0$$

$$\frac{16(-8)}{(-5)(-1)} > 0$$

$$\frac{-128}{5} > 0$$

Since a negative number is not greater than zero, the range $x < -3$ is not part of the solution.

(b) To test if the inequality holds for $-3 < x < 0$, choose a value of x between 0 and -3. We will use -1, and replace x by this value in the inequality.

$$\frac{x^2(x-4)}{(x-1)(x+3)} > 0$$

$$\frac{(-1)^2(-1-4)}{(-1-1)(-1+3)} > 0$$

$$\frac{1(-5)}{(-2)(2)} > 0$$

$$\frac{-5}{-4} > 0$$

$$\frac{5}{4} > 0$$

Since $\dfrac{5}{4}$ is indeed greater than zero, the range $-3 < x < 0$ is part of the solution.

(c) Testing if $0 < x < 1$ is part of the solution, we choose a value of x between 0 and 1. We will use $\dfrac{1}{2}$, and replace x by this value in the inequality.

$$\frac{x^2(x-4)}{(x-1)(x+3)} > 0$$

$$\frac{\left(\dfrac{1}{2}\right)^2\left(\dfrac{1}{2}-4\right)}{\left(\dfrac{1}{2}-1\right)\left(\dfrac{1}{2}+3\right)} > 0$$

$$\frac{\left(\dfrac{1}{4}\right)\left(-3\dfrac{1}{2}\right)}{\left(-\dfrac{1}{2}\right)\left(3\dfrac{1}{2}\right)} > 0$$

$$\frac{\left(\dfrac{1}{4}\right)\left(-\dfrac{7}{2}\right)}{\left(-\dfrac{1}{2}\right)\left(\dfrac{7}{2}\right)} > 0$$

$$\frac{-\dfrac{7}{8}}{-\dfrac{7}{4}} > 0$$

$$-\frac{7}{8}\left(-\frac{4}{7}\right) > 0$$

$$\frac{1}{2} > 0$$

Since $\dfrac{1}{2}$ is indeed greater than zero, the range $0 < x < 1$ is part of the solution.

(d) Testing if $1 < x < 4$ is part of the solution, we choose a value of x between 1 and 4. We will use 2, and replace x by this value in the inequality.

$$\frac{x^2(x-4)}{(x-1)(x+3)} > 0$$

$$\frac{(2)^2(2-4)}{(2-1)(2+3)} > 0$$

$$\frac{4(-2)}{(1)(5)} > 0$$

$$\frac{-8}{5} > 0$$

Since a negative number is not greater than zero, the range $1 < x < 4$ is not part of the solution.

(e) Testing if $x > 4$ is part of the solution, we choose any value of x greater than 5. We will use 5, and replace x by this value in the inequality.

$$\frac{x^2(x-4)}{(x-1)(x+3)} > 0$$

$$\frac{(5)^2(5-4)}{(5-1)(5+3)} > 0$$

$$\frac{25(1)}{(4)(8)} > 0$$

$$\frac{25}{32} > 0$$

Since $\frac{25}{32}$ is indeed greater than zero, the range $x > 4$ is part of the solution.

Thus, the permissible ranges for which the inequality $x - 6 > \dfrac{18 - 15x}{x^2 + 2x - 3}$ holds are $-3 < x < 0$, $0 < x < 1$, and $x > 4$.

● PROBLEM 13-12

Show that $x^3 > y^3$ if $x > y$.

SOLUTION:

If we subtract y^3 from both sides of the inequality $x^3 > y^3$ we obtain:
$$x^3 - y^3 > 0$$
Recall the formula for the difference of two cubes:
$$a^3 - b^3 = (a - b)(a^2 + ab + b^2)$$
Thus, $x^3 - y^3 = (x - y)(x^2 + xy + y^2)$ by substitution.

If $x^3 - y^3 > 0$, then $(x - y)(x^2 + xy + y^2) > 0$ (1)

Since we are given $x > y$, subtracting y from both sides of this inequality we obtain $x - y > 0$.

Now that we know $(x - y) > 0$ we can divide both sides of inequality (1) by $(x - y)$ without reversing the inequality.

$$\frac{(x - y)(x^2 + xy + y^2)}{(x - y)} > \frac{0}{(x - y)}$$

Cancelling $(x - y)$ in the numerator and denominator we arrive at

$$x^2 + xy + y^2 > 0. \tag{2}$$

Note that $\qquad x^2 + xy + y^2 = \left(x + \frac{1}{2}y\right)^2 + \frac{3}{4}y^2;$

thus, we have written inequality (2) as the sum of two squares. The square of any number is positive, and if we add two positives we obtain a positive; hence:

$$x^2 + xy + y^2 = \left(x + \frac{1}{2}y\right)^2 + \frac{3}{4}y^2 > 0.$$

Because inequality (2) is always valid, and the steps are all reversible, the given inequality, $x^3 > y^3$, has been proven.

CHAPTER 14

PROGRESSIONS, SEQUENCES, AND SERIES

If the 6th term of an arithmetic progression is 8 and the 11th term is –2, what is the 1st term? What is the common difference?

SOLUTION:

An arithmetic progression is a sequence of numbers where each term excluding the first is obtained from the preceding one by adding a fixed quantity to it. This constant amount is called the common difference.

Let a = value of first term, and d = common difference

Term of sequence: 1st   2nd   3rd   4th   ...   nth
Value of term: a $a + d$ $a + 2d$ $a + 3d$ ... $a + (n-1)d$

Use the formula for the nth term of the sequence to write equations for the given 6th and 11th terms, to determine a and d.

11th term: $a + (11 - 1)d = -2$
6th term: $a + (6 - 1)d = 8$.

Simplifying the above equations we obtain:

$$a + 10d = -2 \tag{1}$$
$$a + 5d = 8 \tag{2}$$

Subtracting (2) from (1) we get; $5d = -10$
$$d = -2$$

Substituting in (1) $a + 10(-2) = -2$
$$a = 18$$

The first term is 18 and the common difference is –2.

If the first term of an arithmetic progression is 7, and the common difference is –2, find the fifteenth term and the sum of the first fifteen terms.

SOLUTION:

An arithmetic progression is a sequence of numbers, each of which is obtained from the preceding one by adding a constant quantity to it. This quantity is the common difference, d. If we designate the first term by a and the common difference by d, then the terms can be expressed as follows:

terms of series	1	2	3	...	n
value of term	a	$a + d$	$a + 2d$		$\ell = a + (n-1)d$

In this example $a = 7$, and $d = -2$. To find the fifteenth term, we have $n = 15$. The nth term is $\ell = a + (n - 1)d$. For $n = 15$, $\ell = 7 + (15 - 1)(-2) = 7 - 28 = -21$. To find the sum of the first fifteen terms, apply the following formula:

$$S_n = \frac{n}{2}\left(a + \ell\right)$$

$$S_{15} = \frac{15}{2}\left[7 + (-21)\right] = \frac{15}{2}(-14) = -105.$$

Find the sum of the arithmetic series $5 + 9 + 13 + ... + 401$.

SOLUTION:

The common difference is $d = 9 - 5 = 4$, and the nth term, or last term, is $\ell = a + (n - 1)d$, where
a = first term of the progression
n = number of terms.

Hence, $401 = 5 + (n - 1)4$. Solving for this equation in terms of n, we have $n = 100$. The required sum is

$$S = 5 + 9 + 13 + ... + 393 + 397 + 401$$

Written in reverse order, this sum is

$$S = 401 + 397 + 393 + ... + 13 + 9 + 5$$

Adding the two expressions for S, we have

$$2S = (5 + 401) + (9 + 397) + (13 + 393) + ...$$
$$+ (393 + 13) + (397 + 9) + (401 + 5).$$

Each term in parentheses is equal to the sum of the first and last terms; 5 + 401 = 406. There is a parenthetic term corresponding to each term of the original series; that is, there are 100 terms. Hence,

$$2S = 100(5 + 401) = 40,600 \text{ and } S = \frac{40,600}{2} = 20,300.$$

In general, the sum of the first n terms of an arithmetic series is:

$$S = \frac{n}{2}(a + \ell) = \frac{n}{2}\left[2a + (n-1)d\right]$$

For this problem,

$$S = \frac{100}{2}(5 + 401) = \frac{100}{2}\left[2(5) + (100-1)4\right] = 20,300.$$

● PROBLEM 14-4

How many terms of the sequence –9, –6, –3, ... must be taken so that the sum will be 66?

SOLUTION:

To solve this problem we apply the formula for the sum of the first n terms of an arithmetic progression. The formula states

$$S_n = \frac{n}{2}\left[2a + (n-1)d\right], \text{ where}$$

S_n = sum of the first n terms
n = number of terms
a = first term
d = common difference.

We are given all of the above information except n. Therefore, by substituting for S_n, a, and d, we can solve for n. We are given that $S_n = 66$, $a = -9$, and $d = 3$, since $(-6) - (-9) = 3$, $(-3) - (-6) = 3$, ...

Hence, $\qquad \frac{n}{2}\left[-18 + (n-1)3\right] = 66.$

Now, multiplying both sides of the equation by 2 we obtain:
$$n\left[-18 + (n-1)3\right] = 132;$$
and simplifying the expression in brackets, we have:
$$n(-18 + 3n - 3) = 132, \text{ or } n(3n - 21) = 132.$$
Therefore, we have:
$$3n^2 - 21n = 132,$$
and dividing each term by 3 we obtain

106

$$n^2 - 7n - 44 = 0;$$

factoring we have,

$$(n - 11)(n + 4) = 0.$$

Therefore,

$$n = 11 \text{ or } -4.$$

We can reject the negative value because there cannot be a negative number of terms in the sequence, and therefore, 11 terms must be taken so that the sum of the terms is 66.

We can check this by taking 11 terms of the series. Doing this we have:

$$(-9) + (-6) + (-3) + 0 + 3 + 6 + 9 + 12 + 15 + 18 + 21 = 66.$$

● PROBLEM 14-5

If the first term of a geometric progression is 9 and the common ratio is $-\dfrac{2}{3}$, find the first five terms.

SOLUTION:

A geometric progression (G.P.) is a sequence of numbers each of which, except the first, is obtained by multiplying the preceding number by a constant number called the common ratio, r. Thus, a G.P. such as $a_1, a_2, a_3, a_4, a_5, \ldots$ or $a_1, a_1 r, a_2 r, a_3 r, a_4 r, \ldots$ with $a_1 = 9$ and $r = -\dfrac{2}{3}$ is determined as follows:

$$a_1 = 9$$

$$a_2 = 9\left(-\frac{2}{3}\right) = -6$$

$$a_3 = (-6)\left(-\frac{2}{3}\right) = 4$$

$$a_4 = 4\left(-\frac{2}{3}\right) = -\frac{8}{3}$$

$$a_5 = \left(-\frac{8}{3}\right)\left(-\frac{2}{3}\right) = \frac{16}{9}$$

Thus, the first five terms are

$$9, -6, 4, -\frac{8}{3}, \text{ and } \frac{16}{9}.$$

Write the fourth, fifth, and sixth terms of the sequence with the general term:

(a) $\dfrac{2n+1}{n!}$

(b) $(-1)^{2n} \dfrac{x^{n-1}}{(2n)!}$

SOLUTION:

(a) $\dfrac{2n+1}{n!}$, where $n = 4, 5, 6$:

$$\dfrac{2(4)+1}{4!}, \dfrac{2(5)+1}{5!}, \dfrac{2(6)+1}{6!}$$

$$\Rightarrow \dfrac{9}{4 \cdot 3 \cdot 2 \cdot 1}, \dfrac{11}{5 \cdot 4 \cdot 3 \cdot 2 \cdot 1}, \dfrac{13}{6 \cdot 5 \cdot 4 \cdot 3 \cdot 2 \cdot 1}$$

$$\Rightarrow \dfrac{3}{8}, \dfrac{11}{120}, \dfrac{13}{720}$$

(b) $(-1)^{2n} \dfrac{x^{n-1}}{(2n)!}$, where $n = 4, 5, 6$:

$$(-1)^{2 \cdot 4} \dfrac{x^{4-1}}{(2(4))!}, (-1)^{2 \cdot 5} \dfrac{x^{5-1}}{(2(5))!}, (-1)^{2 \cdot 6} \dfrac{x^{6-1}}{(2(6))!}$$

$$\Rightarrow \dfrac{x^3}{8!}, \dfrac{x^4}{10!}, \dfrac{x^5}{12!}$$

The first term of a geometric progression is 27, the nth term is $\dfrac{32}{9}$, and the sum of n terms is $\dfrac{665}{9}$. Find n and r.

SOLUTION:

A geometric progression (G.P.) is a sequence of numbers in which each number, except the first, is obtained by multiplying the preceding number by a constant number called the common ratio, r. The following two formulas for geometric progressions will be helpful in finding n, which is the number of terms, and r, which is the common ratio:

(1) the nth term or last term $= \ell = ar^{n-1}$,

(2) the sum of the first n terms $S_n = \dfrac{a(r^n - 1)}{r - 1}$ where a = first term, r = common ratio, n = number of terms, ℓ = nth term, or last term, and S_n = sum of the first n terms.

In this problem it is given that $\ell = \dfrac{32}{9}$, $a = 27$, and $S_n = \dfrac{665}{9}$. Substituting these values into the formula for the nth term or last term, we get:

$$\frac{32}{9} = 27r^{n-1}. \qquad (1)$$

And substituting into the formula for the sum of the first n terms, we get:

$$\frac{665}{9} = \frac{27(r^{n-1})}{r-1} = \frac{27r^n - 27}{r-1} \qquad (2)$$

Multiply both sides of equation (1) by r:

$$r\left(\frac{32}{9}\right) = r\left(27r^{n-1}\right)$$

$$\frac{32}{9}r = 27r \; r^{n-1}$$

$$\frac{32}{9}r = 27r^{1+n-1}$$

$$\frac{32}{9}r = 27r^n$$

Substitute $\dfrac{32}{9}r$ for $27r^n$ in equation (2):

$$\frac{665}{9} = \frac{32r/9 - 27}{r-1}$$

$$\cancel{9}(r-1)\frac{665}{9} = 9(\cancel{r-1})\left[\frac{32r/9 - 27}{\cancel{r-1}}\right]$$

$$(r-1)665 = 9\left[32r/9 - 27\right]$$

109

Distribute on the right side:
$$(r - 1)665 = 32r - 243$$
Distribute on the left side:
$$665r - 665 = 32r - 243$$
Subtract $32r$ from both sides:
$$665r - 665 - 32r = 32r - 243 - 32r$$
$$633r - 665 = -243$$
Add 665 to both sides:
$$633r - 665 + 665 = -243 + 665$$
$$633r = 422$$
Divide both sides by 633:

$$\frac{633r}{633} = \frac{422}{633}$$

$$r = \frac{422}{633} = \frac{2(211)}{3(211)} = \frac{2}{3}$$

Hence, the common ratio is $r = \frac{2}{3}$. Substituting $\frac{2}{3}$ for r in equation (1):

$$\frac{32}{9} = 27\left(\frac{2}{3}\right)^{n-1}$$

Multiply both sides by $\frac{1}{27}$:

$$\frac{1}{27}\left(\frac{32}{9}\right) = \frac{1}{27}\left[27\left(\frac{2}{3}\right)^{n-1}\right]$$

$$\frac{1}{27}\left(\frac{32}{9}\right) = \left(\frac{2}{3}\right)^{n-1}$$

$$\frac{32}{243} = \left(\frac{2}{3}\right)^{n-1} \tag{3}$$

Express the fraction on the left side as a power of $\frac{2}{3}$. Since $32 = 2^5$ and $243 = 3^5$, equation (3) becomes

$$\frac{32}{243} = \frac{2^5}{3^5} = \left(\frac{2}{3}\right)^5 = \left(\frac{2}{3}\right)^{n-1}.$$

Hence, $5 = n - 1$.

Add 1 to both sides: $\qquad 5 + 1 = n - 1 + 1$
$$6 = n$$
Hence, the number of terms is $n = 6$.

Express $.4\overline{23}$ as a rational fraction.

SOLUTION:

We know that,

$.4\overline{23} = .423232323...$

This is a repeating decimal in which 23 is the repeated portion. This is indicated by the bar above the given decimal.

The decimal .4232323... can be rewritten as

$.4 + .023 + .00023 + .0000023 + ...$

We can easily see this by adding each term in column form:

$$
\begin{array}{r}
.4 \\
.023 \\
.00023 \\
+ \quad .0000023 \\
\vdots \\
\hline
.4232323 \ ;
\end{array}
$$

This sum is the desired result.

Now, $.4 + .023 + .00023 + .0000023 + ...$ can be rewritten as

$$\frac{4}{10} + \frac{23}{1000} + \frac{23}{100000} + \frac{23}{10000000} + ...$$

$$= \frac{4}{10} + \frac{23}{10^3} + \frac{23}{10^5} + \frac{23}{10^7} + ...$$

Factoring $\frac{23}{10^3}$ from all terms except the first, we have

$$.4\overline{23} = \frac{4}{10} + \frac{23}{10^3}\left(1 + \frac{1}{10^2} + \frac{1}{10^4} + ...\right).$$

Notice that the series $1 + \frac{1}{10^2} + \frac{1}{10^4} + ...$ has terms which are in a geometric progression where a = first term = 1, and r = common ratio = $\frac{1}{10^2}$.

Since r is less than 1 and the series is an infinite one, we can state that

$$S = \text{sum} = \frac{a}{1-r}$$

$$= \frac{1}{1 - \frac{1}{10^2}}$$

111

Thus, $.4\overline{23} = \dfrac{4}{10} + \dfrac{23}{10^3} \cdot \dfrac{1}{1 - \dfrac{1}{10^2}}$

Now, we can simplify $\dfrac{1}{1 - \dfrac{1}{10^2}}$ as follows:

$$\dfrac{1}{1 - \dfrac{1}{10^2}} = \dfrac{1}{\left(1 - \dfrac{1}{100}\right)} = \dfrac{1}{\left(\dfrac{100}{100} - \dfrac{1}{100}\right)} = \dfrac{1}{\dfrac{99}{100}} = \dfrac{100}{99}.$$

Thus, substituting $\dfrac{100}{99}$ for $\dfrac{1}{1 - \dfrac{1}{10^2}}$, we have

$$\begin{aligned}
.4\overline{23} &= \dfrac{4}{10} + \dfrac{23}{10^3} \cdot \dfrac{100}{99} \\
&= \dfrac{4}{10} + \left(\dfrac{23}{100} \cdot \dfrac{100}{99}\right) \\
&= \dfrac{4}{10} + \dfrac{23}{990} \\
&= \dfrac{396}{990} + \dfrac{23}{990} \\
&= \dfrac{419}{990}.
\end{aligned}$$

● **PROBLEM 14-9**

Find the ninth term of the harmonic progression $3, 2, \dfrac{3}{2}, \ldots$

SOLUTION:

The terms of a harmonic progression that lie between two given terms are called the harmonic means between these terms. If a single harmonic mean is inserted between two numbers, it is called the harmonic mean of the numbers.

A harmonic progression (H.P.) is a sequence of numbers whose reciprocals are in arithmetic progression (A.P.). The terms of the A.P. are $\dfrac{1}{3}, \dfrac{1}{2}, \dfrac{2}{3}, \ldots$. We

112

find the ninth term of the A.P. and take its reciprocal to find the corresponding term in the H.P. The formula for the nth term, a_n, of an A.P. is $a_1 + (n - 1)d$
where a_1 is the first term and d is the common difference, the constant quantity added to each term to form the progression. Hence, if $a_n = a_1 + (n - 1)d$, a_1
$= \frac{1}{3}$ and $n = 9$, to find d subtract the first term, $\frac{1}{3}$, from the second term, $\frac{1}{2}$:

$$d = \frac{1}{2} - \frac{1}{3} = \frac{3}{6} - \frac{2}{6} = \frac{1}{6}$$

Thus,
$$a_9 = \frac{1}{3} + (9-1)\frac{1}{6} = \frac{1}{3} + 8\left(\frac{1}{6}\right) = \frac{1}{3} + \frac{4}{3} = \frac{5}{3}.$$

Therefore, the ninth term of the harmonic progression is $\frac{3}{5}$.

● PROBLEM 14-10

If a^2, b^2, c^2 are in arithmetic progression, show that $b + c$, $c + a$, $a + b$ are in
harmonic progression.

SOLUTION:

We are given that a^2, b^2, c^2 are in arithmetic progression. By this we mean
that each new term is obtained by adding a constant to the preceding term.
By adding $(ab + ac + bc)$ to each term, we see that
$a^2 + (ab + ac + bc)$, $b^2 + (ab + ac + bc)$, $c^2 + (ab + ac + bc)$
are also in arithmetic progression. These three terms can be rewritten as
$a^2 + ab + ac + bc$, $b^2 + bc + ab + ac$, $c^2 + ac + bc + ab$.
Notice that
$a^2 + ab + ac + bc = (a + b)(a + c)$
$b^2 + bc + ab + ac = (b + c)(b + a)$
$c^2 + ac + bc + ab = (c + a)(c + b)$
Therefore, the three terms can be rewritten as
$(a + b)(a + c)$, $(b + c)(b + a)$, $(c + a)(c + b)$,
which are also in arithmetic progression.
Now, dividing each term by $(a + b)(b + c)(c + a)$, we obtain

$$\frac{1}{b+c}, \frac{1}{c+a}, \frac{1}{a+b},$$ which are in arithmetic progression.

Recall that a sequence of numbers whose reciprocals form an arithmetic progression is called harmonic progression. Thus, since $\dfrac{1}{b+c}, \dfrac{1}{c+a}, \dfrac{1}{a+b}$, is an arithmetic progression, $b + c, c + a, a + b$ are in harmonic progression.

PROBLEM 14-11

Find the numerical value of the following:

(a) $\displaystyle\sum_{j=1}^{7} (2j + 1)$ (b) $\displaystyle\sum_{j=1}^{21} (3j - 2)$

SOLUTION:

If $A(r)$ is some mathematical expression and n is a positive integer, then the symbol $\displaystyle\sum_{r=0}^{n} A(r)$ means "Successively replace the letter r in the expression $A(r)$ with the numbers 0, 1, 2, ..., n and add up the terms. The symbol Σ is the Greek letter sigma and is a shorthand way to denote "the sum." It avoids having to write the sum $A(0) + A(1) + A(2) + ... + A(n)$.

(a)   Successively replace j by 1, ..., 7 and add up the terms.

$$\sum_{j=1}^{7} (2j + 1) = (2(1) + 1) + (2(2) + 1) + (2(3) + 1) + (2(4) + 1) + (2(5) + 1)$$

$$+ (2(6) + 1) + (2(7) + 1)$$
$$= (2 + 1) + (4 + 1) + (6 + 1) + (8 + 1) + (10 + 1) + (12 + 1) + (14 + 1)$$
$$= 3 + 5 + 7 + 9 + 11 + 13 + 15$$
$$= 63$$

(b)   Successively replace j by 1, 2, 3, ..., 21 and add up the terms.

$$\sum_{j=1}^{21} (3j - 2) = (3(1) - 2) + (3(2) - 2) + (3(3) - 2) + (3(4) - 2) + (3(5) - 2) + (3(6) - 2)$$

$$+ (3(7) - 2) + (3(8) - 2) + (3(9) - 2) + (3(10) - 2)$$
$$+ (3(11) - 2) + (3(12) - 2) + (3(13) - 2) + (3(14) - 2)$$
$$+ (3(15) - 2) + (3(16) - 2) + (3(17) - 2) + (3(18) - 2)$$
$$+ (3(19) - 2) + (3(20) - 2) + (3(21) - 2)$$
$$= (3 - 2) + (6 - 2) + (9 - 2) + (12 - 2) + (15 - 2) + (18 - 2)$$
$$+ (21 - 2) + (24 - 2) + (27 - 2) + (30 - 2) + (33 - 2)$$
$$+ (36 - 2) + (39 - 2) + (42 - 2) + (45 - 2) + (48 - 2)$$
$$+ (51 - 2) + (54 - 2) + (57 - 2) + (60 - 2) + (63 - 2)$$

$$= 1 + 4 + 7 + 10 + 13 + 16 + 19 + 22 + 25 + 28 + 31 + 34 + 37$$
$$+ 40 + 43 + 46 + 49 + 52 + 55 + 58 + 61$$
$$= 651$$

● PROBLEM 14-12

Establish the convergence or divergence of the series:

$$\sin\frac{\pi}{2} + \frac{1}{4}\sin\frac{\pi}{4} + \frac{1}{9}\sin\frac{\pi}{6} + \frac{1}{16}\sin\frac{\pi}{8} + \ldots.$$

SOLUTION:

To establish the convergence or divergence of the given series, we first determine the nth term of the series. By studying the law of formation of the terms of the series, we find the nth term to be: $\frac{1}{n^2}\sin\frac{\pi}{2n}$. To determine whether this series is convergent or divergent, we use the comparison test. We choose $\frac{1}{n^2}$, which is a known convergent series, since it is a p-series, $\frac{1}{n^p}$, with $p = 2$. If we can show $\frac{1}{n^2}\sin\frac{\pi}{2n} < \frac{1}{n^2}$, then $\frac{1}{n^2}\sin\frac{\pi}{2n}$ is convergent. But we can see this is true since $\sin\frac{\pi}{2n}$ is less than 1 for $n > 1$. Therefore, the given series is convergent.

● PROBLEM 14-13

Test the series:

$$1 + \frac{2!}{2^2} + \frac{3!}{3^3} + \frac{4!}{4^4} + \ldots$$

for convergence by means of the ratio test. If this test fails, use another test.

SOLUTION:

To make use of the ratio test, we find the nth term of the given series, and the $(n + 1)$th term. If we let the first term $1 = u_1$, then $\frac{2!}{2^2} = u_2$, $\frac{3!}{3^3} = u_3$, etc., up to

115

u_n and u_{n+1}. We examine the terms of the series to find the law of formation, from which we conclude

$$u_n = \frac{n!}{n^n} \text{ and } u_{n+1} = \frac{(n+1)!}{(n+1)^{n+1}}.$$

Forming the ratio $\frac{u_{n+1}}{u_n}$ we obtain

$$\frac{(n+1)!}{(n+1)^{n+1}} \cdot \frac{n^n}{n!}$$

$$= \frac{(n+1)(n!)}{(n+1)^n(n+1)} \cdot \frac{n^n}{n!}$$

$$= \frac{n^n}{(n+1)^n}$$

Now we find $\displaystyle\lim_{n\to\infty}\left|\frac{n^n}{(n+1)^n}\right|$. This can be rewritten as

$$\lim_{n\to\infty} \frac{n^n}{\left[n\left(1+\frac{1}{n}\right)\right]^n} = \lim_{n\to\infty} \frac{n^n}{n^n \cdot \left(1+\frac{1}{n}\right)^n} = \lim_{n\to\infty} \frac{1}{\left(1+\frac{1}{n}\right)^n}.$$

We now use the definition

$$e = \lim_{x\to 0} (1+x)^{\frac{1}{x}}.$$

If we let $x = \dfrac{1}{n}$ in this definition, we have: $\displaystyle\lim_{\frac{1}{n}\to 0}\left(1+\frac{1}{n}\right)^{\frac{1}{\frac{1}{n}}} = \lim_{n\to\infty}\left(1+\frac{1}{n}\right)^n$, which

is what we have above. Therefore, $\displaystyle\lim_{n\to\infty} \frac{1}{\left(1+\frac{1}{n}\right)^n} = \frac{1}{e}$. Since $e \approx 2.7$, $\dfrac{1}{e} \approx \dfrac{1}{2.7}$

which is less than 1. Hence, by the ratio test, the given series is convergent.

Determine whether the following series are convergent for the given values of a, p, and r.

(a) $a + ar + ar^2 + \ldots + ar^{n-1} + \ldots$ where $a = 5$; $r = 9$

(b) $\dfrac{1}{1^p} + \dfrac{1}{2^p} + \dfrac{1}{3^p} + \ldots + \dfrac{1}{n^p} + \ldots$ where $p = 5$

SOLUTION:

(a) $a + ar + ar^2 + \ldots + ar^{n-1} + \ldots$ represents a geometric series.

If $|r| < 1$ then the series is convergent.

If $|r| \geq 1$ then the series is divergent.

In this case, $r = 9$, and $|r| \geq 1$. Therefore, the series diverges.

(b) $\dfrac{1}{1^p} + \dfrac{1}{2^p} + \dfrac{1}{3^p} \ldots$ represents a p-series. If $p > 1$, the series converges.

If $p \leq 1$, the series diverges. In this case, $p = 5$ so $p > 1$. Therefore, the series converges.

● **PROBLEM 14-15**

Test the alternating series: $\dfrac{1+\sqrt{2}}{2} - \dfrac{1+\sqrt{3}}{4} + \dfrac{1+\sqrt{4}}{6} - \dfrac{1+\sqrt{5}}{8} + \ldots$ for convergence.

SOLUTION:

An alternating series is convergent if (a) the terms, after a certain nth term, decrease numerically, i.e., $|u_{n+1}| \leq |u_n|$, and (b) the general term approaches 0 as n becomes infinite. Therefore, we determine the nth term of the given alternating series. By discovering the law of formation, we find that the general term

is $\pm\dfrac{1+\sqrt{n+1}}{2n}$. Therefore, the preceding term is $\mp\dfrac{1+\sqrt{n}}{2(n-1)}$. To satisfy condition

(a) stated above, we must show that:

$$\frac{1+\sqrt{n+1}}{2n} < \frac{1+\sqrt{n}}{2(n-1)}.$$

Obtaining a common denominator for both these terms,

$$\frac{1}{2} \cdot \frac{\left(1 + \sqrt{n+1}\right)(n-1)}{n(n-1)} < \frac{\left(1 + \sqrt{n}\right)(n)}{n(n-1)} \cdot \frac{1}{2}$$

Since the denominators are the same, to prove condition (a) we must show,

$$1 + \sqrt{n+1}(n-1) < \left(1 + \sqrt{n}\right)(n),$$

which is obvious since subtracting 1 from n has a greater effect than adding 1 to $\sqrt{n}$. Since $|u_{n+1}| \leq |u_n|$, we have the first condition for convergence.

Now we must show that

$$\lim_{n \to \infty} \frac{1 + \sqrt{n}}{2n - 2} = 0.$$

We find that $\lim_{n \to \infty} \dfrac{1 + \sqrt{n}}{2n - 2} = \dfrac{\infty}{\infty}$, which is an indeterminate form. We therefore apply L'Hopital's Rule, obtaining:

$$\lim_{n \to \infty} \frac{\frac{1}{2} n^{-\frac{1}{2}}}{2} = \lim_{n \to \infty} \frac{1}{4\sqrt{n}} = 0.$$

Since both conditions hold, the given alternating series is convergent.

● PROBLEM 14-16

Find the limit of the sequence defined by $x_1 = \dfrac{2}{3}$ and $x_{n+1} = \dfrac{x_n + 1}{2x_n + 1}$.

SOLUTION:

We write the first four terms of the sequence $\left\{ \dfrac{2}{3}, \dfrac{5}{7}, \dfrac{12}{17}, \dfrac{29}{41}, \ldots \right\}$.

Note that we pass from $\dfrac{a}{b}$ to

$$\frac{\frac{a}{b} + 1}{\frac{2a}{b} + 1} = \frac{a + b}{2a + b}$$

from one term of the sequence to the next. To find the limit of this sequence, apply Banach's fixed point theorem, which states for the case of one variable:

Let S be a closed nonempty subset of R. Let f be a contraction mapping on S; f maps S into S such that for some k, $0 < k < 1$, and all x and y in S,

$$|f(x) - f(y)| \le k \, |x - y|. \tag{1}$$

Then, there is one and only one point x in S for which $f(x) = x$. In addition, if $x_1 \in S$ and $x_{n+1} = f(x_n)$ for all n, then $x_n \to x$ as $n \to \infty$.

To apply this theorem, first note that for $x \ge 0$,

$$\frac{1}{2} \le f(x) = \frac{x+1}{2x+1} \le 1$$

because

$$1 - \frac{x+1}{2x+1} = \frac{x}{2x+1} \ge 0.$$

Therefore, with

$$S = \left[\frac{1}{2};1\right],$$

f maps S to S and is a contraction. To prove this, note that
$$f(x) - f(y) = f'(z)(x - y)$$
where $x < z < y$, by the Mean Value Theorem. Hence,
$$|f(x) - f(y)| = |f'(z)| \, |x - y| \le k \, |x - y|$$
if $|f'(z)| \le k$. Therefore, to prove that f is a contraction mapping it suffices to show that $|f'(x)| \le k < 1$ where $x \in S$. Since

$$|f'(x)| = \frac{1}{(2x+1)^2} \le \frac{1}{4},$$

(1) is satisfied. Consequently, for $x, y \in S$ we have

$$|f(x) - f(y)| \le \frac{1}{4} \, |x - y|$$

Therefore, by the theorem, $x_n \to x$, where

$$x = f(x) = \frac{x+1}{2x+1} \quad \text{and} \quad \frac{1}{2} \le x \le 1.$$

Hence, since $x = \dfrac{x+1}{2x+1}$, we have

$$2x^2 + x = x + 1 \implies x^2 = \frac{1}{2} \implies x = \left(\frac{1}{2}\right)^{\frac{1}{2}}.$$

x cannot be $\left(\dfrac{1}{2}\right)^{\frac{1}{2}}$, because $\dfrac{1}{2} \le x \le 1$.

Thus, $\displaystyle\lim_{n \to \infty} x_n = x = \left(\frac{1}{2}\right)^{\frac{1}{2}}.$

Determine if the following series are absolutely convergent, conditionally convergent, or divergent.

(a) $\sum_{n=1}^{\infty} \frac{(-1)^{n+1}}{n}$ (b) $\sum_{n=2}^{\infty} (-1)^n \left(\frac{n}{1+n^2} \right)^n$ (c) $\sum_{n=1}^{\infty} \frac{(-1)^n 2^n}{n!}$

SOLUTION:

(a) To determine if the series

$$\sum_{n=1}^{\infty} \frac{(-1)^{n+1}}{n}$$

is convergent or divergent, the following test, called the alternating series test, is used. This test states:

An alternating series

$$a_1 - a_2 + a_3 - a_4 + \ldots = \sum_{n=1}^{\infty} (-1)^{n+1} a_n, \, a_n > 0,$$

converges if the following two conditions are satisfied:

(1) its terms are decreasing in absolute value:

$$|a_{n+1}| \le |a_n| \text{ for } n = 1, 2, \ldots$$

(2) $\lim_{n \to \infty} a_n = 0$

For this series, the terms are decreasing in absolute value since

$$1 > \frac{1}{2} > \frac{1}{3} \ldots$$

Also, the nth term approaches zero so $\lim_{n \to \infty} a_n = 0$.

Hence, the series converges. Next, if $\sum |a_n|$ converges also, then the series $\sum a_n$ is absolutely convergent. But the series of absolute values is the harmonic series $\sum_{n=1}^{\infty} \frac{1}{n}$ which is known to diverge. Hence, $\sum_{n=1}^{\infty} |a_n|$ does not converge and

the series $\sum_{n=1}^{\infty} \frac{(-1)^{n+1}}{n}$ is conditionally convergent.

(b) For the series

$$\sum_{n=2}^{\infty} (-1)^n \left(\frac{n}{1+n^2} \right)^n$$

120

use the root test, which states: Let a series $\sum_{n=1}^{\infty} a_n$ be given and let $\lim_{n \to \infty} \sqrt[n]{|a_n|} = R$

Then if $R < 1$, the series is absolutely convergent. If $R > 1$, the series diverges. If $R = 1$, the test fails.

For this series

$$\lim_{n \to \infty} \sqrt[n]{|a_n|} = \lim_{n \to \infty} \sqrt[n]{\left(\frac{n}{1+n^2}\right)^n} = \lim_{n \to \infty} \frac{n}{1+n^2} = \lim_{n \to \infty} \frac{1}{\frac{1}{n}+n} = 0.$$

Therefore, the series converges absolutely.

(c) For the series

$$\sum_{n=1}^{\infty} \frac{(-1)^n 2^n}{n!}$$

use the ratio test. This states that if $a_n \neq 0$ for $n = 1, 2, \ldots$ and

$$\lim_{n \to \infty} \left| \frac{a_n + 1}{a_n} \right| = L$$

then if $L < 1$, $\sum_{n=1}^{\infty} a_n$ is absolutely convergent, if $L = 1$, the test fails, if $L > 1$,

$\sum_{n=1}^{\infty} a_n$ is divergent.

Here

$$\lim_{n \to \infty} \left| \frac{a_n + 1}{a_n} \right| = \lim_{n \to \infty} \frac{2^{n+1}}{(n+1)!} \cdot \frac{n!}{2^n} = \lim_{n \to \infty} \frac{2^{n+1} 2^{-n} (n!)}{(n!) \cdot (n+1)}$$

$$= \lim_{n \to \infty} \frac{2}{n+1} = 0$$

Hence, $L = 0$ and the series converges absolutely.

(a) Define the general form, radius of convergence, and interval of convergence of a power series.

(b) Given the power series $\sum a_n x^n$, show that the series converges, if given that:

$$(1) \quad R = \frac{1}{L} \text{ where } L = \lim_{n \to \infty} \left| \frac{a_{n+1}}{a_n} \right|$$

exists and $|x| < R$ or

$$(2) \quad R = \frac{1}{\alpha} \text{ where } \alpha = \limsup_{n \to \infty} \sqrt[n]{|a_n|} \text{ and } |x| < R.$$

SOLUTION:

(a) By definition the general form of a power series in powers of $x - x_0$, where x_0 is fixed and x is variable, is

$$\sum_{n=0}^{\infty} a_n (x - x_0)^n = a_0 + a_1 (x - x_0) + a_2 (x - x_0)^2 + \ldots + a_n (x - x_0)^n + \ldots$$

However, in the study of power series it is convenient to look at a series of the form,

$$a_0 + a_1 x + a_2 x^2 + \ldots = \sum_{n=0}^{\infty} a_n x^n$$

This is a power series in x (i.e., $x_0 = 0$). The reason for this is that equation (1) can be reduced to the above form by the substitution $t = x - x_0$.

Furthermore, in general a power series converges absolutely for $|x| < R$ and diverges for $|x| > R$, where the constant R is called the radius of convergence of the series. However, the series may or may not converge at the end points $x = \pm R$. That is, it may converge at both, at just one, or at neither. In addition, the interval of convergence of the series is the interval $-R < x < R$, with the possible inclusion of the endpoints.

(b) For the power series $\sum a_n x^n$ if we are given that

$$(1) \quad R = \frac{1}{L} \text{ where } L = \lim_{n \to \infty} \left| \frac{a_{n+1}}{a_n} \right|$$

exists, for this case let $U_n = a_n x^n$. Then

$$\lim_{n \to \infty} \left| \frac{U_{n+1}}{U_n} \right| = \lim_{n \to \infty} \left| \frac{a_{n+1}}{a_n} x \right| = L |x|.$$

However, by the ratio test, the series $\sum U_n$ converges absolutely if

$$\lim_{n \to \infty} \left| \frac{U_{n+1}}{U_n} \right| < 1,$$

and diverges if

$$\lim_{n \to \infty} \left| \frac{U_{n+1}}{U_n} \right| > 1.$$

Consequently, for convergence

$$L \, |x| = \frac{|x|}{R} < 1.$$

Therefore, the power series converges absolutely if $|x| < R$, diverges if $|x| > R$. Also if $L = 0$ we have $R = +\infty$, and if $L = +\infty$ then R = 0.

(2) For this case, again let $U_n = a_n x^n$. Then

$$\limsup_{n \to \infty} \sqrt[n]{|U_n|} = \limsup_{n \to \infty} \sqrt[n]{|a_n x^n|}$$

$$= |x| \limsup_{n \to \infty} \sqrt[n]{|a_n|}$$

$$= |x| \alpha = \frac{|x|}{R}$$

However, by the root test, the series $\sum U_n$ converges absolutely if

$$\limsup_{n \to \infty} \sqrt[n]{|U_n|} < 1$$

and diverges if $\qquad \displaystyle\limsup_{n \to \infty} \sqrt[n]{|U_n|} > 1.$

Therefore, for convergence of the power series

$$\frac{|x|}{R} < 1 \text{ or } |x| < R \, ;$$

if $|x| > R$, the power series diverges.

In addition, if $\alpha = 0$, $R = +\infty$; if $\alpha = +\infty$, R = 0.

We make note that the second method of finding R is more powerful than the first. That is, the limit

$$\lim_{n \to \infty} \left| \frac{a_{n+1}}{a_n} \right|$$

does not exist for certain power series.

SECTION 2

TRIGONOMETRY

CHAPTER 15

LOGARITHMS AND EXPONENTIALS

Show that $a^{4\log_a b} = b^4$.

SOLUTION:

Let $x = 4\log_a b$.

Thus, $x = \log_a b^4$ Then, using the fact that

$$m = \log_r c \Rightarrow r^m = c,$$

we get $a^x = b^4$

Now, replacing x by $4\log_a b$, we get $a^{4\log_a b} = b^4$.

Express the logarithm of 7 to the base 3 in terms of common logarithms.

SOLUTION:

By definition, if $\log_b a = n$, then $b^n = a$. Therefore, if $\log_3 7 = x$, then $3^x = 7$. Take the logarithm of both sides:

$$\log 3^x = \log 7$$

By the law of the logarithm of a power of a positive number which states that

124

$\log a^n = n \log a$, $\log 3^x = x \log 3$. Hence, $x \log 3 = \log 7$. Divide both sides of this equation by $\log 3$:

$$\frac{x \log 3}{\log 3} = \frac{\log 7}{\log 3}$$

Therefore, $x = \dfrac{\log 7}{\log 3} = \log_3 7$ is the logarithm of 7 to the base 3 expressed in terms of common logarithms.

Express the logarithm $\dfrac{\sqrt{a^3}}{c^5 b^2}$ in terms of $\log a$, $\log b$, and $\log c$.

SOLUTION:

We apply the following properties of logarithms:

$$\log_b(P \cdot Q) = \log_b P + \log_b Q$$

$$\log_b(P/Q) = \log_b P - \log_b Q$$

$$\log_b(P^n) = n \log_b P$$

$$\log_b(\sqrt[n]{P}) = \frac{1}{n} \log_b P$$

Therefore,

$$\log \frac{\sqrt{a^3}}{c^5 b^2} = \log \frac{a^{\frac{3}{2}}}{c^5 b^2}$$

$$= \log a^{\frac{3}{2}} - \log(c^5 b^2)$$

$$= \frac{3}{2} \log a - (\log c^5 + \log b^2)$$

$$= \frac{3}{2} \log a - \log c^5 - \log b^2$$

$$= \frac{3}{2} \log a - 5 \log c - 2 \log b$$

Given that $\log_{10} 2 = 0.3010$ and $\log_{10} 3 = 0.4771$, find $\log_{10} \sqrt{6}$.

SOLUTION:

$\sqrt{6} = 6^{\frac{1}{2}}$, thus $\log_{10} \sqrt{6} = \log_{10} 6^{\frac{1}{2}}$. Since $\log_b x^y = y \log_b x$, $\log_{10} 6^{\frac{1}{2}} = \frac{1}{2} \log_{10} 6$.

$6 = 3 \cdot 2$, hence $\frac{1}{2} \log_{10} 6 = \frac{1}{2} \log_{10}(3 \cdot 2)$. Recall $\log_{10}(a \cdot b) = \log_{10} a + \log_{10} b$.

Thus, $\frac{1}{2} \log_{10}(3 \cdot 2) = \frac{1}{2}(\log_{10} 3 + \log_{10} 2)$. Replace our values for $\log_{10} 3$ and $\log_{10} 2$:

$$\log_{10} \sqrt{6} = \frac{1}{2}(0.4771 + 0.3010)$$

$$= \frac{1}{2}(0.7781)$$

Therefore, $\qquad \log_{10} \sqrt{6} \approx 0.3890$

Find antilog$_{10}$ 0.8762 – 2.

SOLUTION:

Let $N = $ antilog$_{10}$ 0.8762 – 2. The following relationship between log and antilog exists: $\log_{10} x = a$ is the equivalent of $x = $ antilog$_{10}$ a. Therefore,

$$\log_{10} N = 0.8762 - 2$$

The characteristic is –2. The mantissa is 0.8762. The number that corresponds to this mantissa is 7.52. This number is found from a table of common logarithms, base 10. Therefore,

$$N = 7.52 \times 10^{-2}$$

$$= 7.52 \times \left(\frac{1}{10^2}\right)$$

$$= 7.52 \times \left(\frac{1}{100}\right)$$

126

$$= 7.52 \times (.01)$$
$$N = 0.0752$$

Therefore, $N = \text{antilog}_{10}\ 0.8762 - 2 = 0.0752$.

● **PROBLEM 15-6**

Find $\text{antilog}_{10}\ 1.4850$.

SOLUTION:

By definition, $\text{antilog}_{10}\ a = N$ is equivalent to $\log_{10} N = a$. Let $\text{antilog}_{10} 1.4850 = N$. Hence, $\text{antilog}_{10} 1.4850 = N$ is equivalent to $\log_{10} N = 1.4850$. The characteristic is 1. The mantissa is 0.4850.

Therefore, the number that corresponds to this mantissa will be multiplied by 10^1 or 10. The mantissas which appear in a table of common logarithms and are closest to the mantissa 0.4850 are 0.4843 and 0.4857. The number that corresponds to the mantissa 0.4850 will be found by interpolation.

	Number	Logarithms	
d	3.05	0.4843	.0007
	x	0.4850	
.01	3.06	0.4857	.0014

Set up the following proportion:

$$\frac{d}{.01} = \frac{.0007}{.0014}$$

Cross–multiplying, $.0014d = (.01)(.0007)$, or $d = .01\left(\frac{.0007}{.0014}\right)$

$$= \left(1 \times 10^{-2}\right)\left(\frac{7 \times 10^{-4}}{1.4 \times 10^{-3}}\right)$$

$$= \frac{7 \times 10^{-6}}{1.4 \times 10^{-3}} = \frac{7}{1.4} \times \frac{10^{-6}}{10^{-3}} = 5 \times 10^{-6-(-3)}$$

$$= 5 \times 10^{-3} = 5 \times .001 = .005$$

Hence, $\qquad\qquad d = 0.005$

$$x = d + 3.05$$
$$= 0.005 + 3.050$$
$$= 3.055$$

Hence, $N = \text{antilog}_{10} 1.4850 = 3.055 \times 10$
$$= 30.550$$
$$= 30.55$$

Therefore $\text{antilog}_{10} 1.4850 = 30.55$.

● PROBLEM 15-7

Find the value of $(2.154)^5$.

SOLUTION:

We will use logs, to solve the given problem.

Let $x = (2.154)^5$. Now take the log of both sides:

$\log x = \log(2.154)^5$; and now by the rule $\log a^b = b \log a$ we obtain
$$\log x = 5 \log(2.154).$$

Log(2.154) is now found by interpolation, using a table of common logs. Notice 2.154 occurs between 2.150 and 2.160 which have recorded logs.

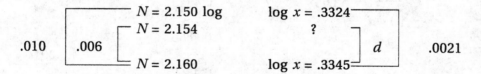

Now set up the proportion and use scientific notation.

$$\frac{.006}{.010} = \frac{d}{.0021}$$

$$\frac{6 \times 10^{-3}}{1 \times 10^{-2}} = \frac{d}{2.1 \times 10^{-3}}$$

$$\left(2.1 \times 10^{-3}\right)\left(\frac{6 \times 10^{-3}}{1 \times 10^{-2}}\right) = \left(\overline{2.1 \times 10^{-3}}\right)\left(\frac{d}{\overline{2.1 \times 10^{-3}}}\right)$$

$$\frac{12.6 \times 10^{-6}}{1 \times 10^{-2}} = d$$

$$12.6 \times 10^{-4} = d$$

$$\left(12.6\right)\left(0.0001\right) = d$$

$$0.00126 = d$$

or $$d \approx 0.0013$$

128

Hence, log 2.154 = .3345 − d = .3345 − .0013

$$\log 2.154 = .3332$$

Therefore,   log x = 5 log(2.154)

$$= 5(.3332)$$

$$\log x = 1.6660$$

The characteristic is 1. Therefore, the number that corresponds to the mantissa 0.6660 will be multiplied by 10^1 or 10. Using a table of common logarithms, the number that approximately corresponds to the mantissa is 4.63. Then,

$$x = (4.63)10 \text{ or } (2.154)^5 = x = 46.3$$

Hence, $(2.154)^5 = 46.3$

● **PROBLEM 15-8**

Find the product 5.06 × 71.32 by using logs and antilogs.

SOLUTION:

By definition, antilog a = N is equivalent to log N = a. Now substitute the value for a in the antilog expression. Therefore, antilog a = N becomes antilog (log N) = N. Let N = 5.06 × 71.32; then, 5.06 × 71.32 = antilog [log(5.06 × 71.32)]. Since 5.06 × 71.32 = 5.06 × 7.132 × 10, we write

5.06 × 71.32 = antilog [log(5.06 × 7.132 × 10)].   (1)

Evaluating the expression in the brackets:

log(5.06 × 7.132 × 10) = log 5.06 + log 7.132 + log 10.

This is true because of the following law of exponents:

log abc = log a + log b + log c.

Using a table of common logarithms to find the value of log 5.06 and noting that log 10 = 1,

log(5.06 × 7.132 × 10) = 0.7042 + (log 7.132) + 1

$$= 1.7042 + \log 7.132 \qquad (2)$$

We now evaluate log 7.132. The numbers that appear in a table of common logarithms which are closest to the number 7.132 are 7.13 and 7.14. The mantissa that corresponds to the number 7.132 will be found by interpolation.

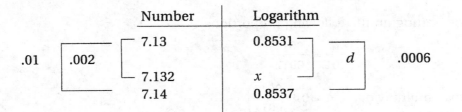

Number	Logarithm
7.13	0.8531
7.132	x
7.14	0.8537

.01   .002 d .0006

Now, setting up the following proportion:

$$\frac{d}{.0006} = \frac{.002}{.01}$$

Cross–multiplying, $\quad d = .0006\left(\dfrac{.002}{.01}\right)$

$$= \left(6 \times 10^{-4}\right)\left(\frac{2 \times 10^{-3}}{1 \times 10^{-2}}\right) = \frac{12 \times 10^{-4+(-3)}}{1 \times 10^{-2}}$$

$$= \frac{12 \times 10^{-7}}{1 \times 10^{-2}} = 12 \times 10^{-7-(-2)}$$

$$= 12 \times 10^{-5}$$

$$= \left(1.2 \times 10^{1}\right) \times 10^{-5} = 1.2 \times 10^{1+(-5)}$$

$$= 1.2 \times 10^{-4}$$

$$= 1.2 \times 0.0001$$

$$= 0.00012$$

$$\approx 0.0001$$

Hence, $\quad \log 7.132 = x \quad = 0.8531 + 0.0001$

$$= 0.8532$$

Therefore, equation (2) becomes

$$\log(5.06 \times 7.132 \times 10) = 1.7042 + 0.8532$$
$$= 2.5574$$

Equation (1) becomes

$$5.06 \times 71.32 = \text{antilog}[2.5574] = M \qquad (3)$$

By definition, antilog[2.5574] is equivalent to log $M = 2.5574$. The characteristic is 2. The mantissa is 0.5574. The number that corresponds to this mantissa will be multiplied to 10^2 or 100. The mantissas which appear in a table of logarithms and are closest to the mantissa 0.5574 are 0.5563 and 0.5575. The number that corresponds to the mantissa 0.5574 can be found by interpolation.

Number	Logarithm
3.60	0.5563
x	0.5574
3.61	0.5575

.01 ⎡ d ⎤   .0011 ⎤ .0012

Now setting up the following proportion:

$$\frac{d}{.01} = \frac{.0011}{.0012}$$

Cross–multiplying, $\quad d = .01\left(\dfrac{.0011}{.0012}\right)$

130

$$= \left(1 \times 10^{-2}\right)\left(\frac{1.1 \times 10^{-3}}{1.2 \times 10^{-3}}\right) = \frac{1.1 \times 10^{-2+(-3)}}{1.2 \times 10^{-3}}$$

$$= \frac{1.1 \times 10^{-5}}{1.2 \times 10^{-3}} = \frac{1.1}{1.2} \times 10^{-5-(-3)}$$

$$= 0.917 \times 10^{-2}$$

$$= 0.917 \times 0.01$$

$$= 0.00917$$

$$\approx 0.009$$

Hence, $x = 3.60 + 0.009$

$$= 3.600 + 0.009$$

$$= 3.609$$

Therefore, $M = 3.609 \times 10^2 = 360.9$. Equation (3) becomes

$$5.06 \times 71.32 = M = 360.9$$

● PROBLEM 15-9

If colog $a = b$, find log a.

SOLUTION:

We will solve this problem for the general case, and then apply it to our specific case.

$$\text{colog } N = \log \frac{1}{N} = \log 1 - \log N$$

$$= 0 - \log N = - \log N$$

$$\text{colog } a = b = - \log a$$

Therefore, log $a = -b$

● PROBLEM 15-10

The graph of an exponential function f contains the point (2, 9). What is the base of f?

SOLUTION:

Since f is an exponential function, we know that $f(x) = b^x$, where b, the base, is a positive number that we are to determine. An exponential function f may also be written as $y = f(x) = b^x$.

131

Since the exponential function f contains the point $(2, 9)$,
$$9 = f(2) = b^2 \text{ or } b^2 = 9$$
$$\sqrt{b^2} = \sqrt{9}$$
$$b = 3$$

Note that only the positive square root was taken, since for the base b, a positive number is desired.

/

Solve for x in the equation $7^{2x-1} - 5^{3x} = 0$.

SOLUTION:

Writing the equation as $7^{2x-1} = 5^{3x}$, and equating logarithms of both members, we have
$$\log 7^{2x-1} = \log 5^{3x}.$$
Recall $\log x^y = y \log x$. Thus,
$$(2x - 1)\log 7 = 3x \log 5.$$
Looking up $\log 7$ and $\log 5$ in our log table and substituting,
$$(2x - 1)(0.8451) = 3x(0.6990).$$
Hence,
$$1.6902x - 0.8451 = 2.097x$$
$$0.4068x = -0.8451$$
$$x = -2.077.$$

Express y in terms of x if $\log_b y = 2x + \log_b x$.

SOLUTION:

Moving $\log_b x$ to the other side of the equation, we have
$$\log_b y - \log_b x = 2x.$$

A property of logarithms is that the logarithm of the quotient of two positive numbers S and T is equal to the difference of the logarithms of the numbers; that is,

$$\log_b \frac{S}{T} = \log_b S - \log_b T.$$

Therefore, $$\log_b \frac{y}{x} = 2x.$$

Now use the definition of logarithm: The logarithm of N to the base b is $x = \log_b N$; and $b^x = N$ is an equivalent statement. Then,

$$2x = \log_b \frac{y}{x} \text{ is equivalent to}$$

$$b^{2x} = \frac{y}{x}.$$

Solving for y we obtain.

$$y = x \cdot b^{2x}$$

● **PROBLEM 15-13**

Find the following by inspection:
(a) $\ln 50067400 - \ln 500674 - 2 \ln 10$

(b) $\ln e^{\left(5x^2 + x\right)}$ where $x = 1$

SOLUTION:

Before we solve either of these problems, a few rules about the natural log which are helpful are

$$\ln a - \ln b = \ln \frac{a}{b}$$

$$\ln a + \ln b = \ln a \cdot b$$
$$\ln e^x = x$$
$$\ln a^n = n \ln a$$

(a) $\ln 50067400 - \ln 500674 - 2 \ln 10$

$$= \ln \frac{50067400}{500674} - 2 \ln 10 = \ln 100 - 2 \ln 10$$

$$= \ln 100 - \ln 10^2 = \ln 100 - \ln 100 = 0$$

(b) $\ln e^{\left(5x^2 + x\right)} = 5x^2 + x = 5(1)^2 + 1 = 6$

Find the inverse of the function

$$y = \ln\left(1 + \sqrt{1 - e^2 x^4}\right) - 2\ln x - 1. \tag{1}$$

SOLUTION:

Transfer all the natural logarithm functions to one side with the variables and constants on the other side. Thus,

$$y + 1 = \ln\left(1 + \sqrt{1 - e^2 x^4}\right) - 2\ln x$$

Recall $a \log b = \log b^a$ thus $2 \ln x = \ln x^2$ and

$$y + 1 = \ln\left(1 + \sqrt{1 - e^2 x^4}\right) - \ln x^2$$

Since $\ln a - \ln b = \ln \dfrac{a}{b}, \ln\left(1 + \sqrt{1 - e^2 x^4}\right) - \ln x^2 = \ln \dfrac{1 + \sqrt{1 - e^2 x^4}}{x^2}$

Thus, $y + 1 = \ln \dfrac{1 + \sqrt{1 - e^2 x^4}}{x^2}$.

The inverse function of the logarithmic function is the exponential function. If $\ln u = v$ then $e^v = u$. Here

$$u = \frac{1 + \sqrt{1 - e^2 x^4}}{x^2}, v = y + 1$$

$$e^{y+1} = \frac{1 + \sqrt{1 - e^2 x^4}}{x^2}$$

Then, multiply by x^2 and subtract 1 from both sides to obtain

$$x^2 e^{y+1} - 1 = \sqrt{1 - e^2 x^4}.$$

Rationalizing this equation, we get by squaring:

$$x^4 e^{2y+2} - 2x^2 e^{y+1} + 1 = 1 - e^2 x^4.$$

Now x must be positive for the term ln x, in equation (1) to have meaning. ln x exists for $x > 0$. In particular, x cannot be zero; hence, after subtracting 1 from each member of the last equation, we may further simplify by dividing by ex^2.

$$x^4 e^{2y+2} - 2x^2 e^{y+1} = -e^2 x^4 \text{ (subtracting 1 from each side)}$$
$$x^2 e^{2y+1} - 2e^y = -ex^2 \text{ (dividing by } ex^2\text{)}$$
$$x^2 e^{2y+1} + ex^2 = 2e^y$$
$$ex^2\left(e^{2y} + 1\right) = 2e^y \text{ (factor out } ex^2\text{)}$$

Solve for x^2.

$$x^2 = \frac{2e^y}{e\left(e^{2y}+1\right)} = \frac{2}{e\left(e^y + e^{-y}\right)}$$

Remembering that x must be positive, we extract only the positive square root to obtain

$$x = \sqrt{\frac{2}{e\left(e^y + e^{-y}\right)}}$$

This is the required inverse function.

The form of relation (2) would seem to indicate that, if $x = x_1$ is the value corresponding to $y = y_1$, then $y = -y_1$ will also yield $x = x_1$. However, equation (1) shows that y cannot be replaced by $-y$ without creating thereby a different functional relation. In fact, y as given by (1) will be non–negative for every real value of x in its permissible range, $0 < x \le e^{-\frac{1}{2}}$. $x = 0$ because ln 0 does not exist. If $x \nleq e^{-\frac{1}{2}}$, for example, $x = e$, then

$$\ln\left(1 + \sqrt{1 - e^2 e^4}\right)$$

does not exist. The functional relation $y = \ln\left(1 + \sqrt{1 - e^2 e^4}\right) - 2\ln x - 1$ yields only non-positive values of y and likewise leads to the same inverse relation (2). If you select an x from the domain $0 < x \le e^{-\frac{1}{2}}$, for example $x = e^{-\frac{1}{2}}$, and substitute it in $y = \ln\left(1 + \sqrt{1 - e^2 x^4}\right) - 2\ln x - 1$, then

$$y = \ln\left(1 + \sqrt{1 - e^2 e^{-\frac{4}{2}}}\right) - 2\ln e^{-\frac{1}{2}} - 1$$

$$= \ln\left(1 + \sqrt{1 - e^0}\right) - 2\left(-\frac{1}{2}\right) - 1$$

$$y = \ln(1) + 1 - 1 = 0.$$

Therefore, y is a non-positive value.
Our example thus illustrates the fact that all conclusions drawn from a deduced inverse function must be checked against the original relation.

CHAPTER 16

ANGLES AND ARCS

Complete the following table:

	1	2	3	4	5	6	7	8	9
Angle measure in radians	0	$\frac{1}{6}\pi$	$\frac{1}{4}\pi$		$\frac{1}{2}\pi$	$\frac{2}{3}\pi$			π
Angle measure in degrees	0°			60°			135°	150°	

SOLUTION:

If an angle has A degrees and also t radians, then the numbers A and t are related by the equation

$$\frac{A}{180°} = \frac{t}{\pi} \qquad (1)$$

Thus, equation (1) can be used to complete the table. For column 2:

$$\frac{A}{180°} = \frac{\frac{1}{6}\pi}{\pi}$$

$$\frac{A}{180°} = \frac{1}{6}$$

Multiply both sides by 180°:

$$180°\left(\frac{A}{180°}\right) = 180°\left(\frac{1}{6}\right)$$

$$A = 30°$$

For column 3:

$$\frac{A}{180°} = \frac{\frac{1}{4}\pi}{\pi}$$

$$\frac{A}{180°} = \frac{1}{4}$$

Multiply both sides by 180°:

$$180°\left(\frac{A}{180°}\right) = 180°\left(\frac{1}{4}\right)$$

$$A = 45°$$

For column 4:

$$\frac{60°}{180°} = \frac{t}{\pi}$$

$$\frac{1}{3} = \frac{t}{\pi}$$

Multiply both sides by π,

$$\pi\left(\frac{1}{3}\right) = \pi\left(\frac{t}{\pi}\right)$$

$$\frac{1}{3}\pi = t$$

For column 5:

$$\frac{A}{180°} = \frac{\frac{1}{2}\pi}{\pi}$$

$$\frac{A}{180°} = \frac{1}{2}$$

Multiply both sides by 180°:

$$180°\left(\frac{A}{180°}\right) = 180°\left(\frac{1}{2}\right)$$

$$A = 90°$$

For column 6:

$$\frac{A}{180°} = \frac{\frac{2}{3}\pi}{\pi}$$

$$\frac{A}{180°} = \frac{2}{3}$$

Multiply both sides by 180°:

$$180°\left(\frac{A}{180°}\right) = 180°\left(\frac{2}{3}\right)$$

$$A = 120°$$

For column 7:
$$\frac{135°}{180°} = \frac{t}{\pi}$$

$$\frac{3}{4} = \frac{t}{\pi}$$

Multiply both sides by π,

$$\pi\left(\frac{3}{4}\right) = \pi\left(\frac{t}{\pi}\right)$$

$$\frac{3}{4}\pi = t$$

For column 8:
$$\frac{150°}{180°} = \frac{t}{\pi}$$

$$\frac{5}{6} = \frac{t}{\pi}$$

Multiply both sides by π,

$$\pi\left(\frac{5}{6}\right) = \pi\left(\frac{t}{\pi}\right)$$

$$\frac{5}{6}\pi = t$$

For column 9:
$$\frac{A}{180°} = \frac{\pi}{\pi}$$

$$\frac{A}{180°} = 1$$

Multiply both sides by 180°:

$$180°\left(\frac{A}{180°}\right) = 180°(1)$$

$$A = 180°$$

All of the computed values are now put into the table as follows:

	1	2	3	4	5	6	7	8	9
Angle measure in radians	0	$\frac{1}{6}\pi$	$\frac{1}{4}\pi$	$\frac{1}{3}\pi$	$\frac{1}{2}\pi$	$\frac{2}{3}\pi$	$\frac{3}{4}\pi$	$\frac{5}{6}\pi$	π
Angle measure in degrees	0°	30°	45°	60°	90°	120°	135°	150°	180°

What primary angle is co-terminal with the angle of –743° ?

SOLUTION:

$$-743° = \alpha - n \cdot 360° \tag{1}$$
$$-743° = \alpha - 3 \cdot 360° = \alpha - 1080° \tag{2}$$

Multiply both sides of equation (2) by –1.

$$-1(-743°) = -1(\alpha - 1080°)$$
$$743° = -\alpha + 1080°$$
$$743° = 1080° - \alpha \tag{3}$$

Note that the positive integer value chosen for n results in an angle (in equation (3)) which is larger than but closest to the angle of 743°. Also,

$$0° \leq \alpha \cdot 360°.$$

From equation (3), $\alpha = 1080° - 743° = 337°$.

What primary angle is co-terminal with the angle of $5\frac{1}{4}\pi$ radians?

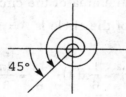

SOLUTION:

The figure illustrates the angle of $5\frac{1}{4}\pi$ radians.

Note that the angle of $5\frac{1}{4}\pi$ radians has a reference angle of 45°. However, we seek a primary angle (an angle between 0° and 360°) which is co-terminal with $5\frac{1}{4}\pi$; that is, which has the same terminal side as an angle of $5\frac{1}{4}\pi$ radians. Also, since a primary angle is a positive angle, its initial side is the positive x-axis and the angle revolves in the counterclockwise direction. Therefore, a primary angle with the same terminal side as an angle of $5\frac{1}{4}\pi$ radians is

$$(180° + 45°) = 225° = (\pi + \frac{\pi}{4}) \text{ radians} = \frac{5}{4}\pi \text{ radians}.$$

● **PROBLEM 16-4**

Find the area of a sector in which the measure of the central angle is 60° and the radius of the circle is 2.

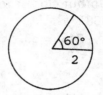

SOLUTION:

Note the diagram.

The central angle, 60°, is $\frac{1}{6} \times (360°)$; that is, $60° = \frac{1}{6} \times$ (circumference of circle). Therefore, one-sixth of the area of the circle is covered. Using the fact that the area of the total area of the circle is $A = \pi r^2$, the area covered by the sector given in this problem is

$$A = \frac{1}{6}\pi r^2 = \frac{1}{6}\pi(2)^2 = \frac{1}{6}\pi(4) = \frac{4\pi}{6} = \frac{2\pi}{3}.$$

● **PROBLEM 16-5**

What length of arc is subtended by a central angle of 75° on a circle 13.7 inches in radius?

SOLUTION:

Let θ denote a central angle in a circle of radius r, and let s be the length of the intercepted arc, measured in the same units as the radius. Then if θ is an angle measured in radians, the length of the arc, s, is $s = r\theta$.

140

We must express the given angle in radians. Since 2π radians = 360° then 1° = $2\pi/360$ radians = $\pi/180$ radians. Thus, 75° = 75 × $\pi/180$ radians = 5/12 π radians.

Substituting this value into the relation $s = r\theta$, we have

$$s = 13.7\left(\frac{5}{12}\pi\right) \text{ inches } = (5.71\pi) \text{ inches}$$

$$= (5.71)(3.14) \text{ inches}$$
$$\approx 17.9 \text{ inches.}$$

● PROBLEM 16-6

In a circle whose radius is 8 inches, find the number of degrees contained in the central angle whose arc length is 2π inches.

SOLUTION:

The measure of a central angle is equal to the measure of the arc it intercepts.

The ratio of arc length to circumference, in linear units, will be equal to the ratio of arc length to circumference as measured in degrees.

If n = the number of degrees in the arc 2π inches long, then

$$\frac{\text{length of arc}}{\text{circumference}} = \frac{n}{360°}$$

By substitution,

$$\frac{2\pi \text{ in.}}{2\pi(8 \text{ in.})} = \frac{n}{360°}$$

$$\frac{1}{8} = \frac{n}{360°}$$
$$360° = 8n$$
$$45° = n$$

Therefore, the central angle contains 45°.

● PROBLEM 16-7

The lengths of the sides of a triangle are 8, 15, and 17. Show that the triangle is a right triangle.

SOLUTION:

This problem requires the use of the converse of the Pythagorean Theorem, which states that if the square of the length of one side of a triangle is equal to the sum of the squares of the lengths of the other two sides, then the triangle is a right triangle.

Let $x = 17$, the longest side of the triangle and let $y = 8$ and $z = 15$.

Then, $\qquad x^2 = (17)^2 = 289$

and $\qquad y^2 + z^2 = (8)^2 + (15)^2 = 64 + 225 = 289$.

Since $17^2 = 8^2 + 15^2$, the triangle is a right triangle.

CHAPTER 17

TRIGONOMETRIC FUNCTIONS

● **PROBLEM 17-1**

Construct a table to indicate the signs of all the trigonometric functions for all four quadrants.

SOLUTION:

Quadrant	sin α	cos α	tan α	cot α	sec α	csc α
I	+	+	+	+	+	+
II	+	−	−	−	−	+
III	−	−	+	+	−	−
IV	−	+	−	−	+	−

Calculate the values of the six trigonometric functions at the point $\frac{1}{3}\pi$.

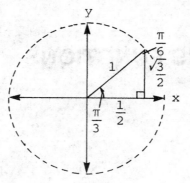

SOLUTION:

To find the trigonometric point $P\left(\frac{1}{3}\pi\right)$, proceed around the unit circle in a counterclockwise direction, since $\frac{\pi}{3}$ is a positive angle. Recall that $\sin 60° = \sin\left(\frac{\pi}{3}\right) = \frac{\sqrt{3}}{2}$. Now, using the Pythagorean theorem and the fact that the hypotenuse is unity because it is a radius of the unit circle we can compute the third side, which we find to be $\frac{1}{2}$ (see figure). Therefore, the coordinates of the trigonometric point $P\left(\frac{1}{3}\pi\right)$ are $\left(\frac{1}{2}, \frac{\sqrt{3}}{2}\right)$. Hence, we apply the following equations:

$$\cos\theta = \frac{\text{adjacent side}}{\text{hypotenuse}} \qquad \sec\theta = \frac{1}{\cos\theta} = \frac{\text{hypotenuse}}{\text{adjacent side}}$$

$$\sin\theta = \frac{\text{opposite side}}{\text{hypotenuse}} \qquad \csc\theta = \frac{1}{\sin\theta} = \frac{\text{hypotenuse}}{\text{opposite side}}$$

$$\tan\theta = \frac{\text{opposite side}}{\text{adjacent side}} \qquad \cot\theta = \frac{\cos\theta}{\sin\theta} = \frac{\text{adjacent side}}{\text{opposite side}}$$

Thus, $\qquad \cos\frac{1}{3}\pi = \frac{1}{2}, \qquad\qquad \sec\frac{1}{3}\pi = 2,$

$$\sin\frac{1}{3}\pi = \frac{1}{2}\sqrt{3}, \quad \csc\frac{1}{3}\pi = \frac{2}{\sqrt{3}} = \frac{2}{\sqrt{3}} \cdot \frac{\sqrt{3}}{\sqrt{3}} = \frac{2}{3}\sqrt{3},$$

$$\tan \frac{1}{3}\pi = \sqrt{3}, \qquad \cot \frac{1}{3}\pi = \frac{1}{\sqrt{3}} = \frac{1}{\sqrt{3}} \cdot \frac{\sqrt{3}}{\sqrt{3}} = \frac{1}{3}\sqrt{3}$$

● **PROBLEM 17-3**

Find the values of the trigonometric functions of an angle of –510°.

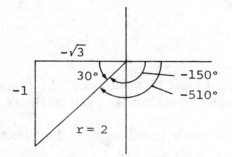

SOLUTION:

We see that angles of –510° and –150° are coterminal angles having the same values for the trigonometric functions. The reference angle of an angle of –150° is an angle of 30° and –150° is a third quadrant angle. In the third quadrant, the tangent and cotangent functions are positive while the other four functions are negative. This yields

$$\sin (-510°) = -\sin 30° = -\frac{1}{2}$$

$$\csc(-510°) = -\csc 30° = -2$$

$$\cos (-510°) = -\cos 30° = -\frac{\sqrt{3}}{2}$$

$$\sec(-510°) = -\sec 30° = \frac{-2}{\sqrt{3}} = \frac{-\sqrt{2}}{3} \times \frac{\sqrt{3}}{\sqrt{3}} = \frac{-2}{3}\sqrt{3}$$

$$\tan (-510°) = \tan 30° = \frac{1}{\sqrt{3}} = \frac{1}{\sqrt{3}} \times \frac{\sqrt{3}}{\sqrt{3}} = \frac{1}{3}\sqrt{3}$$

$$\cot(510°) = \cot 30° = \sqrt{3}$$

Given that tan θ = 2 and cos θ is negative, find the other functions of θ.

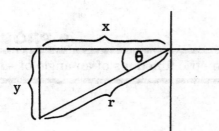

SOLUTION:

Since cos θ is negative, θ must be a second or third quadrant angle. In the second quadrant, the tangent function is negative. Hence, θ must be a third quadrant angle.

In the figure, the trigonometric functions have the following values:

$$\sin \theta = \frac{\text{opposite side}}{\text{hypotenuse}} = \frac{y}{r},$$

$$\cos \theta = \frac{\text{adjacent side}}{\text{hypotenuse}} = \frac{x}{r},$$

$$\tan \theta = \frac{\text{opposite side}}{\text{adjacent side}} = \frac{y}{x},$$

$$\cot \theta = \frac{1}{\tan \theta} = \frac{1}{y/x} = \frac{x}{y},$$

$$\sec \theta = \frac{1}{\cos \theta} = \frac{1}{x/r} = \frac{r}{x}, \text{ and}$$

$$\csc \theta = \frac{1}{\sin \theta} = \frac{1}{y/r} = \frac{r}{y}$$

Therefore, in this problem,

$$\tan \theta = 2 = \frac{-2}{-1} = \frac{y}{x}.$$

Hence, $y = -2$ and $x = -1$. Also, from the figure, $r^2 = x^2 + y^2$ (by the Pythagorean Theorem). So,

$$r^2 = x^2 + y^2 = (-1)^2 + (-2)^2 = 1 + 4 = 5,$$

and $r = \sqrt{5}$. Therefore,

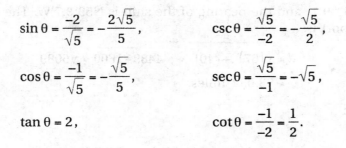

$$\sin\theta = \frac{-2}{\sqrt{5}} = -\frac{2\sqrt{5}}{5}, \qquad \csc\theta = \frac{\sqrt{5}}{-2} = -\frac{\sqrt{5}}{2},$$

$$\cos\theta = \frac{-1}{\sqrt{5}} = -\frac{\sqrt{5}}{5}, \qquad \sec\theta = \frac{\sqrt{5}}{-1} = -\sqrt{5},$$

$$\tan\theta = 2, \qquad \cot\theta = \frac{-1}{-2} = \frac{1}{2}.$$

● PROBLEM 17-5

A ship is 67 miles west and 40 miles north of the port it sailed from, travelling in a straight line. What is the distance and bearing of the ship from the port? (See figure.)

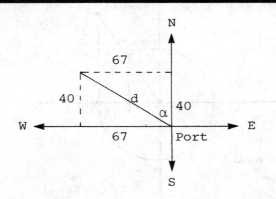

SOLUTION:

In order to specify the bearing of some traveling vehicle, the angle of the direction in which the vehicle is traveling must be discovered. To do this we superimpose our direction upon the coordinate axes by extending a line from the origin to the point (x, y), where x is the distance traveled east or west, and y is the distance traveled north or south. The distance in the direction of travel is determined using the Pythagorean Theorem: $d^2 = x^2 + y^2$. The angle that the direction makes with a north/south line is determined using the form

$$\tan\alpha = \frac{\text{side opposite } \alpha}{\text{side adjacent } \alpha} = \frac{x}{y}$$

$$= \frac{67}{40} = 1.675$$

$$\approx \tan 59°9.7'$$

147

Hence, $\alpha \approx 59°9.7'$ and the bearing of the ship is N59°9.7'W. The distance of the ship from port is:

$$d = \sqrt{(67)^2 + (40)^2} = \sqrt{4489 + 1600} = \sqrt{6089}$$

$$\approx 78.032 \text{ miles.}$$

● PROBLEM 17-6

(a) Show that tan $\alpha = bc$ in figure 1a.
(b) Determine which segment in figure 1a has measure equal to sec α.
(c) Determine which segment in figure 1b has length equal to cot α.
(d) Determine which segment in figure 1b has measure equal to csc α.

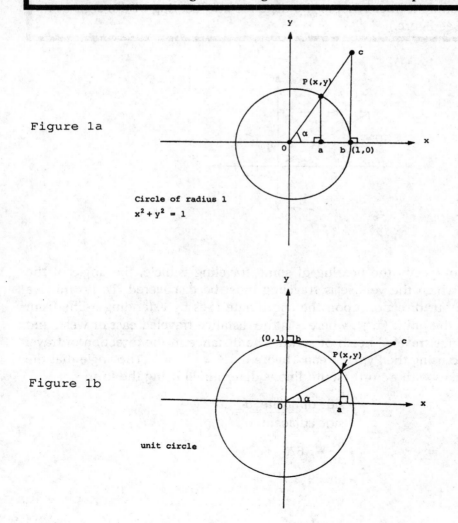

Figure 1a

Circle of radius 1
$x^2 + y^2 = 1$

Figure 1b

unit circle

SOLUTION:

(a) By definition, $\tan \alpha = \dfrac{aP}{ao}$.

From figure 1a, $\angle Poa = \angle cob = \alpha$ and $\angle Pao = \angle cbo = 90°$.
By the Angle-Angle Similarity Theorem we have $\Delta aoP \sim \Delta boc$.

Hence $\dfrac{ao}{bo} = \dfrac{aP}{bc} = \dfrac{oP}{oc}$, which gives $\dfrac{aP}{ao} = \dfrac{bc}{bo} = \tan \alpha$.

Since $bo = 1$, $\tan \alpha = \dfrac{bc}{bo} = bc$.

(b) By definition, $\sec \alpha = \dfrac{oP}{ao}$. From part (a), one has $\dfrac{ao}{bo} = \dfrac{oP}{oc}$,

which gives $\dfrac{oP}{ao} = \dfrac{oc}{bo} = \dfrac{oc}{1} = \sec \alpha$, i.e., $\sec \alpha = oc$.

(c) From figure 1b, one has $\angle Pao = \angle obc = 90°$, thus $bc /\!/ ao$. Then $\angle Poa = \angle ocb = \alpha$. Therefore, $\Delta bco \sim \Delta aoP$.

Since $\Delta bco \sim \Delta aoP$, $\dfrac{ao}{bc} = \dfrac{aP}{bo} = \dfrac{oP}{co}$ and $\cot \alpha = \dfrac{ao}{aP} = \dfrac{bc}{bo} = \dfrac{bc}{1} = bc$.

(d) $\csc \alpha = \dfrac{oP}{aP}$ Using the result from part (c), one obtains

$$\dfrac{oP}{aP} = \dfrac{co}{bo}$$

$$\csc \alpha = \dfrac{oP}{aP} = \dfrac{co}{bo} = \dfrac{co}{1} = co.$$

By the same technique used here, one can represent all the trigonometric functions of any angle θ by a line segment, i.e., the line representation of the trigonometric functions.

149

CHAPTER 18

TABLES AND LOGARITHMS OF TRIGONOMETRIC FUNCTIONS

● **PROBLEM 18-1**

Find cos 37°12'.

SOLUTION:

See a table of natural trigonometric functions, which is constructed in terms of multiples of ten minutes. The cosine of 37°12' lies between 37°10' and 37° 20'. Therefore, we must interpolate. The cosine decreases as the angle increases, so we form our proportion as follows, where

x = the cosine of the angle 37°12'
d = the difference between cos 37°10' and cos 37°12'

$$10' \begin{bmatrix} 2' \begin{bmatrix} \cos 37°10' = 0.7969 \\ \cos 37°12' = x \end{bmatrix} d \\ \cos 37°20' = 0.7951 \end{bmatrix} -0.0018$$

$$\frac{2}{10} = \frac{d}{-0.0018}$$

Cross-multiply to obtain

$$10d = 2(-0.0018)$$
$$d = .2(-0.0018)$$
$$= -0.00036$$
$$d \approx -0.0004$$

150

Thus,
$$x = 0.7969 - 0.0004$$
$$= 0.7965$$

Since the cosine is positive in the first quadrant,
$$\cos 37°12' = 0.7965$$

Remember that results obtained by interpolation are approximations. You should not use an answer that is more accurate than the original data, in this case, four significant digits.

● PROBLEM 18-2

Find the value of tan 38°46' by use of interpolation.

SOLUTION:

Since 38°46' is between 38°40' and 38°50', we assume that tan 38°36' is between tan 38°40' and tan 38°50'. In fact, since 38°46' is six–tenths of the way from 38°40' toward 38°50', we assume that tan 38°46' is six–tenths of the way from tan 38°40' = .8002 toward tan 38°50' = .8050. Using these assumptions we perform the following interpolation:

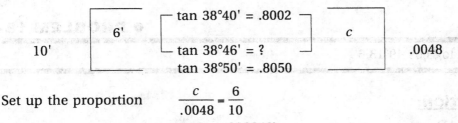

Set up the proportion $\dfrac{c}{.0048} = \dfrac{6}{10}$

$$10c = 6(.0048)$$

$$c = \frac{6}{10}(.0048) = .0029$$

$$\tan 38°46' = .8002 + .0029 = .8031$$

Therefore, c was added because tan θ increases from θ = 38°40' to θ = 38°50'.

● PROBLEM 18-3

Find log sin 36°41'.

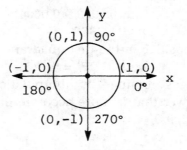

SOLUTION:

From a table of logarithms of trigonometric functions we find log sin 36°40' and log sin 36°50'. Then, by the process of interpolation we find: log sin 36° 41' = 9.77626 − 10. Since all values of the sine function for acute angles are in the range of $0 \le \sin x \le 1$, the characteristic is negative. (Recall that for a number less than one, the characteristic is negative.) The range of sine can be seen by inspecting the accompanying figure. Sine is given by the y coordinate; cos is given by the x coordinate. Observe that y value varies from 0 to 1, as the angle varies from 0° to 90°.

● PROBLEM 18-4

Find log cos 49°13.6'.

SOLUTION:

First consult a table of logarithms of trigonometric functions.

Notice that 49°13.6' lies between 49°10' and 49°20', so that the log of 49°13.6' will occur between the logs of 49°10' and 49°20' and can be determined by interpolation.

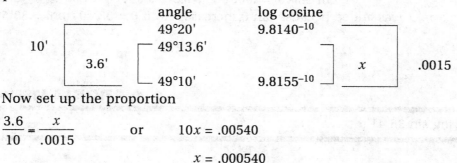

Now set up the proportion

$$\frac{3.6}{10} = \frac{x}{.0015} \qquad \text{or} \qquad 10x = .00540$$

$$x = .000540$$

152

Since cos decreases on the interval $0 \le \theta < \dfrac{\pi}{2}$, subtract x from the log cosine of 49°10'.

$$\begin{array}{r} 9.8155 \\ -\ .000540 \\ \hline 9.814960 \end{array}$$

Thus, log cosine 49°13.6' is 9.81496 − 10.

CHAPTER 19

TRIGONOMETRIC IDENTITIES AND FORMULAS

Derive the formulas for

(a) $\cot 2\alpha$ in terms of $\cot \alpha$

(b) $\sin \dfrac{1}{2}\alpha$ in terms of $\cos \theta$

(c) $\tan \dfrac{1}{2}\alpha$ in terms of $\cos \theta$

SOLUTION:

(a) $\quad \cot 2\alpha = \dfrac{\cos 2\alpha}{\sin 2\alpha} = \dfrac{\cos(\alpha + \alpha)}{\sin(\alpha + \alpha)}$

$$= \dfrac{\cos\alpha\cos\alpha - \sin\alpha\sin\alpha}{\sin\alpha\cos\alpha + \cos\alpha\sin\alpha}$$

Dividing both numerator and denominator by $\sin^2 \alpha$, one obtains

$$\cot 2\alpha = \dfrac{\dfrac{\cos^2\alpha}{\sin^2\alpha} - 1}{\dfrac{\cos\alpha}{\sin\alpha} + \dfrac{\cos\alpha}{\sin\alpha}} = \dfrac{\cot\alpha^2 - 1}{2\cot\alpha}$$

(b) $\quad \cos 2\theta = 1 - 2\sin^2\theta$. Let $\theta = \dfrac{\alpha}{2}$. Then,

154

$$\cos 2\left(\frac{\alpha}{2}\right) = \cos \alpha = 1 - 2\sin^2 \frac{\alpha}{2}$$

$$\sin^2 \frac{\alpha}{2} = \frac{1}{2}\left[1 - \cos \alpha\right]$$

$$\sin \frac{\alpha}{2} = \pm\sqrt{\frac{1 - \cos \alpha}{2}}$$

(c) $\cos 2\theta = 2\cos^2 \theta - 1$. Letting $\theta = \frac{\alpha}{2}$, one can obtain $\cos \frac{\alpha}{2} = \pm\sqrt{\frac{\cos \alpha + 1}{2}}$

by the same method as in part (2).

Now, $$\tan \frac{\alpha}{2} = \frac{\sin \frac{\alpha}{2}}{\cos \frac{\alpha}{2}} = \pm\sqrt{\frac{\frac{1 - \cos \alpha}{2}}{\frac{1 + \cos \alpha}{2}}} = \pm\sqrt{\frac{1 - \cos \alpha}{1 + \cos \alpha}}$$

● PROBLEM 19-2

Find the exact value for
(a) sin 37.5° sin 7.5°
(b) sin 52.5° cos 7.5°

SOLUTION:

Use the formulas for the products of sines and cosines.
(a) sin 37.5° sin 7.5°

$$= -\frac{1}{2}\left[\cos(37.5° + 7.5°) - \cos(37.5° - 7.5°)\right]$$

$$= -\frac{1}{2}\left[\cos 45° - \cos 30°\right]$$

$$= -\frac{1}{2}\left(\frac{\sqrt{2}}{2} - \frac{\sqrt{3}}{2}\right) = -\left(\frac{\sqrt{2} - \sqrt{3}}{4}\right) = \frac{\sqrt{3} - \sqrt{2}}{4}$$

(b) sin 52.5° cos 7.5°

$$= \frac{1}{2}\left[\sin(52.5° + 7.5°) + \sin(52.5° - 7.5°)\right]$$

$$= \frac{1}{2} \ (\sin 60° + \sin 45°) = \frac{1}{2} \left(\frac{\sqrt{3}}{2} + \frac{\sqrt{2}}{2} \right)$$

$$= \frac{\sqrt{3} + \sqrt{2}}{4}.$$

● PROBLEM 19-3

Find the exact value for
(a) sin 75° – sin 15°
(b) sin² 22.5°
(c) tan² 15°

SOLUTION:

(a) By use of the formula for the difference of sines, one obtains

$$\sin 75° - \sin 15° = 2 \ \cos \frac{1}{2}(75° + 15°)\sin \frac{1}{2}(75° - 15°)$$

$$= 2 \ \cos\left(\frac{90°}{2}\right) \sin\left(\frac{60°}{2}\right) = 2 \ \cos 45° \sin 30°$$

$$= 2\left(\frac{\sqrt{2}}{2}\right)\left(\frac{1}{2}\right) = \frac{2\sqrt{2}}{4} = \frac{\sqrt{2}}{2}$$

(b) Since $\qquad \cos 2\alpha = 1 - 2 \sin^2\alpha,$

$$\sin^2\alpha = \frac{1 - \cos 2\alpha}{2}.$$

Then, $\qquad \sin^2 22.5° = \dfrac{1 - \cos 2 \times 22.5°}{2}$

$$= \frac{1}{2} - \frac{1}{2}\cos 45° = \frac{1}{2} - \frac{1}{2}\left(\frac{\sqrt{2}}{2}\right) = \frac{1}{2} - \frac{\sqrt{2}}{4}$$

(c) Using the double angle formula

$$\cos 2\alpha = 2 \cos^2\alpha - 1, \text{ one gets } \cos^2\alpha = \frac{1}{2}(\cos 2\alpha + 1).$$

Now $\qquad \tan^2 \alpha = \dfrac{\sin^2 \alpha}{\cos^2 \alpha} = \dfrac{\dfrac{1 - \cos 2\alpha}{2}}{\dfrac{1 + \cos 2\alpha}{2}} = \dfrac{1 - \cos 2\alpha}{1 + \cos 2\alpha}$

so
$$\tan^2 15° = \frac{1 - \cos 2 \times 15°}{1 + \cos 2 \times 15°} = \frac{1 - \cos 30°}{1 + \cos 30°}$$

$$= \frac{1 - \dfrac{\sqrt{3}}{2}}{1 + \dfrac{\sqrt{3}}{2}} = \frac{2 - \sqrt{3}}{2 + \sqrt{3}}$$

● **PROBLEM 19-4**

Simplify $\dfrac{\frac{1}{2}\left(\cos 3\alpha + \cos \alpha\right)}{\sin \alpha - \sin\left(-3\alpha\right)}$

SOLUTION:

$$\frac{\frac{1}{2}\left(\cos 3\alpha + \cos \alpha\right)}{\sin \alpha - \sin\left(-3\alpha\right)} = \frac{\cos 3\alpha + \cos \alpha}{2\left(\sin \alpha + \sin 3\alpha\right)}$$

By the sum of cosines formula

$$\cos A + \cos B = 2 \cos \frac{1}{2}(A + B) \cos \frac{1}{2}(A - B)$$

and the sum of sines formula

$$\sin A + \sin B = 2 \sin \frac{1}{2}(A + B) \cos \frac{1}{2}(A - B),$$

one gets

$$= \frac{2 \cos \dfrac{1}{2}\left(3\alpha + \alpha\right)\cos \dfrac{1}{2}\left(3\alpha - \alpha\right)}{2\left(2 \sin \dfrac{1}{2}\left(\alpha + 3\alpha\right)\cos \dfrac{1}{2}\left(\alpha - 3\alpha\right)\right)}$$

$$= \left(\frac{1}{2}\right)\frac{\cos 2\alpha \cos \alpha}{\sin 2\alpha \cos(-\alpha)} = \left(\frac{1}{2}\right)\frac{\cos 2\alpha \cos \alpha}{\sin 2\alpha \cos \alpha}$$

$$= \left(\frac{1}{2}\right)\frac{\cos 2\alpha}{\sin 2\alpha} = \frac{1}{2}\cot 2\alpha.$$

157

Change $4 + (\tan \theta - \cot \theta)^2$ to $\sec^2 \theta + \csc^2 \theta$.

SOLUTION:

If we square the binomial in the first expression, we have

$$4 + (\tan \theta - \cot \theta)^2 = 4 + (\tan \theta - \cot \theta)(\tan \theta - \cot \theta)$$
$$= 4 + \tan^2 \theta - 2 \tan \theta \cot \theta + \cot^2 \theta$$

Since $\cot \theta = \dfrac{1}{\tan \theta}$ the term $-2 \tan \theta \cot \theta = -2 \tan \theta \left(\dfrac{1}{\tan \theta}\right) = -2(1) = -2$.

Thus $\quad 4 + (\tan \theta - \cot \theta)^2 = 4 + \tan^2 \theta - 2 + \cot^2 \theta$
$$= 2 + \tan^2 \theta + \cot^2 \theta$$

Since $2 = 1 + 1$, $\qquad\qquad\quad = 1 + \tan^2 \theta + 1 + \cot^2 \theta$

Recall $1 + \tan^2 \theta = \sec^2 \theta$ and $1 + \cot^2 \theta = \csc^2 \theta$. Replacing these values we obtain

$$4 + (\tan \theta - \cot \theta)^2 = \sec^2 \theta + \csc^2 \theta$$

Change $\tan \theta (\sin \theta + \cot \theta \cos \theta)$ to $\sec \theta$.

SOLUTION:

Distribute to obtain

$$\tan \theta (\sin \theta + \cot \theta \cos \theta) = \tan \theta \sin \theta + \tan \theta \cot \theta \cos \theta.$$

Recall that $\cot \theta = \dfrac{1}{\tan \theta}$, and replace $\cot \theta$ by $\dfrac{1}{\tan \theta}$:

$$= \tan \theta \sin \theta + \tan \theta \left(\dfrac{1}{\tan \theta}\right) \cos \theta$$

$$= \tan \theta \sin \theta + \cos \theta.$$

Since $\tan \theta = \dfrac{\sin \theta}{\cos \theta}$ we may replace $\tan \theta$ by $\dfrac{\sin \theta}{\cos \theta}$:

$$= \dfrac{\sin \theta}{\cos \theta} \sin \theta + \cos \theta$$

$$= \dfrac{\sin^2 \theta}{\cos \theta} + \cos \theta$$

To combine terms, we convert cos θ into a fraction whose denominator is cos θ, thus

$$= \frac{\sin^2 \theta}{\cos \theta} + \left(\frac{\cos \theta}{\cos \theta} \right) \cdot \cos \theta.$$

(Note that $\dfrac{\cos \theta}{\cos \theta}$ equals one, so the equation is unaltered.)

$$= \frac{\sin^2 \theta}{\cos \theta} + \frac{\cos^2 \theta}{\cos \theta}$$

$$= \frac{\sin^2 \theta + \cos^2 \theta}{\cos \theta} .$$

Recall the identity $\sin^2 \theta + \cos^2 \theta = 1$; hence,

$$= \frac{1}{\cos \theta}$$

$$= \sec \theta .$$

● PROBLEM 19-7

Find sin 105° without the use of a trigonometric table.

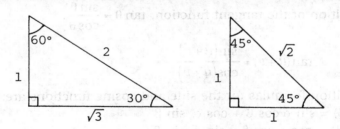

SOLUTION:

We note that 105° = 60° + 45° and find the sine of the sum of two angles.
$$\sin 105° = \sin(60° + 45°)$$
Using the formula for the sine of the sum of two numbers,
$$\sin(x + y) = \sin x \cos y + \cos x \sin y,$$
$$\sin(60° + 45°) = \sin 60° \cos 45° + \cos 60° \sin 45°$$
Now we must find the values of sin 60°, cos 45°, cos 60°, and sin 45°. Observing a 30–60 and 45–45 right triangle we note

$$\sin = \frac{\text{opposite}}{\text{hypotenuse}} ; \text{ thus, } \quad \sin 60° = \frac{\sqrt{3}}{2}$$

$$\sin 45° = \frac{1}{\sqrt{2}} = \frac{\sqrt{2}}{2}$$

$$\cos = \frac{\text{adjacent}}{\text{hypotenuse}}; \text{ thus, } \cos 45° = \frac{1}{\sqrt{2}} = \frac{\sqrt{2}}{2}$$

$$\cos 60° = \frac{1}{2}$$

Substituting, we obtain $\quad \sin (105°) = \frac{\sqrt{3}}{2} \cdot \frac{\sqrt{2}}{2} + \frac{1}{2} \cdot \frac{\sqrt{2}}{2}.$

Multiply the fractions (recall $\sqrt{a} \cdot \sqrt{b} = \sqrt{ab}$) to obtain $\frac{\sqrt{6}}{4} + \frac{\sqrt{2}}{4} = \frac{\sqrt{6} + \sqrt{2}}{4}.$

Therefore, $\sin 105° = \frac{\sqrt{6} + \sqrt{2}}{4}.$

● PROBLEM 19-8

Find an expression for $\tan(u + v)$.

SOLUTION:

By definition of the tangent function, $\tan \theta = \frac{\sin \theta}{\cos \theta}.$

Then, $\qquad \tan(u + v) = \frac{\sin(u + v)}{\cos(u + v)}$ $\qquad\qquad$ (1)

The addition formulas for the sine and cosine functions are:

$\sin(\alpha + \beta) = \sin \alpha \cos \beta + \cos \alpha \sin \beta$

$\cos(\alpha + \beta) = \cos \alpha \cos \beta - \sin \alpha \sin \beta$

Replacing α by u and β by v, and using these addition formulas, equation (1) becomes

$$\tan(u + v) = \frac{\sin(u + v)}{\cos(u + v)} = \frac{\sin u \cos v + \cos u \sin v}{\cos u \cos v - \sin u \sin v}$$

If neither $\cos u = 0$ nor $\cos v = 0$, we can divide both the numerator and the denominator of this fraction by the product $\cos u \cos v$ to obtain a formula that involves only the tangent function:

$$\tan(u + v) = \frac{\dfrac{\sin u \cos v + \cos u \sin v}{\cos u \cos v}}{\dfrac{\cos u \cos v - \sin u \sin v}{\cos u \cos v}}$$

$$= \frac{\dfrac{\sin u \cos v}{\cos u \cos v} + \dfrac{\cos u \sin v}{\cos u \cos v}}{\dfrac{\cos u \cos v}{\cos u \cos v} - \dfrac{\sin u \sin v}{\cos u \cos v}}$$

$$= \frac{\dfrac{\sin u}{\cos u} + \dfrac{\sin v}{\cos v}}{1 - \dfrac{\sin u \sin v}{\cos u \cos v}}$$

$$\tan(u + v) = \frac{\tan u + \tan v}{1 - \tan u \tan v}$$

● PROBLEM 19-9

Prove the identity $\dfrac{1 - \cos\theta}{\sin\theta} = \dfrac{\sin\theta}{1 + \cos\theta}$.

SOLUTION:

One side of this identity is as complicated as the other so that it makes no difference which side is used. The illustration uses both sides.

(a)
$$\frac{1 - \cos\theta}{\sin\theta} = \frac{(1 - \cos\theta)}{\sin\theta}\frac{(1 + \cos\theta)}{(1 + \cos\theta)}$$

$$= \frac{1 - \cos\theta + \cos\theta - \cos^2\theta}{\sin\theta(1 + \cos\theta)}$$

$$= \frac{1 - \cos^2\theta}{\sin\theta(1 + \cos\theta)}$$

Since $\cos^2\theta + \sin^2\theta = 1$ or $\sin^2\theta = 1 - \cos^2\theta$, then

$$\frac{1 - \cos\theta}{\sin\theta} = \frac{1 - \cos^2\theta}{\sin\theta(1 + \cos\theta)} = \frac{\sin^2\theta}{\sin\theta(1 + \cos\theta)}$$

$$= \frac{\sin\theta}{1 + \cos\theta}.$$

Note that this method starts with the left side of the identity to be proved. The following is another method which can be used to prove the identity.

(b) $$\frac{\sin\theta}{1+\cos\theta} = \frac{\sin\theta(1-\cos\theta)}{(1+\cos\theta)(1-\cos\theta)}$$

$$= \frac{\sin\theta(1-\cos\theta)}{1+\cos\theta-\cos\theta-\cos^2\theta}$$

$$= \frac{\sin\theta(1-\cos\theta)}{1-\cos^2\theta}$$

Again, since $\sin^2\theta = 1 - \cos^2\theta$,

$$\frac{\sin\theta}{1+\cos\theta} = \frac{\sin\theta(1-\cos\theta)}{1-\cos^2\theta}$$

$$= \frac{\sin\theta(1-\cos\theta)}{\sin^2\theta}$$

$$= \frac{1-\cos\theta}{\sin\theta}.$$

Note that this second method starts with the right side of the identity to be proved.

● PROBLEM 19-10

Prove the identity: $\sec A \csc A = \tan A + \cot A$.

SOLUTION:

One approach to the proof of identities, when many functions are involved, is to express the given functions in terms of fewer functions. In this case, suppose we express each of the given trigonometric functions in terms of sine and cosine functions. We will work in parallel columns, with each side of the given equation.

Since $\sec A = \dfrac{1}{\cos A}$ and $\csc A = \dfrac{1}{\sin A}$, $\sec A \csc A$

$$= \frac{1}{\cos A} \cdot \frac{1}{\sin A} = \frac{1}{\cos A \sin A}$$

Since $\tan A = \dfrac{\sin A}{\cos A}$ and $\cot A = \dfrac{1}{\tan A} = \dfrac{1}{\sin A/\cos A} = \dfrac{\cos A}{\sin A}$, so $\tan A + \cot A$

$$= \frac{\sin A}{\cos A} + \frac{\cos A}{\sin A}.$$

162

To combine these fractions, we convert them into fractions with the least common denominator (LCD) cos A sin A; thus

$$= \left(\frac{\sin A}{\sin A} \frac{\sin A}{\sin A} \right) + \left(\frac{\cos A}{\cos A} \frac{\cos A}{\sin A} \right)$$

$$= \frac{\sin^2 A + \cos^2 A}{\cos A \sin A}$$

Recall the trigonometric identity $\sin^2 A + \cos^2 A = 1$; replacing $\sin^2 A + \cos^2 A$ by 1 we obtain

$$= \frac{1}{\cos A \sin A}$$

Now, since we have proved that both sides of the given equation are equal to the same expression, we are tempted to say that they are therefore equal to each other, and that we have therefore proved what we set out to prove.

We have indeed, except for one detail. We have not considered the values of A for which the given expressions and those which we substituted are meaningful.

This aspect of the proof of a trigonometric identity rarely leads to trouble, and may therefore usually be omitted. The careful student, however, will want to be prepared to investigate this question.

Thus we note that sec A and tan A are defined if and only if A is a real number of degrees not an odd multiple of 90; csc A and cot A are defined if and only if A is a real number of degrees not an even multiple of 90. Both sides of the equation are therefore defined if and only if A is a real number of degrees not an integer multiple of 90.

Each of the substitutions made in the parallel columns above is valid if A is such a number. Therefore, sec A csc A and tan A cot A are equal whenever both are defined, and the equation sec A csc A = tan A + cot A is an identity.

● PROBLEM 19-11

Prove the identity $\tan\left(\dfrac{\pi}{4} + \dfrac{\theta}{2}\right) = \sec\theta + \tan\theta$.

SOLUTION:

Factor out $\frac{1}{2}$.

$$\tan\left(\frac{\pi}{4}+\frac{\theta}{2}\right)=\tan\frac{1}{2}\left(\frac{\pi}{2}+\theta\right).$$

Then, apply the half-angle formula for the tangent.

$$\tan\frac{1}{2}\theta_1=\pm\sqrt{\frac{1-\cos\theta_1}{1+\cos\theta_1}}.$$

Rationalize the denominator to obtain

$$\tan\frac{1}{2}\theta_1=\pm\sqrt{\frac{1-\cos\theta_1}{1+\cos\theta_1}}\frac{\sqrt{1-\cos\theta_1}}{\sqrt{1-\cos\theta_1}}=\frac{1-\cos\theta_1}{\pm\sqrt{1-\cos^2\theta_1}}$$

$$=\frac{1-\cos\theta_1}{\sqrt{\sin^2\theta_1}}$$

$$\tan\frac{1}{2}\theta_1=\frac{1-\cos\theta_1}{\sin\theta_1}$$

Replace θ_1 by $\frac{\pi}{2}+\theta$.

$$\tan\frac{1}{2}\left(\frac{\pi}{2}+\theta\right)=\frac{1-\cos\left(\frac{\pi}{2}+\theta\right)}{\sin\left(\frac{\pi}{2}+\theta\right)}$$

Apply the formula for the sum of the sine of two angles and the cosine of the sum of two angles.

$\cos(\alpha+\beta)=\cos\alpha\cos\beta-\sin\alpha\sin\beta$

$\sin(\alpha+\beta)=\sin\alpha\cos\beta+\cos\alpha\sin\beta$

$\cos\left(\frac{\pi}{2}+\theta\right)=\cos\frac{\pi}{2}\cos\theta-\sin\frac{\pi}{2}\sin\theta$

$\quad\quad\quad\quad=0(\cos\theta)-1(\sin\theta)$

$\quad\quad\quad\quad=-\sin\theta$

$\sin\left(\frac{\pi}{2}+\theta\right)=\sin\frac{\pi}{2}\cos\theta+\cos\frac{\pi}{2}\sin\theta$

$\quad\quad\quad\quad=1(\cos\theta)+0(\sin\theta)$

$\quad\quad\quad\quad=\cos\theta$

Substitute these two results.

$$\tan\frac{1}{2}\left(\frac{\pi}{2}+\theta\right)=\frac{1-\cos\left(\frac{\pi}{2}+\theta\right)}{\sin\left(\frac{\pi}{2}+\theta\right)}$$

$$=\frac{1-\left(-\sin\theta\right)}{\cos\theta}+\frac{1+\sin\theta}{\cos\theta}$$

$$=\frac{1}{\cos\theta}+\frac{\sin\theta}{\cos\theta}$$

$$=\sec\theta+\tan\theta$$

CHAPTER 20

SOLVING TRIANGLES

● PROBLEM 20-1

Solve the oblique triangle *ABC* for side *c*, and the two unknown angles, where $a = 20$, $b = 40$, $\alpha = 30$; and α is the angle between sides *b* and *c*.

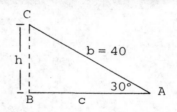

SOLUTION:

If we draw an altitude *h* from *b* to *c*, as in the accompanying diagram, we can find the length of this altitude by trigonometry.

$$\sin 30° = \frac{h}{b}$$

$$h = b \sin 30°$$

Since $\sin 30° = \frac{1}{2}$, and $b = 40$, $h = 40\left(\frac{1}{2}\right) = 20 = $ side *a*.

Thus, the triangle must have the altitude as one of its sides; therefore, we have a right triangle with angles 30°, 60°, and 90°. Sides of such right triangles are in proportion $1 : \sqrt{3} : 2$, and the lengths are therefore $20 : 20\sqrt{3} : 40$.

Hence, $c = 20\sqrt{3}$, and the two unknown angles are 60° and 90°.

Given $a = 8$, $c = 7$, $\beta = 135°$, find b.

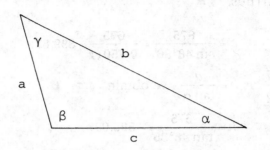

SOLUTION:

Use the law of cosines to find one side given two sides and an included angle.

$$b^2 = a^2 + c^2 - 2ac \cos \text{(included angle)}$$

where the included angle is the angle between the two given sides.

$$b^2 = a^2 + c^2 - 2ac \cos \beta$$
$$b^2 = 64 + 49 - 2 \cdot 8 \cdot 7 \cos 135°$$

$$= 113 - 112 \cdot \left(-\frac{\sqrt{2}}{2}\right) = 113 + 79.196$$

$$= 192.196$$
$$b = 13.863$$

In right triangle ABC, if $a = 675$, $\alpha = 48° 36'$, find b, c, β.

SOLUTION:

If we wish to work with α, the functions of α involving a and one other side are

$$\sin \alpha = \frac{\text{opposite}}{\text{hypotenuse}} = \frac{a}{c}$$

$$\tan \alpha = \frac{\text{opposite}}{\text{adjacent}} = \frac{a}{b}$$

$$\cot \alpha = \frac{1}{\tan \alpha} = \frac{\text{adjacent}}{\text{opposite}} = \frac{b}{a}.$$

Any of these ratios can be chosen. If the first is chosen, $\sin \alpha = \dfrac{a}{c}$ or $c \sin \alpha$

$= a$ and $c = \dfrac{a}{\sin \alpha}$. Thus,

$$c = \frac{675}{\sin 48° 36'} = \frac{675}{0.75011} = 899.87.$$

Using $\tan \alpha = \dfrac{a}{b}$ or $b = \dfrac{a}{\tan \alpha}$, we obtain

$$b = \frac{675}{\tan 48° 36'} = 595.09.$$

To find β,

$$\alpha + \beta + 90° = 180°$$
$$\alpha + \beta = 180° - 90° = 90°$$
$$\beta = 90° - \alpha = 90° - 48°36'$$
$$\beta = 41°24'$$

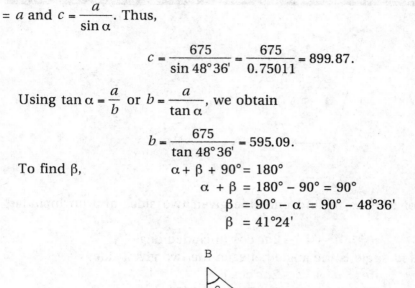

● **PROBLEM 20-4**

Show that in any triangle ABC

$$\frac{a+b}{c} = \frac{\cos \frac{1}{2}(A - B)}{\sin \frac{1}{2} C},$$

and

$$\frac{a-b}{c} = \frac{\sin \frac{1}{2}(A - B)}{\cos \frac{1}{2} C}.$$

SOLUTION:

By the law of sines, one has $\dfrac{a}{c} = \dfrac{\sin A}{\sin C}$ and $\dfrac{b}{c} = \dfrac{\sin B}{\sin C}$.

Adding these two equations together, one has

$$\frac{a}{c} + \frac{b}{c} = \frac{\sin A}{\sin C} + \frac{\sin B}{\sin C}$$

so that

$$\frac{a+b}{c} = \frac{\sin A + \sin B}{\sin C}.$$

Using the formula for the sum of sines, one obtains

$$\frac{a+b}{c} = \frac{2\sin\frac{1}{2}(A+B)\cos\frac{1}{2}(A-B)}{\sin C}.$$

$\sin C$ may be written as

$$\sin 2\left(\frac{C}{2}\right) = 2\sin\frac{C}{2}\cos\frac{C}{2}.$$

Hence,

$$\frac{a+b}{c} = \frac{2\sin\left(\dfrac{A+B}{2}\right)\cos\left(\dfrac{A-B}{2}\right)}{2\sin\dfrac{C}{2}\cos\dfrac{C}{2}}$$

$$= \frac{\sin\left(\dfrac{A+B}{2}\right)\cos\left(\dfrac{A-B}{2}\right)}{\sin\dfrac{C}{2}\cos\dfrac{C}{2}}.$$

Since

$$A + B + C = 180°,$$

$$A + B = 180° - C, \quad \frac{A+B}{2} = 90° - \frac{C}{2}$$

$$\sin\left(\frac{A+B}{2}\right) = \sin\left(90° - \frac{C}{2}\right) = \cos\frac{C}{2}.$$

Therefore,

$$\frac{a+b}{c} = \frac{\sin\left(\dfrac{A+B}{2}\right)\cos\left(\dfrac{A-B}{2}\right)}{\sin\dfrac{C}{2}\cos\dfrac{C}{2}}$$

$$= \frac{\cos\dfrac{C}{2}\cos\left(\dfrac{A-B}{2}\right)}{\sin\dfrac{C}{2}\cos\dfrac{C}{2}}$$

$$= \frac{\cos\left(\dfrac{A-B}{2}\right)}{\sin\dfrac{C}{2}} = \frac{\cos\dfrac{1}{2}(A-B)}{\sin\dfrac{1}{2}C}$$

Similarly, one obtains

$$\frac{a}{c} = \frac{\sin A}{\sin C}, \frac{b}{c} = \frac{\sin B}{\sin C}, \frac{a-b}{c} = \frac{\sin A - \sin B}{\sin C}$$

$$\frac{a-b}{c} = \frac{2\cos\dfrac{1}{2}(A+B)\sin\dfrac{1}{2}(A-B)}{2\sin\dfrac{C}{2}\cos\dfrac{C}{2}} = \frac{\sin\dfrac{1}{2}(A-B)}{\cos\dfrac{C}{2}}$$

These two equations, which were just verified, are a pair of Mollweide's formulas. Mollweide's formulas are the following, for any triangle ABC:

$$\frac{a+b}{c} = \frac{\cos\dfrac{1}{2}(A-B)}{\sin\dfrac{C}{2}}, \quad \frac{a-b}{c} = \frac{\sin\dfrac{1}{2}(A-B)}{\cos\dfrac{C}{2}}$$

$$\frac{b+c}{a} = \frac{\cos\dfrac{1}{2}(B-C)}{\sin\dfrac{A}{2}}, \quad \frac{b-c}{a} = \frac{\sin\dfrac{1}{2}(B-C)}{\cos\dfrac{A}{2}}$$

$$\frac{c+a}{b} = \frac{\cos\dfrac{1}{2}(C-A)}{\sin\dfrac{B}{2}}, \quad \frac{c-a}{b} = \frac{\sin\dfrac{1}{2}(C-A)}{\cos\dfrac{B}{2}}$$

CHAPTER 21

INVERSE TRIGONOMETRIC FUNCTIONS

● **PROBLEM 21-1**

Calculate the following numbers:

(a) Arctan $\sqrt{3}$ (c) Tan^{-1} 1.871

(b) Tan^{-1} .2027

SOLUTION:

(a) The expression $\tan y = x$ is equivalent to arctan $x = \tan^{-1} x = y$. Let the expression arctan $\sqrt{3} = y$. Hence, the expression arctan $\sqrt{3} = y$ is equivalent to $\tan y = \sqrt{3} = 1.7321$. In a table of trigonometric functions, the number y that corresponds to $\tan y = 1.7321$ is approximately 1.05.

(b) Note that the expression $\tan^{-1}$ .2027 = arctan .2027. Let the expression $\tan^{-1}$ .2027 = y. Hence, the expression $\tan^{-1}$ .2027 = arctan .2027 = y is equivalent to $\tan y = .2027$. In a table of trigonometric functions, the number y that corresponds to $\tan y = .2027$ is .20.

(c) Note that the expression $\tan^{-1}$ 1.871 = arctan 1.871. Let the expression $\tan^{-1}$ 1.871 = y. Hence, the expression $\tan^{-1}$ 1.871 = arctan 1.871 = y is equivalent to $\tan y = 1.871$. In a table of trigonometric functions, the number y that corresponds to $\tan y = 1.871$ is 1.08.

In $\triangle ABC$, $A = \arccos\left(-\dfrac{\sqrt{3}}{2}\right)$. What is the value of A expressed in radians?

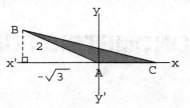

SOLUTION:

The expression "$\arccos\left(-\dfrac{\sqrt{3}}{2}\right)$" means "the angle whose cosine equals $-\dfrac{\sqrt{3}}{2}$."

Angles whose cosine equals $-\dfrac{\sqrt{3}}{2}$ are 150°, 210°, –150°, and –210°.

Since the principal value of an arc cosine of an angle is the positive angle having the smallest numerical value 150°, or $\dfrac{5\pi}{6}$ is the principal value of angle A.

● PROBLEM 21-3

Evaluate: (a) $\sin^{-1}\dfrac{\sqrt{3}}{2}$, (b) $\tan^{-1}\left(-\sqrt{3}\right)$.

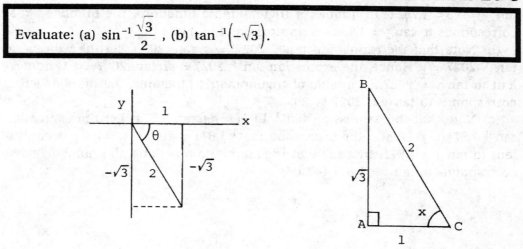

SOLUTION:

(a) Recall that inverse sines are angles. Thus, we are looking for the angle whose sin is $\frac{\sqrt{3}}{2}$. $\sin^{-1} \frac{\sqrt{3}}{2} = x$ means $\sin x = \frac{\sqrt{3}}{2}$ where $\sin = \frac{\text{opposite}}{\text{hypotenuse}}$.

We note that triangle ABC is a 30–60 right triangle, and angle $x = 60°$. Since $\sin 60° = \frac{\sqrt{3}}{2}$, $\sin^{-1} \frac{\sqrt{3}}{2} = 60°$.

(b) Recall that inverse tangents are angles. Thus, we are looking for the angle whose tangent is $-\sqrt{3}$. $\text{Tan}^{-1}\left(-\sqrt{3}\right) = \theta$ means $\tan \theta = -\sqrt{3}$ where $\tan = \frac{\text{opposite}}{\text{adjacent}}$.

Since tangent is negative in the 4th quadrant, we draw our triangle there, and note it is a 30–60 right triangle, and angle $\theta = (-60°)$. Since $\tan(-60°) = \frac{-\sqrt{3}}{1}$, $\tan^{-1}\left(-\sqrt{3}\right) = -60°$.

● **PROBLEM 21-4**

Find $\sin \arccos \frac{4}{5}$, if $\arccos \frac{4}{5}$ is in quadrant I.

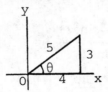

SOLUTION:

Let $\theta = \arccos \frac{4}{5}$; then $\cos \theta = \frac{4}{5}$. We can then construct the triangle of the figure. From the triangle we get $\sin \theta = \frac{3}{5}$; therefore, $\sin \arccos \frac{4}{5} = \frac{3}{5}$.

173

Find sin(arctan x), where x may be any real number.

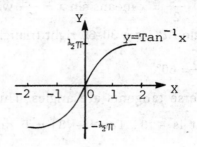

SOLUTION:

Let $t = $ arctan x. Then tan $t = x$, and $-\frac{1}{2}\pi < t < \frac{1}{2}\pi$. Also t and x have the same sign (see figure). Now, we express sin t in terms of x as follows:

since

$$\tan t = x = \frac{\sin t}{\cos t},$$

and

$$\sin t = \frac{\sin t}{\cos t} \cdot \cos t,$$

we write

$$\sin t = x \cos t$$

and by the identity

$$\sin^2 t = x^2 \cos^2 t$$

$$\sin^2 t + \cos^2 t = 1,$$
$$\sin^2 t = x^2(1 - \sin^2 t).$$

Solving for $\sin^2 t$,

$$1 = \frac{x^2\left(1 - \sin^2 t\right)}{\sin^2 t}$$

$$1 = \frac{x^2 - x^2 \sin^2 t}{\sin^2 t}$$

$$1 = \frac{x^2}{\sin^2 t} - \frac{x^2 \sin^2 t}{\sin^2 t}$$

$$1 = \frac{x^2}{\sin^2 t} - x^2$$

$$1 + x^2 = \frac{x^2}{\sin^2 t}$$

$$\sin^2 t\,(1 + x^2) = x^2$$

$$\sin^2 t = \frac{x^2}{1+x^2}$$

Hence, $\qquad \sin t = \dfrac{x}{\sqrt{1+x^2}}$ or $\dfrac{-x}{\sqrt{1+x^2}}$.

Since $-\dfrac{1}{2}\pi < t < \dfrac{1}{2}\pi$, $\sin t$ and t have the same sign. From above we know that t and x have the same sign. Thus, $\sin t$ and x must have the same sign.

Now $\dfrac{x}{\sqrt{1+x^2}}$ has the same sign as x, while $\dfrac{-x}{\sqrt{1+x^2}}$ has the opposite sign; thus

$$\sin t = \sin(\arctan x) = \frac{x}{\sqrt{1+x^2}}.$$

● PROBLEM 21-6

Solve the equation arcsin x + arccos $(1 - x) = 0$.

SOLUTION:

Let $\alpha = \arcsin x$, $\beta = \arccos (1 - x)$. Then we must solve the equation
$$\alpha + \beta = 0,$$
where $\sin \alpha = x$ and $\cos \beta = 1 - x$. Now, by use of the identity $\sin^2 a + \cos^2 a = 1$ we obtain:

$$\cos \alpha = \pm\sqrt{1 - \sin^2 \alpha} = \pm\sqrt{1 - x^2}, \text{ and}$$

$$\sin \beta = \pm\sqrt{1 - \cos^2 \beta} = \pm\sqrt{1 - (1 - x)^2} = \pm\sqrt{2x - x^2}.$$

We now make use of the formula for the sine of the sum of two angles which states,
$$\sin(\alpha + \beta) = \sin \alpha \cos \beta + \cos \alpha \sin \beta;$$
and this equals 0 since $\alpha + \beta = 0$, and $\sin 0 = 0$. Substituting the above values for $\sin \alpha$, $\cos \beta$, $\cos \alpha$, $\sin \beta$ we have

$$\sin \alpha \cos \beta + \cos \alpha \sin \beta = 0$$

$$x(1 - x) \pm \sqrt{1 - x^2}\sqrt{2x - x^2} = 0$$

$$x^2(1 - x)^2 = (1 - x^2)(2x - x^2)$$

$$x^2(1 - 2x + x^2) = (1 - x^2)(2x - x^2)$$

Observe that $x = 0$ satisfies this equation. Substituting this value in the given equation we obtain:
$$\arcsin 0 + \arccos(1 - 0) = 0.$$
Now, since $\arcsin 0 = 0$ and $\arccos 1 = 0$ we have:
$$0 + 0 = 0$$
$$0 = 0$$
Thus this value of x also satisfies the original equation. Removing the factor x from $x^2(1 - 2x + x^2) = (1 - x^2)(2x - x^2)$ yields:
$$x^2(1 - 2x + x^2) = (1 - x^2)(2 - x)x$$
$$x(1 - 2x + x^2) = (1 - x^2)(2 - x)$$
$$x - 2x^2 + x^3 = 2 - x - 2x^2 + x^3$$
$$2x = 2$$
$$x = 1$$
Thus, $x = 1$ is another possible solution to the original equation. But $\arcsin 1 = \dfrac{\pi}{2}$ and $\arccos 0 = \dfrac{\pi}{2}$, thus

$$\arcsin 1 + \arccos(1 - 1) = \frac{\pi}{2} + \frac{\pi}{2} = \pi \neq 0.$$

Thus, $x = 1$ does not satisfy the given equation. (Notice that outside the restricted values for arccos we have $\arccos 0 = -\dfrac{\pi}{2}$ also, which, together with

$\arcsin 1 = \dfrac{\pi}{2}$, makes $x = 1$ a solution.)

Hence, $x = 0$ is the only solution of the given equation when only the restricted values are permitted (recall that for the inverse sine function,

$$-\frac{\pi}{2} \leq (\arcsin x = \alpha) \leq \frac{\pi}{2}$$

and for the inverse cosine function
$$0 \leq (\arccos(1 - x) = \beta) \leq \pi).$$

CHAPTER 22

TRIGONOMETRIC EQUATIONS

Find the solution set on $[0, 2\pi]$ of the equation $\sqrt{1 + \sin^2 x} = \sqrt{2} \sin x$.

SOLUTION:

Since the unknown quantity is involved in the radicand, squaring of both sides to eliminate the radical is suggested. Thus, we obtain $1 + \sin^2 x = 2 \sin^2 x$. Hence, $\sin^2 x - 1 = 0$, or $\sin^2 x = 1$

$$\sqrt{\sin^2 x} = \pm\sqrt{1}$$
$$\sin x = \pm 1.$$

When $\sin x = 1$ on $[0, 2\pi]$, $x = \dfrac{\pi}{2}$. When $\sin x = -1$ on $[0, 2\pi]$, $x = \dfrac{3\pi}{2}$.

The complete solution set seems to be $\left\{\dfrac{\pi}{2}, \dfrac{3\pi}{2}\right\}$. Since we squared both sides of the equation, we should try each element in the original equation. When $x = \dfrac{\pi}{2}$, we obtain $\sqrt{1+1} = \sqrt{2} \cdot 1$. When $x = \dfrac{3\pi}{2}$, we obtain $\sqrt{1+1} = \sqrt{2}(-1)$. The second element does not satisfy the original equation, hence does not belong to the solution set. An extraneous root was introduced by squaring the equation, it would seem. Thus, the solution set is $\left\{\dfrac{\pi}{2}\right\}$.

Find the solution set on $[0, \pi]$ for the equation
$$\tan x \sin x - \sin x - \tan x + 1 = 0.$$

SOLUTION:

This equation can be factored to obtain
$$(\sin x - 1)(\tan x - 1) = 0.$$
The values of x satisfying this equation may be found by setting each factor equal to zero.

$$\sin x - 1 = 0 \; ; \; \tan x - 1 = 0$$
or $$\sin x = 1 \; ; \quad \tan x = 1$$

Keeping in mind that our solution set cannot contain values exceeding π or less than zero. We find that $x = \dfrac{\pi}{2}$, is our only acceptable solution for the first equation and $x = \dfrac{\pi}{4}$ is the only acceptable solution for the second, i.e.,

$$\sin\left(k \cdot \frac{\pi}{2}\right) = 1 \text{ where } k = 1, 5, 9,\ldots \text{ but } k = 5, 9, \ldots \text{ are unacceptable}$$

$$\tan\left(\frac{k\pi}{4}\right) = \frac{\sin\left(k \cdot \dfrac{\pi}{4}\right)}{\cos\left(k \cdot \dfrac{\pi}{4}\right)} = \frac{\pm\dfrac{\sqrt{2}}{2}}{\pm\dfrac{\sqrt{2}}{2}}, \; k = 1, 5, 9 \ldots \text{ but } k = 5, 9, \ldots \text{are also unacceptable.}$$

By substituting $\dfrac{\pi}{2}$ into $(\sin x - 1)(\tan x - 1) = 0$ we arrive at the undefined quantity $0 \cdot \left(\dfrac{1}{0} - 1\right)$ so we must specify that $\dfrac{\pi}{4}$ is our only solution, as its substitution leads to a valid identity.

Find the solution set of $\sin^2 \theta + \sin \theta = 0$.

SOLUTION:

Factoring the left side of the equation, obtain $\sin \theta (\sin \theta + 1) = 0$. Setting each factor equal to zero and solving for $\sin \theta$, obtain $\sin \theta = 0$ and $\sin \theta = -1$.

For $\sin \theta = 0$, $\theta = 0$, π, ... and all integral multiples of π.

For $\sin \theta = -1$, note that the sign is negative and that the absolute value of the sine is one. Thus, $\theta = \dfrac{3\pi}{2}$ and all integral multiples of 2π plus $\dfrac{3\pi}{2}$.
Therefore, from the first equation, the solution set contains the elements $n\pi$, $n = 0, \pm 1$, ... From the second, the solution set contains the elements $\dfrac{3\pi}{2} + 2n\pi$, $n = 0, \pm 1$, ... The solution set of the original equation is then

$$\{\theta \mid \theta = n\pi, \text{ or } \frac{3\pi}{2} + 2n\pi, n = 0, \pm 1, \pm 2, ...\}.$$

● PROBLEM 22-4

Find the solution set on $[0, 2\pi)$ of $2 \tan x + \sqrt{3} \sin x \sec^2 x = 0$.

SOLUTION:

Use the following facts concerning trigonometric functions to rewrite the given equation:

$$\tan x = \frac{\sin x}{\cos x}, \ \sec x = \frac{1}{\cos x}.$$

Therefore, the given equation becomes

$$2 \tan x + \sqrt{3} \sin x \sec^2 x = \frac{2 \sin x}{\cos x} + \frac{\sqrt{3} \sin x}{\cos^2 x} = 0 \qquad (1)$$

Multiply both sides of equation (1) by $\cos^2 x$. Hence, equation (1) becomes

$$\cos^2 x \left[\frac{2 \sin x}{\cos x} + \frac{\sqrt{3} \sin x}{\cos^2 x} \right] = \cos^2 x \, (0)$$

or $\qquad 2 \sin x \cos x + \sqrt{3} \sin x = 0$

or $\qquad \sin x (2 \cos x + \sqrt{3}) = 0.$

Therefore, $\quad \sin x = 0$ or $2 \cos x + \sqrt{3} = 0$

$$2 \cos x = -\sqrt{3}$$

$$\cos x = \frac{-\sqrt{3}}{2}.$$

179

When $\sin x = 0$ on $[0, 2\pi)$, $x = 0$ or $x = \pi$. When $\cos x = \dfrac{-\sqrt{3}}{2}$ on $[0, 2\pi)$, $x =$

$\dfrac{5\pi}{6}$ or $x = \dfrac{7\pi}{6}$. Therefore, the complete solution set is $\{0, \dfrac{5\pi}{6}, \pi, \dfrac{7\pi}{6}\}$.

● **PROBLEM 22-5**

Determine all angles x, $0° \le x < 360°$, such that $\sin 2x = -\dfrac{1}{2}$.

SOLUTION:

To determine all values of x such that $0° \le x < 360°$ and $\sin 2x = -\dfrac{1}{2}$, we must

determine all values of $2x$ such that

$$2 \cdot 0° \le 2 \cdot x < 2 \cdot 360° \text{ and } \sin 2x = -\dfrac{1}{2},$$

or all values of $2x$ must be determined such that

$$0° \le 2x < 720° \text{ and } \sin 2x = -\dfrac{1}{2}.$$

Since the sine function is negative in only the third and fourth quadrants,

the angle $2x$ may lie in only these two quadrants. Also, since $\sin 30° = -\dfrac{1}{2}$ in the

third and fourth quadrants, any angle with a reference angle of $30°$ will satisfy

the equation $2x = -\dfrac{1}{2}$. The angles that satisfy this equation and which are

in the range of $0° \le 2x < 720°$ are $180° + 30° = 210°$, $360° - 30° = 330°$,

180

$360° + 210° = 570°$, and $720° - 30° = 690°$ (see diagram). Therefore, $2x = 210°$ or $x = 105°$, $2x = 330°$ or $x = 165°$, $2x = 570°$ or $x = 285°$, and $2x = 690°$ or $x = 345°$. Hence, the solutions of the equation are $x = 105°$, $x = 165°$, $x = 285°$, and $x = 345°$. These solutions are checked by substituting each of them into the equation.

$$\sin 2(105°) = \sin 210° = \sin 30° = -\frac{1}{2} \checkmark$$

$$\sin 2(165°) = \sin 330° = \sin 30° = -\frac{1}{2} \checkmark$$

$$\sin 2(285°) = \sin 570° = \sin 30° = -\frac{1}{2} \checkmark$$

$$\sin 2(345°) = \sin 690° = \sin 30° = -\frac{1}{2} \checkmark$$

Note that the angles 210°, 330°, 570°, and 690° lie in either the third or fourth quadrant, in which the sine function is always negative.

● PROBLEM 22-6

Determine the non-negative values of x less than 2π for which

$$2 \cos^2 x + \sin x - 2 > 0.$$

SOLUTION:

We first transform the left member by means of the identity $\sin^2 x + \cos^2 x = 1$, thus

$$\cos^2 x = 1 - \sin^2 x$$
$$2 \cos^2 x + \sin x - 2 > 0$$
$$2(1 - \sin^2 x) + \sin x - 2 > 0$$
$$2 - 2 \sin^2 x + \sin x - 2 > 0$$

a relation involving only one trigonometric function. Multiplying by –1 (or transposing), we have

$$2 \sin^2 x - \sin x < 0, \text{ or}$$
$$(\sin x)(2 \sin x - 1) < 0.$$

Now for a product to be negative, then one factor must be negative and the other must be positive. There are two cases to be considered.

Case I		Case II
$\sin x > 0$	or	$\sin x < 0$
$2 \sin x - 1 < 0$		$2 \sin x - 1 > 0.$

For Case I, when $\sin x > 0$, the angle is in quadrant I or II and $x > 0$. Con-

181

sider the second restriction, $2 \sin x - 1 < 0$. Then $\sin x < \dfrac{1}{2}$. Thus, $x < \dfrac{\pi}{6}$.

Combine these two restrictions: $0 < x < \dfrac{\pi}{6}$. Since $\dfrac{\pi}{6}$ is a reference angle in

quadrant II, then $\dfrac{5}{6} < x < \pi$ since $0 < \sin x < \dfrac{1}{2}$.

Case II is impossible; the first restriction says that $\sin x < 0$, and the second

restriction says that $\sin x > \dfrac{1}{2}$. Both of these conditions cannot occur. Thus, the

entire solution set is $0 < x < \dfrac{\pi}{6}$ and $\dfrac{5\pi}{6} < x < \pi$.

CHAPTER 23

HYPERBOLIC AND INVERSE HYPERBOLIC FUNCTIONS

● **PROBLEM 23-1**

Calculate   (a) coth 4
             (b) csch 4
             (c) sech 4
             (d) sinh^{-1} 4
             (e) cosh^{-1} 4

SOLUTION:

(a) $\coth = \dfrac{\cosh x}{\sinh x} = \dfrac{e^x + e^{-x}}{e^x - e^{-x}}$

       $\coth 4 = \dfrac{e^4 + e^{-4}}{e^4 - e^{-4}} \approx 1.0007$

(b) $\text{csch } 4 = \dfrac{1}{\sinh 4} = \dfrac{2}{e^4 - e^{-4}}$

       ≈ 0.0366

(c) $\text{sech } x = \dfrac{1}{\cosh x} = \dfrac{2}{e^x + e^{-x}}$

       $\text{sech } 4 = \dfrac{2}{e^4 + e^{-4}} \approx 0.0366$

(d) $\sinh^{-1} x = \ln\left(x + \sqrt{x^2 + 1}\right)$

$\sinh^{-1} 4 = \ln\left(4 + \sqrt{4^2 + 1}\right) = 2.0947$

(e) $\cosh^{-1} x = \pm\ln\left(x + \sqrt{x^2 - 1}\right)$

$\cosh^{-1} 4 = \pm\ln\left(4 + \sqrt{4^2 - 1}\right)$

$= \pm 2.0634$

● **PROBLEM 23-2**

Show that (a) $\cosh^2 x - \sinh^2 x = 1$
(b) $\sinh(x + y) = \sinh x \cosh y + \cosh x \sinh y$

SOLUTION:

(a) $\cosh x = \dfrac{e^x + e^{-x}}{2}$

$\sinh x = \dfrac{e^x - e^{-x}}{2}$

$\cosh^2 x - \sinh^2 x = \left(\dfrac{e^x + e^{-x}}{2}\right)^2 - \left(\dfrac{e^x - e^{-x}}{2}\right)^2$

$= \dfrac{\left(e^{2x} + 2e^x e^{-x} + e^{-2x}\right) - \left(e^{2x} - 2e^x e^{-x} + e^{-2x}\right)}{4}$

$= \dfrac{4e^x e^{-x}}{4} = e^x e^{-x} = e^{x-x} = e^0 = 1$

(b) $\sinh x \cosh y + \cosh x \sinh y$

$= \left(\dfrac{e^x - e^{-x}}{2}\right)\left(\dfrac{e^y + e^{-y}}{2}\right) + \left(\dfrac{e^x + e^{-x}}{2}\right)\left(\dfrac{e^y - e^{-y}}{2}\right)$

$= \left[\dfrac{e^x e^y + e^x e^{-y} - e^{-x} e^y - e^{-x} e^{-y}}{4}\right] + \left[\dfrac{e^x e^y - e^x e^{-y} + e^{-x} e^y - e^{-x} e^{-y}}{4}\right]$

$= \dfrac{2e^x e^y - 2e^{-x} e^{-y}}{4} = \dfrac{e^x e^y - e^{-x} e^{-y}}{2}$

184

$$= \frac{e^{(x+y)} - e^{-x-y}}{2} = \frac{e^{(x+y)} - e^{-(x+y)}}{2} = \sinh(x+y)$$

If $y = \sinh x = \frac{1}{2}(e^x - e^{-x})$, the inverse function is written $x = \sinh^{-1} y$. Similar notations are employed for the inverses of the remaining hyperbolic functions. Show that

(a) $\sinh^{-1} y = \ln\left(y + \sqrt{1+y^2}\right)$

(b) $\cosh^{-1} y = \pm\ln\left(y + \sqrt{y^2 - 1}\right)$

(c) $\tanh^{-1} y = \frac{1}{2}\ln\frac{1+y}{1-y}$

SOLUTION:

(a) To show that $\sinh^{-1} y = \ln\left(y + \sqrt{1+y^2}\right)$, we solve for x in the equation

$$y = \frac{e^x - e^{-x}}{2}$$

We have

$$2y = e^x - e^{-x}$$

$$2y = e^x - \frac{1}{e^x}$$

$$2ye^x = e^{2x} - 1$$

$$e^{2x} - 2ye^x - 1 = 0$$

To solve for e^x, we use the quadratic formula, with $a = 1$, $b = -2y$, and $c = -1$, obtaining

$$e^x = \frac{2y \pm \sqrt{4y^2 + 4}}{2} = y + \sqrt{1+y^2}.$$

Therefore,

$$x = \ln\left(y + \sqrt{1+y^2}\right) = \sinh^{-1} y.$$

(b) If $y = \cosh x = \dfrac{e^x + e^{-x}}{2}$, solving for x gives $\cosh^{-1} y$. We have

$$y = \frac{e^x + e^{-x}}{2}$$
$$2y = e^x + e^{-x}$$
$$2y = e^x + \frac{1}{e^x}$$
$$2ye^x = e^{2x} + 1$$
$$e^{2x} - 2ye^x + 1 = 0$$

We use the quadratic formula to solve for e^x, letting $a = 1$, $b = -2y$, and $c = 1$, obtaining

$$e^x = \frac{2y \pm \sqrt{4y^2 - 4}}{2} = y \pm \sqrt{y^2 - 1}.$$

Therefore, $\qquad x = \ln\left(y \pm \sqrt{y^2 - 1}\right) = \cosh^{-1} y$

(c) If $y = \tanh x = \dfrac{e^x - e^{-x}}{e^x + e^{-x}}$ solving for x gives $\tanh^{-1} y$. We have

$$y = \frac{e^x - e^{-x}}{e^x + e^{-x}}$$
$$y\left(e^x + \frac{1}{e^x}\right) = e^x - \frac{1}{e^x}$$
$$ye^x + \frac{y}{e^x} = e^x - \frac{1}{e^x}$$
$$ye^{2x} + y = e^{2x} - 1$$
$$ye^{2x} - e^{2x} = -y - 1$$
$$e^{2x}(y - 1) = -y - 1$$
$$e^{2x} = \frac{-y - 1}{y - 1}$$
$$2x = \ln\left(\frac{-y - 1}{y - 1}\right)$$

Then $\qquad x = \dfrac{1}{2}\ln\dfrac{1 + y}{1 - y} = \tanh^{-1} y.$

SECTION 3

GRAPHING

CHAPTER 24

PROJECTIONS, MIDPOINTS, AND THE DISTANCE FORMULA

● **PROBLEM 24-1**

Find the projection of AB on the coordinate axes where the coordinates of the points A and B are (4, 4) and (9, 10), respectively.

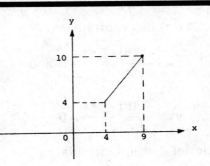

SOLUTION:

By definition, the projection of the line segment joining points $P_1(x_1, y_1)$ and $P_2(x_2, y_2)$ onto the x–axis or onto any line parallel to the x-axis is $(x_2 - x_1)$, and the projection of $P_1 P_2$ onto the y-axis or any line parallel to the y-axis is $(y_2 - y_1)$.

Therefore, the projection of AB onto the x-axis is $(9 - 4) = 5$, and the projection of AB onto the y-axis is $(10 - 4) = 6$.

Find the coordinates of the point $P(x, y)$ which divides the following segments into the given ratios:

(a) $P_1(4, 4)$, $P_2(8, 8)$, $r_1 : r_2 = -1 : 2$

(b) $P_1(4, 9)$, $P_2(9, 10)$, $r_1 : r_2 = 0 : a$ where a is a real constant.

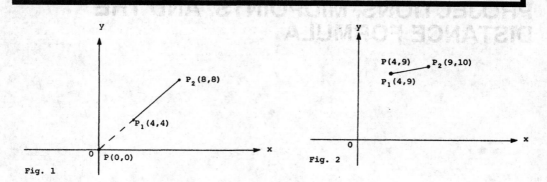

Fig. 1

Fig. 2

SOLUTION:

(a) The point of division formula is

$$x = \frac{r_1 x_2 + r_2 x_1}{r_1 + r_2}, \quad y = \frac{r_1 y_2 + r_2 y_1}{r_1 + r_2}$$

Hence, the point $P(x, y)$ has coordinates

$$x = \frac{(-1)(8) + 2 \cdot 4}{(-1) + 2} = 0 \text{ and}$$

$$y = \frac{(-1)(8) + 2 \cdot 4}{(-1) + 2} = 0$$

(b) Using the point of division formula,

$$x = \frac{0 \cdot 9 + a \cdot 4}{0 + a} = \frac{0 + 4a}{a} = \frac{4a}{a} = 4 = x_1$$

$$y = \frac{0 \cdot 10 + a \cdot 9}{0 + a} = 9 = y_1$$

So $P(x, y) = (4, 9) = P_1(x_1, y_1)$. Note that if $r_1 : r_2 = a : 0$, $P(x, y) = P_2(x_2, y_2)$.

Find the midpoint of the segment from $R(-3, 5)$ to $S(2, -8)$.

SOLUTION:

The midpoint of a line segment from (x_1, y_1) to (x_2, y_2) is given by

$$\left(\frac{x_1 + x_2}{2}, \frac{y_1 + y_2}{2}\right)$$

the abscissa being half the sum of the abscissas of the endpoints and the ordinate half the sum of the ordinates of the endpoints. Let the coordinates of the midpoint be $P(x_0, y_0)$. Then,

$$x_0 = \frac{1}{2}(-3 + 2) = -\frac{1}{2}, \quad y_0 = \frac{1}{2}\left[5 + (-8)\right] = \frac{1}{2}(-3) = -\frac{3}{2}.$$

Thus, the midpoint is $P\left(-\frac{1}{2}, -\frac{3}{2}\right)$.

A line segment AB is $7\frac{1}{2}$ inches long. Locate the point C between A and B so that AC is $\frac{3}{2}$ inches shorter than twice CB.

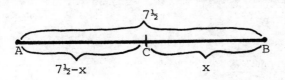

SOLUTION:

See the accompanying figure. Let x = the length of CB in inches. Then $7\frac{1}{2} - x$ is the length of AC. We are told AC is $\frac{3}{2}$ inches shorter than twice CB. Thus, $AC = 2x - \frac{3}{2}$. Therefore,

$$7\frac{1}{2} - x = 2x - \frac{3}{2}$$

$$\frac{15}{2} - x = 2x - \frac{3}{2}$$

Multiplying both members by 2,

$$15 - 2x = 4x - 3$$
$$-6x = -18$$
$$x = 3$$

Therefore, $CB = 3$ and $AC = 7\frac{1}{2} - 3 = 4\frac{1}{2}$. Hence, C is located $4\frac{1}{2}$ inches from A and 3 inches from B.

● **PROBLEM 24-5**

Find the distance from the origin to the point (x, y).

SOLUTION:

If P_1 is $(0, 0)$ and P_2 is (x, y), then to find the distance from the origin, which is the point $(0, 0)$, and the point (x, y), apply the distance formula:

$$d = \sqrt{\left(x_2 - x_1\right)^2 + \left(y_2 - y_1\right)^2}$$

$$d = \sqrt{\left(x - 0\right)^2 + \left(y - 0\right)^2}$$

$$d = \sqrt{x^2 + y^2}$$

Find the distance between the given pair of points, and find the slope of the line segment joining them: (3, –5), (2, 4)

SOLUTION:

Let (3, –5) be P_1 : (x_1, y_1) and let (2, 4) be P_2 : (x_2, y_2). By the distance formula,

$$d = \sqrt{(x_2 - x_1)^2 + (y_2 - y_1)^2}$$

the distance between the points (3, –5) and (2, 4) is

$$d = \sqrt{(2-3)^2 + (4-(-5))^2}$$
$$= \sqrt{(-1)^2 + (4+5)^2}$$
$$= \sqrt{1 + (9)^2}$$
$$= \sqrt{1 + 81}$$
$$= \sqrt{82}.$$

The slope of the line joining the points (3, –5) and (2, 4) is given by the formula:

$$\text{slope} = m = \frac{y_2 - y_1}{x_2 - x_1}$$

Again, let (3, –5) be P_1 : (x_1, y_1) and let (2, 4) be P_2 : (x_2, y_2). Then the slope is

$$m = \frac{4 - (-5)}{2 - 3}$$
$$= \frac{4 + 5}{-1}$$
$$= \frac{9}{-1}$$
$$= -9.$$

Show that the triangle with (–3, 2), (1, 1), and (–4, –2) as vertices is an isosceles triangle.

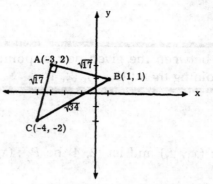

SOLUTION:

If we can show that two sides of the triangle are equal in length, then the triangle is isosceles. This can be done by applying the formula for the distance between two points, (x_1, y_1) and (x_2, y_2):

$$d = \sqrt{(x_2 - x_1)^2 + (y_2 - y_1)^2}$$

Let the given points be designated as A, B, and C, respectively. Then

$$|AB| = \sqrt{(1+3)^2 + (1-2)^2} = \sqrt{17}$$

$$|AC| = \sqrt{(-4+3)^2 + (-2-2)^2} = \sqrt{17}$$

Hence $|AB| = |AC|$, and the triangle is isosceles. Furthermore,

$$|BC| = \sqrt{(-4-1)^2 + (-2-1)^2} = \sqrt{34}$$

Since $|BC|^2 = |AB|^2 + |AC|^2 \left(\sqrt{34}^2 = \sqrt{17}^2 + \sqrt{17}^2 \text{ or } 34 = 17 + 17 \right)$, the Theorem of

Pythagoras holds, and ABC is a right triangle, with the right angle at A. (See figure.)

● **PROBLEM 24-8**

Find the equation for the set of points the sum of whose distances from (4, 0) and from (–4, 0) is 10.

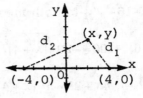

SOLUTION:

We find the desired equation by choosing an arbitrary point (x, y) and computing the sum of its distances from $(4, 0)$ and $(-4, 0)$ (see accompanying figure). Applying the distance formula for the distance between two points (a_1, b_1) and (a_2, b_2), $d = \sqrt{(a_1 - a_2)^2 + (b_1 - b_2)^2}$, we find that the distance from (x, y) to $(4, 0)$ is

$$d_1 = \sqrt{(x - 4)^2 + y^2}$$

and the distance from (x, y) to $(-4, 0)$ is

$$d_2 = \sqrt{(x + 4)^2 + y^2}.$$

We are given that the sum of the distances $d_1 + d_2 = 10$. Hence, the required equation for the set of points is

$$\sqrt{(x - 4)^2 + y^2} + \sqrt{(x + 4)^2 + y^2} = 10$$

$$\sqrt{(x - 4)^2 + y^2} = 10 - \sqrt{(x + 4)^2 + y^2}$$

Squaring both sides,

$$\left(\sqrt{(x - 4)^2 + y^2}\right)^2 = \left(10 - \sqrt{(x + 4)^2 + y^2}\right)^2.$$

Since $\left(\sqrt{a}\right)^2 = \sqrt{a}\sqrt{a} = \sqrt{a \bullet a} = \sqrt{a^2} = a$,

$$\left(\sqrt{(x - 4)^2 + y^2}\right)^2 = (x - 4)^2 + y^2.$$

Thus,

$$(x - 4)^2 + y^2 = 100 - 20\sqrt{(x + 4)^2 + y^2} + (x + 4)^2 + y^2$$

$$x^2 - 8x + 16 + y^2 = 100 - 20\sqrt{(x + 4)^2 + y^2} + x^2 + 8x + 16 + y^2.$$

Adding $-\left(100 + x^2 + 8x + 16 + y^2\right)$ to both members,

$$-16x - 100 = -20\sqrt{\left(x+4\right)^2 + y^2}.$$

Dividing both sides by -4, $4x + 25 = 5\sqrt{\left(x+4\right)^2 + y^2}$.

Squaring again,

$$\left(4x + 25\right)\left(4x + 25\right) = \left(5\sqrt{\left(x+4\right)^2 + y^2}\right)^2$$

$$16x^2 + 200x + 625 = 25\left(\sqrt{\left(x+4\right)^2 + y^2}\right)^2$$

$$16x^2 + 200x + 625 = 25\left[\left(x+4\right)^2 + y^2\right]$$

$$16x^2 + 200x + 625 = 25\left(x^2 + 8x + 16 + y^2\right)$$

$$16x^2 + 200x + 625 = 25x^2 + 200x + 400 + 25y^2.$$

Adding $-\left(16x^2 + 200x + 400\right)$ to both members,

$$225 = 9x^2 + 25y^2$$

Dividing both members by 225, we can write the last equation in the form

$$\frac{9x^2}{225} + \frac{25y^2}{225} = \frac{225}{225}, \text{ or}$$

$$\frac{x^2}{25} + \frac{y^2}{9} = 1,$$

which is the standard form of the equation of an ellipse. This is the desired equation.

● PROBLEM 24-9

Find the interior angles of $\triangle ABC$, which has vertices $A(0, 0)$, $B(4, -2)$, and $C(9, 4)$. Find the area of $\triangle ABC$.

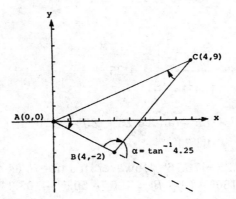

SOLUTION:

$\triangle ABC$ is shown in the figure. First, find the slope of each side of $\triangle ABC$ using the formula $k = \dfrac{y_2 - y_1}{x_2 - x_1}$, where (x_1, y_1) and (x_2, y_2) are any two points on a side of $\triangle ABC$. Therefore,

$$k_{AB} = \frac{y_B - y_A}{x_B - x_A} = \frac{-2 - 0}{4 - 0} = -\frac{1}{2}$$

$$k_{AC} = \frac{4 - 0}{9 - 0} = \frac{4}{9}, \quad k_{BC} = \frac{4 - (-2)}{9 - 4} = \frac{6}{5}.$$

Next, draw curved arrows to indicate the positive direction about each vertex as shown in the figure. The head of the arrow is on the side whose slope is to be taken as k_1 in the formula $\tan \theta = \dfrac{k_1 - k_2}{1 + k_1 k_2}$, and the tail of the arrow is on the side whose slope is k_2. θ is the angle between these two sides.

The interior angles are then found as the following:

$$\tan A = \frac{k_1 - k_2}{1 + k_1 k_2} = \frac{k_{AB} - k_{AC}}{1 + k_{AB} k_{AC}} = \frac{-\dfrac{1}{2} - \dfrac{4}{9}}{1 + \left(-\dfrac{1}{2}\right)\dfrac{4}{9}} = -\frac{17}{14}$$

$$\tan^{-1} -\frac{17}{14} = 50.5°$$

$$A = 50.5°$$

195

$$\tan B = \frac{\frac{6}{5} - \left(-\frac{1}{2}\right)}{1 + \frac{6}{5}\left(-\frac{1}{2}\right)} = 4.25$$

$$B = 180° - \tan^{-1} 4.25 = 180° - 76.76°$$
$$= 103.24°$$

Note that $\tan^{-1} 4.25 = 76.76°$. However, it's not B, as one can see from Fig. 1.

$$C = 180° - (A + B) = 180° - 50.5° - 103.24° = 26.26°$$

Finally, the area of any triangle whose vertices are $P_1(x_1, y_1)$, $P_2(x_2, y_2)$, $P_3(x_3, y_3)$ is

$$A = \frac{1}{2}(x_1 y_2 + x_2 y_3 + x_3 y_1 - x_1 y_3 - x_2 y_1 - x_3 y_2).$$

Therefore, the area of $\triangle ABC$ is

$$A = \frac{1}{2} (0 \times (-2) + 4 \times 4 + 9 \times 0 - 0 \times 4 - 4 \times 0 - 9 \times (-2)) = 17.$$

CHAPTER 25

STRAIGHT LINES AND FAMILIES OF STRAIGHT LINES

● **PROBLEM 25-1**

Find the slope of $f(x) = 3x + 4$.

SOLUTION:

Two points on the line determined by $f(x) = 3x + 4$ are $A(0, 4)$ and $B(1, 7)$.

$$\frac{\text{difference of ordinates}}{\text{difference of abscissas}} = \frac{7-4}{1-0} = 3$$

Note that the ordinates are the y-coordinates and the abscissas are the x-coordinates. The slope determined by points A and B is 3. Hence, the slope of $f(x) = 3x + 4$ is 3. In general, the slope of a linear function of the form $f(x) = mx + b$ is m.

● **PROBLEM 25-2**

Show that the slope of the segment joining $(1, 2)$ and $(2, 6)$ is equal to the slope of the segment joining $(5, 15)$ and $(10, 35)$.

SOLUTION:

The slope of the line segment, m, joining the points (x_1, y_1) and (x_2, y_2) is given by the formula

197

$$m = \frac{(y_2 - y_1)}{(x_2 - x_1)}.$$

Therefore, the slope of the segment joining (1, 2) and (2, 6) is

$$\frac{6-2}{2-1} = \frac{4}{1} = 4.$$

The slope of the segment joining (5, 15) and (10, 35) is

$$\frac{35-15}{10-5} = \frac{20}{5} = 4.$$

Thus, the slopes of the two segments are equal.

● PROBLEM 25-3

Find the slope, the y-intercept, and the x-intercept of the equation $2x - 3y - 18 = 0$.

SOLUTION:

The equation $2x - 3y - 18 = 0$ can be written in the form of the general linear equation, $ax + by = c$.

$$2x - 3y - 18 = 0$$
$$2x - 3y = 18$$

To find the slope and y-intercept we derive them from the formula of the general linear equation $ax + by = c$. Dividing by b and solving for y we obtain:

$$\frac{a}{b}x + y = \frac{c}{b}$$

$$y = \frac{c}{b} - \frac{a}{b}x$$

where $-\frac{a}{b}$ = slope and $\frac{c}{b}$ = y-intercept.

To find the x-intercept, solve for x and let $y = 0$:

$$x = \frac{c}{a} - \frac{b}{a}y$$

$$x = \frac{c}{a}$$

In this form we have $a = 2$, $b = -3$, and $c = 18$. Thus,

$$\text{slope} = -\frac{a}{b} = -\frac{2}{-3} = \frac{2}{3}$$

$$y\text{-intercept} = \frac{c}{b} = \frac{18}{-3} = -6$$

$$x\text{-intercept} = \frac{c}{a} = \frac{18}{2} = 9$$

● PROBLEM 25-4

Write the equation of a line passing through points $P_1(5, 10)$ and $P_2(0, 4)$ in
(a) Point-slope form
(b) Slope-intercept form
(c) Two-point form
(d) Intercept form
(e) Form of general equation for straight lines

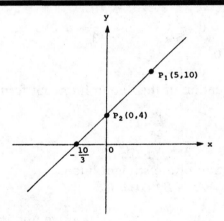

SOLUTION:

Since we are given two points on the line, the equation of the line in two-point form is the most easily obtained.

The two-point form is

$$y - y_1 = \frac{y_2 - y_1}{x_2 - x_1}(x - x_1).$$

Hence,

$$y - 10 = \frac{4 - 10}{0 - 5}(x - 5) = \frac{-6}{-5}(x - 5) = \frac{6}{5}(x - 5)$$

$$(y-10) = \frac{6}{5}(x-5)$$

is the equation of the straight line in the point-slope form, where the slope of the line is $\frac{6}{5}$.

To obtain the slope-intercept form of the line, $y = kx + b$,

$$y - 10 = \frac{6}{5}x - 6$$

$$y = \frac{6}{5}x - 6 + 10 = \frac{6}{5}x + 4$$

i.e.,
$$y = \frac{6}{5}x + 4.$$

The intercept form of the equation of the line is $\frac{x}{a} + \frac{y}{b} = 1$, where a and b are, respectively, the x-intercept and the y-intercept of the line.

To find a, let $y = 0$.

$$0 = \frac{6}{5}x + 4, \; x = -\frac{10}{3} = a$$

To find b, let $x = 0$.

$$y = 0 + 4 = 4 = b$$

Therefore, the equation of the line in intercept form is

$$\frac{x}{-\frac{10}{3}} + \frac{y}{4} = 1.$$

The general equation of the straight line is

$$Ax + By + C = 0 .$$

From
$$y = \frac{6}{5}x + 4, \text{ we obtain}$$

$$5y = 6x + 20,$$

$$6x - 5y + 20 = 0.$$

● **PROBLEM 25-5**

Determine the constant A so that the lines $3x - 4y = 12$ and $Ax + 6y = -9$ are parallel.

SOLUTION:

If two non-vertical lines are parallel, their slopes are equal. Thus, the lines

$Ax + By + C = 0$ and $Ax + By + D = 0$ are parallel (since both have slope $= -\dfrac{A}{B}$).

We are given two lines:

$$3 - 4y = 12 \qquad\qquad (1)$$
$$Ax + 6y = -9 \qquad\qquad (2)$$

We must make the coefficients of y the same for both equations in order to

equate the coefficients of x. Multiply (1) by $-\dfrac{3}{2}$ to obtain

$$\frac{-3}{2}(3x - 4y) = -\frac{3}{2}(12)$$

$$-\frac{9}{2}x + 6y = -18 \qquad\qquad (3)$$

$$Ax + 6y = -9 \qquad\qquad (2)$$

Transpose the constant terms of (3) and (2) to the other side.

Adding 18 to both sides, $\quad -\dfrac{9}{2}x + 6y + 18 = 0 \qquad\qquad (4)$

Adding 9 to both sides $\quad Ax + 6y + 9 = 0 \qquad\qquad (5)$

(4) and (5) will now be parallel if the coefficients of the x-terms are the same.

Thus, the constant $A = -\dfrac{9}{2}$. Then equation (5) becomes $-\dfrac{9}{2}x + 6y + 9 = 0$. We

can also express (5) in its given form, $Ax + 6y = -9$ or $-\dfrac{9}{2}x + 6y = -9$.

We also can write it in a form that has the same coefficient of x as (1), which clearly shows that they have equal slopes.

$$3x - 4y = 12 \qquad\qquad (1)$$

$$-\frac{9}{2}x + 6y = -9$$

Multiply the second equation by $-\dfrac{2}{3}$ to obtain a coefficient of x equal to 3.

$$-\frac{2}{3}\left(\frac{-9}{2}x + 6y\right) = -\frac{2}{3}(-9)$$

$$3x - 4y = 6$$

Now equations (1), $3x - 4y = 12$, and the equation $3x - 4y = 6$ are parallel since the coefficients of x and y are identical.

Find the equation for the line passing through (3, 5) and (–1, 2).

SOLUTION:

We use the two-point form with (x_1, y_1) = (3, 5) and (x_2, y_2) = (–1, 2). Then

$$\frac{y - y_1}{x - x_1} = m = \frac{y_2 - y_1}{x_2 - x_1}$$

$$\frac{y_2 - y_1}{x_2 - x_1} = \frac{2 - 5}{-1 - 3}, \text{ thus } \frac{y - 5}{x - 3} = \frac{-3}{-4}.$$

Cross multiply, $-4(y - 5) = -3(x - 3)$. Distributing, $-4y + 20 = -3x + 9$, which gives us the general form equation $3x - 4y = -11$.

(a) Find the equation of a line that is parallel to $Ax + By + C = 0$, where A, B, and C are arbitrary constants.

(b) Prove that if two lines ℓ_1 and ℓ_2 are perpendicular to each other, then the slopes of the two lines have the following relationship: $k_1 k_2 = -1$.

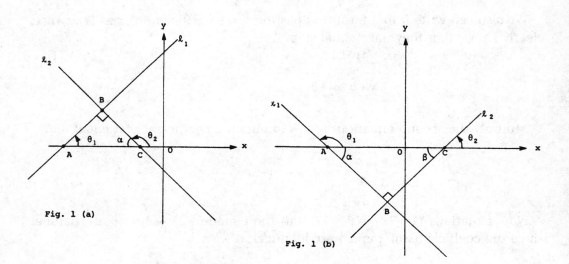

Fig. 1 (a)

Fig. 1 (b)

SOLUTION:

(a) Any line that is parallel to $Ax + By + C = 0$ must have the same slope as $Ax + By + C = 0$, which is $k = -\dfrac{A}{B}$.

Therefore, the equation of the lines which are parallel to $Ax + By + C = 0$ is $Ax + By + D = 0$, where D is an arbitrary constant.

(b) Let $k_1 = \tan\theta_1$ and $k_2 = \tan\theta_2$ (see Fig.1). From Fig.1(a), one has in $\triangle ABC$

$$\alpha = 180° - \theta_2 \quad \text{and} \quad \theta_1 + \alpha = 90°$$

That is,

$$\theta_1 + (180° - \theta_2) = 90°$$

$$\theta_1 = \theta_2 - 90°$$

$$
\begin{aligned}
k_1 = \tan\theta_1 &= \tan(\theta_2 - 90°)\\
&= \tan[-(90° - \theta_2)]\\
&= -[\tan(90° - \theta_2)] = -[\cot\theta_2]\\
&= -\frac{1}{\tan\theta_2} = -\frac{1}{k_2}
\end{aligned}
$$

Therefore, $k_1 k_2 = -1$.
Similarly, from Fig. 1(b), in $\triangle ABC$

$$\beta = \theta_2, \quad \alpha = 180° - \theta_1$$

$$\beta + \alpha = 90° = \theta_2 + 180° - \theta_1$$

$$\theta_1 = \theta_2 + 90°$$

$$k_1 = \tan\theta_1 = \tan(90° + \theta_2) = \cot\theta_2$$

$$= -\frac{1}{\tan\theta_2} = -\frac{1}{k_2}$$

● PROBLEM 25-8

Find the equation of the line ℓ which is equidistant from $\ell_1 : x + y + 2 = 0$ and $\ell_2 : x + y - 2 = 0$.

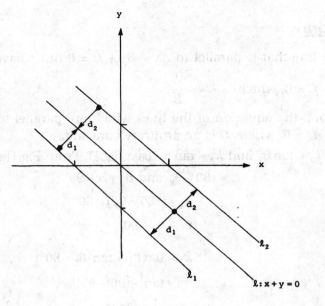

$\ell : x + y = 0$

SOLUTION:

As one sees from the figure, ℓ_1 and ℓ_2 are parallel, ℓ must be between ℓ_1 and ℓ_2, and parallel to both ℓ_1 and ℓ_2. Furthermore, observe that the directed distances between ℓ_1 and ℓ, ℓ and ℓ_2 have the same magnitude but opposite sign, i.e., $d_1 = -d_2$.

Let a point $P(x_0, y_0)$ be a point on the line ℓ.

$$d_1 = \frac{1 \bullet x_0 + 1 \bullet y_0 + 2}{\sqrt{1^2 + 1^2}} = -d_2 = -\frac{1 \bullet x_0 + 1 \bullet y_0}{\sqrt{1^2 + 1^2}}$$

$$\frac{x_0 + y_0 + 2}{\sqrt{2}} = -\frac{x_0 + y_0 - 2}{\sqrt{2}}$$

$$(x_0 + y_0 + 2) = -(x_0 + y_0 - 2)$$

$$x_0 + y_0 = 0$$

Since $P(x_0, y_0)$ can be any point on ℓ, one can replace $P(x_0, y_0)$ by $P(x, y)$ to obtain the equation for ℓ, i.e., $x + y = 0$.

Find the equation of the family of lines that satisfy the conditions

(a) parallel to $\ell_0 : x + 2y + 4 = 0$

(b) passing through the point $P_0(4, 9)$.

SOLUTION:

(a) The slope of ℓ_0 is $-\dfrac{1}{2}$. Hence, all lines with slope $-\dfrac{1}{2}$ will be in the family whose equation is required.

$y = -\dfrac{1}{2}x + b$ is the equation of the family of lines that are parallel to ℓ_0, where b is the parameter.

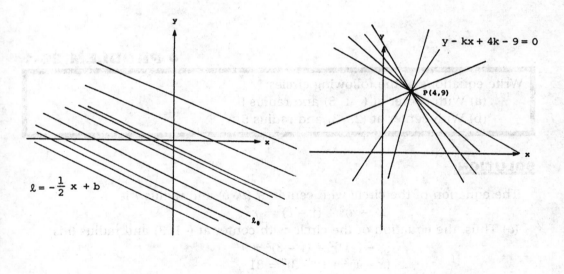

(b) The equation of the family of lines passing through $P_0(4, 9)$ is

$$y - 9 = k(x - 4)$$

with parameter k (the slope of the line). The equation can be written as

$$y - kx + 4k - 9 = 0.$$

CHAPTER 26

CIRCLES, PARABOLAS, ELLIPSES, AND HYPERBOLAS

● **PROBLEM 26-1**

Write equations of the following circles:
   (a) With center at (–1, 3) and radius 9.
   (b) With center at (2, –3) and radius 5.

SOLUTION:

The equation of the circle with center at (a, b) and radius r is
$$(x - a)^2 + (y - b)^2 = r^2.$$
(a) Thus, the equation of the circle with center at (–1, 3) and radius 9 is
$$[x - (-1)]^2 + (y - 3)^2 = 9^2$$
$$(x + 1)^2 + (y - 3)^2 = 81$$
(b) Similarly, the equation of the circle with center at (2, –3) and radius 5 is
$$(x - 2)^2 + [y - (-3)^2] = 5^2$$
$$(x - 2)^2 + (y + 3)^2 = 25$$

● **PROBLEM 26-2**

Find the center and radius of the circle
$$x^2 - 4x + y^2 + 8y - 5 = 0 \qquad (1)$$

SOLUTION:

We can find the radius and the coordinates of the center by completing the square in both x and y. To complete the square in either variable, take half the coefficient of the variable term (i.e., the x term or the y term) and then square this value. The resulting number is then added to both sides of the equation. Completing the square in x:

$$\left[\frac{1}{2}(-4)\right]^2 = \left[-2\right]^2 = 4$$

Then equation (1) becomes

$$(x^2 - 4x + 4) + y^2 + 8y - 5 = 0 + 4,$$

or

$$(x - 2)^2 + y^2 + 8y - 5 = 4 \tag{2}$$

Before completing the square in y, add 5 to both sides of equation (2):

$$(x - 2)^2 + y^2 + 8y - 5 + 5 = 4 + 5$$

$$(x - 2)^2 + y^2 + 8y = 9 \tag{3}$$

Now, completing the square in y:

$$\left[\frac{1}{2}(8)\right]^2 = \left[4\right]^2 = 16$$

Then equation (3) becomes

$$(x - 2)^2 + (y^2 + 8y + 16) = 9 + 16,$$

or

$$(x - 2)^2 + (y + 4)^2 = 25 \tag{4}$$

Note that the equation of a circle is

$$(x - h)^2 + (y - k)^2 = r^2$$

where (h, k) is the center of the circle and r is the radius of the circle. Equation (4) is in the form of the equation of a circle. Hence, equation (4) represents a circle with center $(2, -4)$ and radius = 5.

● PROBLEM 26-3

Find the equation of the circle that goes through the points $(1, 3)$, $(-8, 0)$, and $(0, 6)$.

SOLUTION:

We are asked to find the equation of a circle. There are two forms: (1) the standard form $(x - h)^2 + (y - k)^2 = a^2$; (2) the general form $x^2 + y^2 + Dx + Ey + F = 0$. Both are equivalent; however, the standard form is more convenient when we are dealing with the coordinates of the center point (h, k) or the length of the radius a. As we can see, all three numbers, h, k, and a, can be readily obtained given the standard form. The drawback of the standard form is its factored format which, in problems which do not ask for the center co-ordinates or the radius, is just extra work to calculate. In these cases, the multiplied out form, the general form, is more convenient.

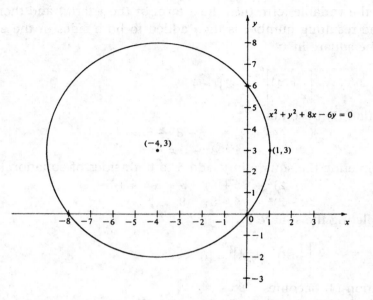

Here we are asked to find the equation given three points. We are given three pairs of (x, y), and asked to find the three equation unknowns. If we were to use standard form, the unknowns would be h, k, and a. The unknowns would be squared. Moreover, to solve the equations we would have to multiply out the $(x - h)^2$ and $(y - h)^2$ terms. It would be long and difficult.

If we use the second method, however, the unknowns would be the unsquared terms D, E, and F. Furthermore, there are no multiplications (other than x^2 and y^2) necessary. Thus, even though we may wish to express the equation of the circle in standard form later on, it is easier to solve for the general form equation first.

Suppose the equation of the circle is $x^2 + y^2 + Dx + Ey + F = 0$. Because point $(1, 3)$ is on the circle it must satisfy the equation. Then,

(i)	$1^2 + 3^2 + D(1) + E(3) + F = 0$
or	$D + 3E + F = -10$.

Similarly, since $(-8, 0)$ and $(0, 6)$ are also points on the circle, we have

(ii) $(-8)^2 + 0^2 + D(-8) + E(0) + F = 0$ or

        $-8D + F = -64$.

(iii) $0^2 + 6^2 + D(0) + E(6) + F = 0$ or $6E + F = -36$.

We thus have three equations and three unknowns.

(iv) $D + 3E + F = -10$

(v) $-8D + F = -64$

(vi) $6E + F = -36$

We make this system a system of two equations and two unknowns by eliminating D. Multiply (iv) by 8 and add it to (v). We have

(vii) $24E + 9F = -144$

(viii) $6E + F = -36$ (see (vi))

Now eliminate E to form one equation and one unknown. Multiply (viii) by -4 and add the result to (vii) to obtain

(ix) $5F = 0$ or $F = 0$.

Substituting this result in (viii), we find E. Since $6E + F = -36$, then $6E + 0 = -36$ or $E = \dfrac{-36}{6} = -6$. Substituting the value for F in (v), we find $-8D + F = -64$.

Thus, $-8D = -64$ or $D = \dfrac{-64}{-8} = 8$. The general form of the equation is

(x) $x^2 + y^2 + 8x - 6y = 0$.

Usually, it is standard practice to give the equation in standard form.

(xi) $(x^2 + 8x) + (y^2 - 6y) = 0$

(xii) $(x^2 + 8x + 16) + (y^2 - 6y + 9) - 16 - 9 = 0$

(xiii) $(x + 4)^2 + (y - 3)^2 = 25$

● PROBLEM 26-4

Find the equation of the circle of radius $r = 9$, with center on $\ell: y = x$ and tangent to both coordinate axes.

SOLUTION:

As seen in Fig. 1, there are two such circles, 0 and 0'. Let the centers of 0 and 0' be (a, b) and (c, d), respectively.

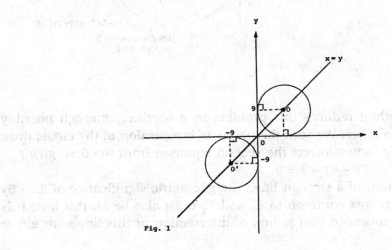

Fig. 1

209

Since points (a, b) and (c, d) are on ℓ: $y = x$, one has $a = b$ and $c = d$. The equations will be

$$(x - a)^2 + (y - a)^2 = 9^2$$

and

$$(x - c)^2 + (y - c)^2 = 9^2$$

Because the circles are tangent to both coordinate axes, one obtains $a = 9 = b$ and $c = -9 = d$. (See Fig. 1.) Therefore, the equations are

$$(x - 9)^2 + (y - 9)^2 = 81 \text{ and}$$
$$(x + 9)^2 + (y + 9)^2 = 81$$

● PROBLEM 26-5

Find the points of intersection (if any) of the circles C_1 and C_2 where

$$C_1: x^2 + y^2 - 4x - 2y + 1 = 0$$
$$C_2: x^2 + y^2 - 6x + 4y + 4 = 0$$

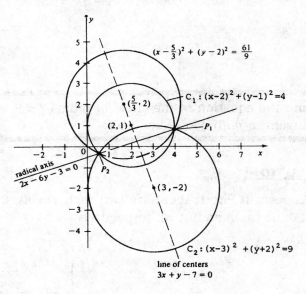

SOLUTION:

The analytic method reduces this problem to a routine, although possibly messy, problem in algebra. We seek the points of intersection of the circle; thus, an obvious first step is to subtract the second equation from the first, giving

$$2x - 6y - 3 = 0.$$

This is the equation of a straight line. The geometric significance of $2x - 6y - 3 = 0$ is that any points common to C_1 and C_2 must also lie on this line. It is a straightforward process to find points of intersection of this line with either

210

C_1 or C_2. We can solve for x in terms of y,

$$x = 3y + \frac{3}{2}$$

substitute back into the equation C_1, find the two real values of y, then use $x = 3y + \frac{3}{2}$ again to find the corresponding values of x. Using this or an equivalent procedure, we obtain as points of intersection

$$P_1\left(\frac{9}{4} + \frac{3\sqrt{135}}{20}, \frac{1}{4} + \frac{\sqrt{135}}{20}\right) \approx (3.99, 0.83) \text{ and}$$

$$P_2\left(\frac{9}{4} - \frac{3\sqrt{135}}{20}, \frac{1}{4} - \frac{\sqrt{135}}{20}\right) \approx (0.51, -0.33)$$

● **PROBLEM 26-6**

Show that the quadratic equation $y = 2x^2 - 20x + 25$ is the equation of a parabola.

SOLUTION:

If we can write $y = 2x^2 - 20x + 25$ in the standard form $y = a(x - h)^2 + k$, we will show that its graph is a parabola. The axis of symmetry will be the line $x = h$. The vertex will be at (h, k). Notice that the standard form has a term with a perfect square in it. We use a method known as completing the square to rewrite

$$y = 2x^2 - 20x + 25$$

(a) Subtract the constant term, 25, from both members.

$$y - 25 = 2x^2 - 20x$$

(b) Factor 2 from the right member.

$$y - 25 = 2(x^2 - 10x)$$

(c) We need to add 25 within the parentheses since 25 is the square of one-half the coefficient of the term in x. If we do, then we must add 50 to the left member to maintain equality, since we have in fact added two times the quantity added in the parentheses ($2 \times 25 = 50$) to the right member.

$$y + 25 = 2(x^2 - 10x + 25)$$

(d) The expression within the parentheses is now a perfect square.

$$y + 25 = 2(x - 5)^2$$

(e) Next we subtract 25 from each member.

$$y = 2(x - 5)^2 - 25$$

211

This is now in standard form $y = a(x - h)^2 + k$. Here $a = 2$, $h = 5$, and $k = -25$. Thus, the graph of $y = 2x^2 - 20x + 25$ is a parabola. Its axis of symmetry is the line $x = 5$; its vertex is at $(5, -25)$.

Find the equation of the tangent to the parabola $y = x^2 - 6x + 9$, if the slope of the tangent equals 2.

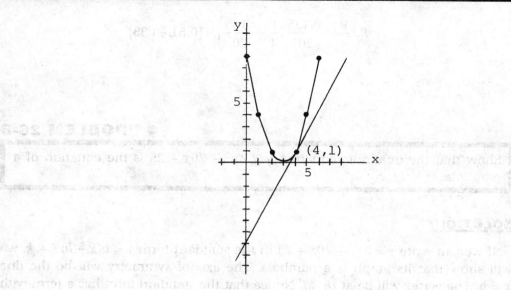

SOLUTION:

The equation of a straight line is $y = mx + k$, where m is the slope and k is the y-intercept. The equation

$$y = 2x + k \tag{1}$$

represents a family of parallel lines with slope 2, some of which intersect the parabola in two points, others which have no point of intersection with the parabola, and just one which intersects the parabola in only one point. The problem is to find the value of k so that the graph of equation (1) intersects the parabola in just one point. If we solve the system

$$y = 2x + k \tag{1}$$
$$y = x^2 - 6x + 9 \tag{2}$$

by substitution, we get for the first step

$$2x + k = x^2 - 6x + 9 \text{ or}$$
$$x^2 - 8x + 9 - k = 0 \tag{3}$$

This is a quadratic equation of the form $ax^2 + bx + c = 0$. The discriminant determines the nature of the roots when $ax^2 + bx + c = 0$. The condition that equation (3) has but one solution is that the discriminant, $b^2 - 4ac$ equals 0. Therefore, if $a = 1$, $b = -8$, $c = 9 - k$, then $b^2 - 4ac = 64 - 4(9 - k) = 0$ or $k = -7$.

Substituting this value of k in equation (1), we have $y = 2x - 7$ which is the equation of the tangent to the given parabola when the slope of the tangent is equal to 2. The figure is the graph of the parabola and the tangent. The student may verify that the point of contact is (4, 1). This is shown by substituting (4, 1) into

$$y = 2x - 7 = x^2 - 6x + 9$$
$$1 = 2(4) - 7 = 4^2 - 6(4) + 9$$
$$1 = 1 = 1$$

● **PROBLEM 26-8**

Write the equation of the parabola whose focus has coordinates (0, 2) and whose directrix has equation $y = -2$. (See figure.)

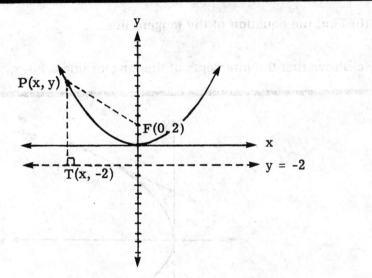

SOLUTION:

Since, by definition, each point lying on a parabola is equidistant from both the focus and directrix of the parabola, the origin must lie on the specific parabola described in the statement of the problem (see figure).

To find the equation of the parabola, choose a point $P(x, y)$ lying on the parabola (see figure). By definition, then, the distance PT must equal the distance PF, where T lies on the directrix, directly below P. Since T also lies on $y = -2$, it

213

has coordinates $(x, -2)$. Using the distance formula, we find $PF = PT$

$$\sqrt{x^2 + (y-2)^2} = \sqrt{(y+2)^2}$$

Squaring both sides of this equation, we obtain

$$x^2 + (y-2)^2 = (y+2)^2.$$

● **PROBLEM 26-9**

Consider the parabola $y^2 = 4px$. A tangent to the parabola at point $P_1\ (x_1, y_1)$ is defined as the line that intersects the parabola at point P_1 and nowhere else.

(a) Show that the slope of the tangent line is $\dfrac{2p}{y_1}$.

[Hint: Let the slope be m. Find the equation of the line passing through P_1 with slope m. What are the points of intersection of the tangent line and the parabola? For what values of m, would there be only one intersection point?]

(b) Find the equation of the tangent line.

(c) Prove that the intercepts of the tangent line are $(-x_1, 0)$ and $\left(0, \dfrac{1}{2}y_1\right)$.

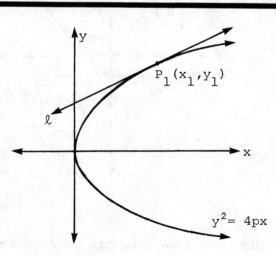

$P_1\,(x_1, y_1)$

ℓ

$y^2 = 4px$

SOLUTION:

(a) We know three things about the tangent line ℓ. First, ℓ is a line, therefore, its equation is of the form $y = mx + b$. Second, P_1 is on ℓ. Therefore, $(x_1,$

y_1) must satisfy the equation for ℓ. Therefore, $y_1 = mx_1 + b$. Third, ℓ is tangent to the parabola at point P_1. This implies two things: (1) P_1 is a point on the parabola. Thus, $y_1^2 = 4px_1$; and (2) P_1 is the only point common to both ℓ and the parabola.

To determine the line we must find m and b.

We first wish to find m. We know that ℓ and $y^2 = 4px$ intersect at only one point. Therefore, we solve for the intersection points of ℓ and $y^2 = 4px$ in terms of m. The value of m that permits only one point of intersection is the correct one.

Any point (x, y) that is a point of intersection of the line and the parabola must satisfy the equations

$$\text{(i)} \qquad y = mx + b$$
$$\text{(ii)} \qquad y^2 = 4px$$

We have two equations in two unknowns x and y. The first expresses y in terms of x. Substituting this expression in (ii) does not change the validity of the second equation. In addition, it makes the second equation a single equation with a single unknown.

$$\text{(iii)} \qquad (mx + b)^2 = 4px$$

Multiplying out and simplifying, we obtain

$$\text{(iv)} \qquad m^2 x^2 + (2mb - 4p)\,x + b^2 = 0$$

Then, by the quadratic formula, we can obtain a value for x in terms of m, p, and b.

$$\text{(v)} \qquad x = \frac{-(2mb - 4p) \pm \sqrt{(2mb - 4p)^2 - 4m^2 b^2}}{2m^2}$$

Because ℓ is a tangent, there should exist only one possible intersection point and, therefore, only one value of x. For equation (v) to have a single value, $\sqrt{(2mb - 4p)^2 - 4m^2 b^2}$ must equal 0. In other words, for ℓ to be a tangent line,

$$\text{(vi)} \qquad (2mb - 4p)^2 - 4m^2 b^2 = 0$$
$$\text{(vii)} \qquad 4m^2 b^2 - 16mbp + 16p^2 - 4m^2 b^2 = 0$$
$$\text{(viii)} \qquad 16p^2 = 16mbp \ \text{ or } \ p = bm$$

Thus, we know $p = mb$. p is known; m and b are what we are solving for. To find values for m and b, we find another relationship between m and b.

Note that point $P_1(x_1, y_1)$ is a point on ℓ. Therefore, $y_1 = mx_1 + b$.

With this second set of simultaneous equations, $p = mb$ and $y_1 = mx_1 + b$, we can solve for m. Since $p = mb$, $b = \dfrac{p}{m}$. Substituting this in $y_1 = mx_1 + b$, we obtain $y_1 = mx_1 + \dfrac{p}{m}$. Multiplying by m, we obtain the expression $m^2 x_1 - my_1$

$+p = 0$. By the quadratic formula, we have $m = \dfrac{y_1 \pm \sqrt{y_1^2 - 4x_1p}}{2x_1}$.

Note that (x_1, y_1) are points on the parabola; and therefore, $y_1^2 - 4x_1p = 0$. The radical $\sqrt{y_1^2 - 4x_1p} = 0$, and thus $m = \dfrac{y_1}{2x_1}$.

We are asked to show, though, that $m = \dfrac{2p}{y_1}$. Although not immediately obvious, this is the same as our answer

$$m = \frac{y_1}{2x_1} = \frac{y_1}{2x_1} \cdot \frac{\frac{y_1}{4x_1}}{\frac{y_1}{4x_1}} = \frac{\frac{y_1^2}{4x_1}}{\frac{y_1}{2}} \left(\text{since } y_1^2 = 4px_1, p = \frac{y_1^2}{4x_1} \right)$$

$$m = \frac{p}{\frac{y_1}{2}} = \frac{2p}{y_1}$$

Thus, the slope m of the tangent of the parabola $y^2 = 4px$ at point $P_1(x_1, y_1)$ is $\dfrac{2p}{y_1}$.

(b) The equation of the tangent line ℓ is $y = mx + b$. From part (a), we know $m = \dfrac{2p}{y_1}$. Furthermore, we know from part (a) that $p = mb$. Thus, $b = \dfrac{p}{m} = \dfrac{p}{\left(\frac{2p}{y_1}\right)} = \dfrac{y_1}{2}$, and the equation of ℓ becomes $y = \left(\dfrac{2p}{y_1}\right)x + \left(\dfrac{y_1}{2}\right)$. Another

acceptable form of the equation is obtained by letting $p = \dfrac{y_1^2}{4x_1}$: $y = \left(\dfrac{y_1}{2x_1}\right)x + \dfrac{y_1}{2}$.

(c) Given the equation in part (b), we know that the y-intercept is given by b. Since $b = \dfrac{y_1}{2}$, the y-intercept is $\left(0, \dfrac{y_1}{2}\right)$. [An alternate method is to realize that

the y-intercept is obtained by setting $x = 0$. Thus, $y = \left(\dfrac{y_1}{2x_1}\right) \cdot 0 + \left(\dfrac{y_1}{2}\right) = \dfrac{y_1}{2}$].

To find the x-intercept, we set $y = 0$. Thus, $0 = \left(\dfrac{y_1}{2x_1}\right)x + \left(\dfrac{y_1}{2}\right)$, or

$$\left(\frac{y_1}{2x_1}\right)x = -\frac{y_1}{2}.$$

Dividing by $\frac{y_1}{2}$ and multiplying by x_1, we obtain $x = -x_1$. Thus, $(-x_1, 0)$ is the x-intercept.

● PROBLEM 26-10

In the equation of an ellipse, $4x^2 + 9y^2 - 16x + 18y - 11 = 0$, determine the standard form of the equation, and find the values of a, b, c, and e.

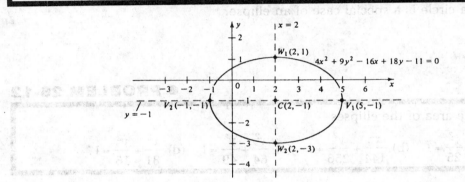

SOLUTION:

By completing the squares, we can arrive at the standard form of the equation, from which the values of the parameters can be determined. Thus,

$$4(x^2 - 4x + 4) + 9(y^2 + 2y + 1) = 36$$

or
$$4(x - 2)^2 + 9(y + 1)^2 = 36. \text{ Dividing by } 36,$$

$$\frac{(x-2)^2}{9} + \frac{(y+1)^2}{4} = 1$$

Thus, the center of the ellipse is at $(2, -1)$. Comparing this equation with the general form,

$\frac{x^2}{a^2} + \frac{y^2}{b^2} = 1$, where $a > b$, we see that $a = 3$, $b = 2$.

$c = \sqrt{a^2 - b^2} = \sqrt{5}$.

Finally, $e = \frac{c}{a} = \frac{\sqrt{5}}{3} \approx 0.745$.

The equation of an ellipse is $\dfrac{x^2}{a^2}+\dfrac{y^2}{b^2}=1$. Discuss what happens if $a = b = r$.

SOLUTION:

If $a = b = r$, the given equation becomes

$$\frac{x^2}{a^2}+\frac{y^2}{b^2}=\frac{x^2}{r^2}+\frac{y^2}{r^2}=1 \tag{1}$$

Multiplying the last branch of the equality in equation (1) by r^2 yields
$$x^2 + y^2 = r^2 \tag{2}$$
This is the equation of a circle with center at $C(0, 0)$ and radius r. Hence, we see that a circle is a special case of an ellipse.

Find the area of the ellipses

(a) $\dfrac{x^2}{9}+\dfrac{y^2}{25}=1$ (b) $\dfrac{x^2}{144}+\dfrac{y^2}{256}=1$ (c) $\dfrac{x^2}{64}+\dfrac{y^2}{49}=1$ (d) $\dfrac{x^2}{81}+\dfrac{y^2}{16}=1$.

SOLUTION:

The area of an ellipse whose equation is $\dfrac{x^2}{a^2}+\dfrac{y^2}{b^2}=1$ is πab. Applying this fact to the given equations, we find

(a) $\dfrac{x^2}{9}+\dfrac{y^2}{25}=1,$ $a^2 = 9,$ $a = 3$

$b^2 = 25,$ $b = 5$
Area $= \pi ab = 15\pi$

(b) $\dfrac{x^2}{144}+\dfrac{y^2}{256}=1,$ $a^2 = 144,$ $a = 12$

$b^2 = 256,$ $b = 16$
Area $= \pi ab = 192\pi$

(c) $\dfrac{x^2}{64}+\dfrac{y^2}{49}=1,$ $a^2 = 64,$ $a = 8$

$b^2 = 49,$ $b = 7$
Area $= \pi ab = 56\pi$

(d) $\dfrac{x^2}{81} + \dfrac{y^2}{16} = 1$, $a^2 = 81$, $a = 9$

$b^2 = 16$, $b = 4$

Area $= \pi ab = 36\pi$

Consider the equation

$$x^2 - 4y^2 + 4x + 8y + 4 = 0.$$

Express this equation in standard form, and determine the center, the vertices, the foci, and the eccentricity of this hyperbola. Describe the fundamental rectangle and find the equations of the two asymptotes.

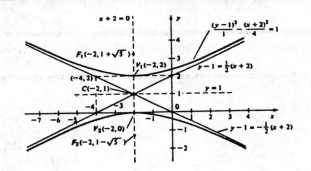

SOLUTION:

Rewrite the equation by completing the squares, i.e.,

$$(x^2 + 4x + 4) - 4(y^2 - 2y + 1) = -4$$

or

$$(x + 2)^2 - 4(y - 1)^2 = -4$$

or, by dividing and rearranging terms,

$$\frac{(y-1)^2}{1} - \frac{(x+2)^2}{4} = 1$$

The center, located at (h, k) in the equation

$$\frac{(y-k)^2}{a^2} - \frac{(x-h)^2}{b^2} = 1 \text{ is, therefore, at } (-2, 1). \text{ Furthermore,}$$

$a = 1$, $b = 2$. Thus,

$$c = \sqrt{1^2 + 2^2} = \sqrt{5}, \text{ and } e = \sqrt{5}.$$

The vertices are displaced $\pm a$ from the center while the foci are displaced $\pm c$ (along the transverse axis). Therefore, the vertices are $(-2, 1 \pm 1)$ and the foci

219

are $(-2, 1 \pm \sqrt{5})$.

By definition, the fundamental rectangle is the rectangle whose vertices are at $(h \pm b, k \pm a)$. Hence, in this example, the coordinates of the vertices of the rectangle are $(0, 2)$, $(-4, 2)$, $(-4, 0)$, and $(0, 0)$. The equations of the two asymptotes are determined by finding the slopes of the lines passing through the center of the hyperbola and two of the vertices of its fundamental rectangle (see figure). Then,

$$m = \frac{\Delta y}{\Delta x} = \pm \frac{1}{2}$$

gives the two slopes and the point-slope form, choosing the point $(-2, 1)$ which is common to both asymptotes, gives

$$y - 1 = \pm \frac{1}{2}(x + 2).$$

● **PROBLEM 26-14**

Find the equation of the hyperbola with vertices V_1 (8, 0), V_2 (2, 0) and eccentricity $e = 2$.

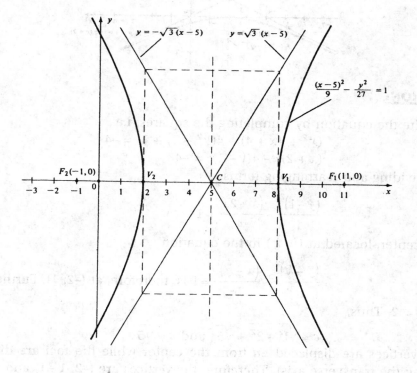

220

SOLUTION:

There are two basic forms of the equation of an hyperbola that is not rotated with respect to the coordinate axes,

$$\frac{(x-h)^2}{a^2} - \frac{(y-k)^2}{b^2} = 1 \text{ and } \frac{(y-k)^2}{a^2} - \frac{(x-h)^2}{b^2} = 1.$$

Which form is appropriate depends upon whether the transverse axis is parallel to the x-axis or to the y-axis, respectively. To determine the equation of an hyperbola, then, it is necessary to first discover which equation applies, then to solve for the constants h, k, a, c. The information about the vertices implies that the transverse axis is the x-axis.

Thus, the first form of the equation for an hyperbola applies. In this case, the center, which is the average of the vertices, is at (5, 0). The distance between the vertices is $2a = 6$; therefore, $a = 3$. In order to determine the value of b, we use the relation between eccentricity, e, c, and a: $e = \frac{c}{a}$. Thus, $c = e \times a$

$= 2 \times 3 = 6.$

But $b = \sqrt{c^2 - a^2} = \sqrt{6^2 - 3^2} = \sqrt{27} \approx 5.2$

Substituting for h, k, a, b, we have $\frac{(x-5)^2}{9} - \frac{y^2}{27} = 1$, or $3x^2 - y^2 - 30x + 48 = 0$.

● PROBLEM 26-15

Find the equation of the conjugate of the hyperbola $4x^2 - y^2 - 40 = 0$.

SOLUTION:

From $4x^2 - y^2 - 40 = 0$, one has

$$4x^2 - y^2 = 40, \quad \frac{x^2}{10} - \frac{y^2}{40} = 1,$$

that is, $a = \sqrt{10}$, $b = 2\sqrt{10}$. Two hyperbolas having the transverse axis of each as the conjugate axis of the other are called conjugate hyperbolas. They have the same center, the same asymptotes, and their foci lie on a circle whose center is the common center of the hyperbolas.

The center of $\frac{x^2}{10} - \frac{y^2}{40} = 1$ is at $0(0, 0)$, and the asymptotes are $y = \pm\frac{b}{a}x$, i.e.,

$y = \pm 2x.$

The conjugate of $4x^2 - y^2 - 40 = 0$ is easily obtained by switching the signs of $\dfrac{x^2}{a^2}$ and $\dfrac{y^2}{b^2}$. For example, we are given $+\dfrac{x^2}{10} - \dfrac{y^2}{40} = 1$. The conjugate is then

$-\dfrac{x^2}{10} + \dfrac{y^2}{40} = 1$, i.e., $\dfrac{y^2}{40} - \dfrac{x^2}{10} = 1$.

This may be obtained directly from the conjugate of $4x^2 - y^2 - 40 = 0$, which is $-4x^2 + y^2 - 40 = 0$.

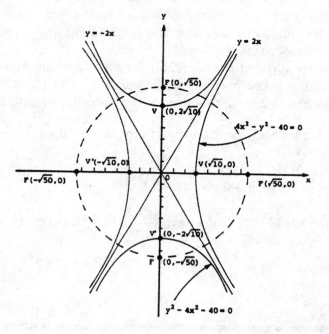

● PROBLEM 26-16

By definition, if an hyperbola has foci $F_1(-c, 0)$ and $F_2(c, 0)$, and $P(x, y)$ is a point on the hyperbola, then $|PF_1 - PF_2| = k$, where k is a constant such that $k < F_1 F_2 = 2c$.

Assuming that the above holds, and defining a constant such that $a = \dfrac{k}{2}$, and a constant b such that $b^2 = c^2 - a^2$, prove that the equation of the hyperbola is $\dfrac{x^2}{a^2} - \dfrac{y^2}{b^2} = 1$.

SOLUTION:

From the given facts,
$$|PF_1 - PF_2| = k = 2a. \tag{1}$$
By the distance formula,

$$PF_1 = \sqrt{(x+c)^2 + y^2} \tag{2}$$

$$PF_2 = \sqrt{(x-c)^2 + y^2} \tag{3}$$

Using (3) and (2) in (1), we obtain

$$\left|\sqrt{(x+c)^2 + y^2} - \sqrt{(x-c)^2 + y^2}\right| = 2a \tag{4}$$

Since any real number (positive or negative) times itself must be positive, we may write, using equation (4)

$$\left(\left|\sqrt{(x+c)^2 + y^2} - \sqrt{(x-c)^2 + y^2}\right|\right)^2 = \left(\sqrt{(x+c)^2 + y^2} - \sqrt{(x-c)^2 + y^2}\right)^2 = 4a^2$$

Expanding the last branch of the last equation

$$(x+c)^2 + y^2 + (x-c)^2 + y^2 - 2\sqrt{\left((x+c)^2 + y^2\right)\left((x-c)^2 + y^2\right)} = 4a^2$$

Expanding the last equation again, and regrouping terms

$$2x^2 + 2y^2 + 2c^2 - 2\sqrt{\left((x+c)^2 + y^2\right)\left((x-c)^2 + y^2\right)} = 4a^2$$

Subtracting $-2\sqrt{\left((x+c)^2 + y^2\right)\left((x-c)^2 + y^2\right)}$ and $4a^2$ from both sides of the last equation yields

$$2x^2 + 2y^2 + 2c^2 - 4a^2 = 2\sqrt{\left((x+c)^2 + y^2\right)\left((x-c)^2 + y^2\right)}$$

Dividing both sides by 2

$$x^2 + y^2 + c^2 - 2a^2 = \sqrt{\left((x+c)^2 + y^2\right)\left((x-c)^2 + y^2\right)}$$

Squaring both sides

$$\left(x^2 + y^2 + c^2 - 2a^2\right)^2 = \left((x+c)^2 + y^2\right)\left((x-c)^2 + y^2\right)$$

Expanding the right side

$$\left(x^2 + y^2 + c^2 - 2a^2\right)^2 = \left(x^2 + y^2 + c^2 + 2cx\right)\left(x^2 + y^2 + c^2 - 2cx\right)$$

Expanding both sides using the distributive law

$$\left(x^2 + y^2 + c^2\right)^2 + 4a^4 - 4a^2\left(x^2 + y^2 + c^2\right) = \left(x^2 + y^2 + c^2\right)^2 - 4c^2x^2$$

Cancelling like terms on both sides and expanding the remaining terms on the left side of the last equation, we find

$$4a^4 - 4a^2x^2 - 4a^2y^2 - 4a^2c^2 = -4c^2x^2 \tag{5}$$

But, we know that

$$c^2 - a^2 = b^2$$

Adding a^2 to both sides of this equation,

$$c^2 = a^2 + b^2 \tag{6}$$

Using equation (6) in equation (5)

$$4a^4 - 4a^2x^2 - 4a^2y^2 - 4a^4 - 4a^2b^2 = -4a^2x^2 - 4b^2x^2$$

Subtracting $-4a^2x^2$ and $-4b^2x^2$ from both sides of the last equation

$$-4a^2y^2 - 4a^2b^2 + 4b^2x^2 = 0$$

Dividing through by $4a^2b^2$ gives

$$-\frac{y^2}{b^2} - 1 + \frac{x^2}{a^2} = 0$$

Adding 1 to both sides of the last equation yields the desired result

$$\frac{x^2}{a^2} - \frac{y^2}{b^2} = 1.$$

CHAPTER 27

TRANSFORMATION OF COORDINATES

Transform each of the following equations into another form, such that the new form of the equation contains no terms of the first degree.

(a) $x^2 + y^2 - 4x + 10y = 0$

(b) $xy + 4x - 2y + 10 = 0$

SOLUTION:

(a) By means of translation of the coordinate axes, one can find the required equations.

METHOD 1.

$x^2 + y^2 - 4x + 10y$

$= (x^2 - 4x) + (y^2 + 10y)$. Now, it is necessary to complete the square.

$(x^2 - 4x + 2^2) + (y^2 + 10y + 5^2) - 4 - 25$

$= (x - 2)^2 + (y + 5)^2 - 29 = 0$

Using the transformation

$\begin{cases} x' = x - 2 \\ y' = y + 5 \end{cases}$ one obtains $x'^2 + y'^2 = 29$ as the required equation.

METHOD 2.

Let $\quad x' = x - a$

$y' = y - b$, and substitute

$x = x' + a$, $y = y' + b$ into the equation. Then

$(x' + a)^2 + (y' + b)^2 - 4(x' + a) + 10(y' + b)$

$= x'^2 + 2ax' + a^2 + y'^2 + 2by' + b^2 - 4x' - 4a + 10y' + 10b$

225

$$= x'^2 + y'^2 + (2a - 4)x' + (2b + 10)y' + 10b - 4a + a^2 + b^2 = 0$$

Setting

$$2a - 4 = 0$$
$$2b + 10 = 0$$

so that the above equation will contain no terms of first degree as required, one has $a = 2$, $b = 5$.

Therefore, by replacing x by $x' + 2$ and y by $y' - 5$, one can obtain the equation

$$x'^2 + y'^2 = 29$$

(b) Let

$$x = x' + a$$
$$y = y' + b$$
$$xy + 4x - 2y + 10 = 0 \text{ becomes}$$
$$(x' + a)(y' + b) + 4(x' + a) - 2(y' + b) + 10$$
$$= x'y' + bx' + ay' + ab + 4x' + 4a - 2y' - 2b + 10$$
$$= x'y' + (b + 4)x' + (a - 2)y' + ab + 4a - 2b + 10$$
$$= 0$$

Setting $b + 4 = 0$ and $a - 2 = 0$ so that the above equation will have no terms of first degree, or $b = -4$ and $a = 2$, the transformation

$$x = x' + 2, \ y = y' - 4 \text{ or}$$
$$x' = x - 2, \ y' = y + 4 \text{ reduces the given equation to } x'y' + 18 = 0.$$

Transform the equation $x^3 - 3x^2 - y^2 + 3x + 4y - 5 = 0$ by translating the coordinate axes to a new origin at $(1, 2)$. Plot the locus and show both sets of axes.

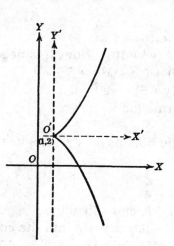

SOLUTION:

When translating the coordinate axes, each variable in the original equation becomes a function of the translation. If the axes are translated to a new origin at, say, (h, k) and any point P has coordinates of (x, y) before the translation and (x', y') after the translation, then we know $x = x' + h$ and $y = y' + k$.

These equations of transformation tell us that for every x and y in the original equation we can substitute $x' + h$ and $y' + k$, respectively, to find the equivalent equation on the translated axes.

If we proceed with the substitution of x and y into the given equation, we obtain

$$(x' + 1)^3 - 3(x' + 1)^2 - (y' + 2)^2 + 3(x' + 1) +$$
$$4(y' + 2) - 5 = 0$$
$$x'^3 + 3x'^2 + 3x' + 1 - (3x'^2 + 6x' + 3) - (y'^2 + 4y' + 4) +$$
$$3x' + 3 + 4y' + 8 - 5 = 0$$
$$x'^3 - y'^2 = 0$$

This is an easier equation to plot. Select several points in the (x', y') system that satisfy the equation so that we can observe the shape of the locus.

x'	0	1	1	2	2
y'	0	1	-1	$\sqrt{8}$	$-\sqrt{8}$

This locus is shown on the accompanying graph. Notice that it is symmetric around the x'-axis.

This is also the graph of the original equation relative to the x and y axes.

● PROBLEM 27-3

By a rotation of the coordinate axes, transform the equation
$$9x^2 - 24xy + 16y^2 - 40x - 30y = 0$$
into another equation lacking the cross product term. (Plot the locus and draw both sets of axes.)

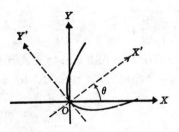

227

SOLUTION:

In a problem of this type where rotation of axes are required, we must apply the formulas

$$x = x' \cos \theta - y' \sin \theta \text{ and } y = x' \sin \theta + y' \cos \theta$$

where θ is the angle through which the axes are rotated and (x, y) and (x', y') are the coordinates of the point P before and after rotation, respectively. (This procedure is used principally to eliminate cross-terms in second degree equations.)

We are not given the required angle of rotation and must devise a procedure to transform the equation without this fact.

If we let θ = the angle of rotation, then by substitution into the original equation, we obtain

$$9(x' \cos \theta - y' \sin \theta)^2 - 24(x' \cos \theta - y' \sin \theta) \times$$
$$(x' \sin \theta + y' \cos \theta) + 16(x' \sin \theta + y' \cos \theta)^2$$
$$- 40(x' \cos \theta - y' \sin \theta) - 30(x' \sin \theta + y' \cos \theta) = 0$$

After expansion and collection of terms, the equation assumes the form

$$* \ (9 \cos^2 \theta - 24 \cos \theta \sin \theta + 16 \sin^2 \theta)x'^2$$
$$+ (14 \sin \theta \cos \theta + 24 \sin^2 \theta - 24 \cos^2 \theta)x'y'$$
$$+ (9 \sin^2 \theta + 24 \sin \theta \cos \theta + 16 \cos^2 \theta)y'^2$$
$$- (40 \cos \theta + 30 \sin \theta)x' + (40 \sin \theta - 30 \cos \theta)y' = 0$$

We are told that this equation is not supposed to have an $x'y'$ term. Therefore,

$$14 \sin \theta \cos \theta + 24 \sin^2 \theta - 24 \cos^2 \theta = 0$$

Two standard trigonometric identities tell us $2 \sin \theta \cos \theta = \sin 2\theta$ and $\sin^2 \theta - \cos^2 \theta = -\cos 2\theta$. Hence, by substitution,

$$14 \sin \theta \cos \theta + 24 (\sin^2 \theta - \cos^2 \theta) = 7 \sin 2\theta - 24 \cos 2\theta = 0.$$

and $\dfrac{\sin 2\theta}{\cos 2\theta} = \dfrac{24}{7}$ or $\tan 2\theta = \dfrac{24}{7}$.

All angles of rotation are between 0 and 90°. Hence, $0 < 2\theta < 180°$, and tangent and cosine will agree in sign.

Again, by trigonometric identity,

$$\frac{1}{\cos^2 2\theta} = 1 + \tan^2 2\theta = 1 + \left(\frac{24}{7}\right)^2$$

$$\cos 2\theta = \sqrt{\dfrac{1}{\dfrac{49}{49} + \dfrac{576}{49}}} = \sqrt{\dfrac{1}{\dfrac{625}{49}}} = \dfrac{7}{25}$$

We can now make use of the half angle formulas of trigonometry to find the values of $\sin \theta$ and $\cos \theta$ which are needed to evaluate (*) and find the transformed equation.

$$\sin \theta = \sqrt{\frac{1 - \cos 2\theta}{2}} = \sqrt{\frac{1 - \dfrac{7}{25}}{2}} = \frac{3}{5}$$

228

$$\cos\theta = \sqrt{\frac{1+\cos 2\theta}{2}} = \sqrt{\frac{1+\frac{7}{25}}{2}} = \frac{4}{5}$$

If these values of sin θ and cos θ are substituted in (*), we have

$$\left(9\left(\frac{4}{5}\right)^2 - 24\left(\frac{3}{5}\right)\left(\frac{4}{5}\right) + 16\left(\frac{3}{5}\right)^2\right)x'^2$$

$$+\left(14\left(\frac{4}{5}\right)\left(\frac{3}{5}\right) + 24\left(\frac{3}{5}\right)^2 - 24\left(\frac{4}{5}\right)^2\right)x'y'$$

$$+\left(9\left(\frac{3}{5}\right)^2 + 24\left(\frac{3}{5}\right)\left(\frac{4}{5}\right) + 16\left(\frac{4}{5}\right)^2\right)y'^2$$

$$-\left(40\left(\frac{4}{5}\right) + 30\left(\frac{3}{5}\right)\right)x' + \left(40\left(\frac{3}{5}\right) - 30\left(\frac{4}{5}\right)\right)y' = 0$$

Hence, the required equation in reduced form is
$$25y'^2 - 50x' = 0 \text{ or } y'^2 - 2x' = 0$$
This equation is in the standard form for a parabola. The parabola and axes are drawn on the accompanying coordinate grid.

● **PROBLEM 27-4**

Transform the equation $2x^2 + \sqrt{3}\,xy + y^2 = 4$ by rotating the coordinate axes through an angle of 30°. Plot the locus and show both sets of axes.

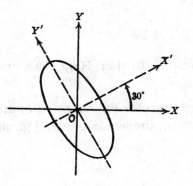

SOLUTION:

In this problem we will have to call on several formulas derived with the help of certain key trigonometric identities.

When the axes are rotated through an angle θ about the origin as a fixed point and the coordinates of any point $P(x, y)$ are transformed into (x', y') then the equations of transformation from the old to the new coordinates are given by

$$x = x' \cos \theta - y' \sin \theta$$
$$y = x' \sin \theta - y' \cos \theta.$$

The expression for x and y can be substituted into the given equation to perform the transformation. In this problem, $\theta = 30°$. Hence, since

$$x = x' \cos 30° - y' \sin 30° = \frac{\sqrt{3}}{2}x' - \frac{1}{2}y'$$

and

$$y = x' \sin 30° + y' \cos 30° = \frac{1}{2}x' + \frac{\sqrt{3}}{2}y',$$

by substitution, we obtain

$$2\left(\frac{\sqrt{3}}{2}x' - \frac{1}{2}y'\right)^2 + \sqrt{3}\left(\frac{\sqrt{3}}{2}x' - \frac{1}{2}y'\right)\left(\frac{1}{2}x' + \frac{\sqrt{3}}{2}y'\right)$$

$$+\left(\frac{1}{2}x' + \frac{\sqrt{3}}{2}y'\right)^2 = 4$$

Expanding this gives us

$$2\left(\frac{3}{4}x'^2 - \frac{\sqrt{3}}{2}x'y' + \frac{1}{4}y'^2\right) + \sqrt{3}\left(\frac{\sqrt{3}}{4}x'^2 + \frac{1}{2}x'y' - \frac{\sqrt{3}}{4}y'^2\right)$$

$$+\left(\frac{1}{4}x'^2 + \frac{\sqrt{3}}{2}x'y' + \frac{3}{4}y'^2\right) = 4$$

which reduces to

$$\frac{10}{4}x'^2 + \frac{1}{2}y'^2 = 4.$$

Multiply by 2 to simplify further. Hence, we obtain

$$5x'^2 + y'^2 = 8.$$

This is the standard form for the equation of an ellipse. The ellipse and both sets of axes are shown on the accompanying graph.

CHAPTER 28

POLAR COORDINATES AND PARAMETRIC EQUATIONS

Transform the equation $x^2 + y^2 - x + 3y = 3$ to a polar equation.

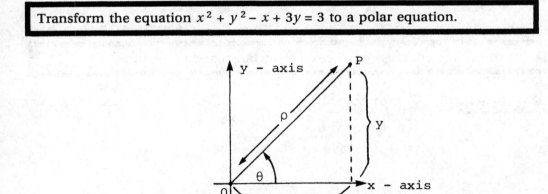

SOLUTION:

Ordinarily, when we wish to locate a point in a plane, we draw a pair of perpendicular axes and measure specified signed distances from the axes. The points are designated by pairs in terms of (x, y). These are called rectangular coordinates.

Another way is to designate a point in terms of polar coordinates. (ρ, θ) are the polar coordinates of a point P where ρ is the radius vector of P and θ is the angle that is made with the positive x-axis and the radius vector, OP. (See diagram.)

If P is designated by the coordinates (x, y) in rectangular coordinates and by (ρ, θ) in polar coordinates, then the following relationships hold:

$$\cos\theta = \frac{\text{adjacent side}}{\text{hypotenuse}} = \frac{x}{\rho} \text{ or } x = \rho\cos\theta$$

$$\sin\theta = \frac{\text{opposite side}}{\text{hypotenuse}} = \frac{y}{\rho} \text{ or } y = \rho\sin\theta$$

Now in this example, we replace x by $\rho\cos\theta$ and y by $\rho\sin\theta$ to obtain

$$\left(\rho\cos\theta\right)^2 + \left(\rho\sin\theta\right)^2 - \left(\rho\cos\theta\right) + 3\left(\rho\sin\theta\right) = 3$$

$$\rho^2\cos^2\theta + \rho^2\sin^2\theta - \rho\cos\theta + 3\rho\sin\theta = 3$$

Factor out ρ^2 and $-\rho$.

$$\rho^2\left(\cos^2\theta + \sin^2\theta\right) - \rho\left(\cos\theta - 3\sin\theta\right) = 3$$

Apply the identity $\cos^2\theta + \sin^2\theta = 1$. Then,

$$\rho^2 - \rho\left(\cos\theta - 3\sin\theta\right) = 3$$

● **PROBLEM 28-2**

Transform the equation $\rho = 2\cos\theta$ to rectangular coordinates.

SOLUTION:

$$\rho = \sqrt{x^2 + y^2}, \quad \cos\theta = \frac{x}{\rho} = \frac{x}{\sqrt{x^2 + y^2}}$$

$$\rho = 2\cos\theta$$

$$\sqrt{x^2 + y^2} = \frac{2x}{\sqrt{x^2 + y^2}}$$

$$x^2 + y^2 = 2x$$

● **PROBLEM 28-3**

Transform the equation $r = \dfrac{4}{(2 - 3\sin\theta)}$ to an equation in Cartesian coordinates.

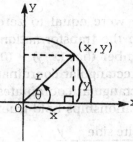

SOLUTION:

The given equation is in polar coordinates. This is another system of coordinates where a point (x, y) lies on a circle of radius r whose center is the origin (see figure).

We want to replace r and $\sin \theta$ by rectangular coordinates. Observe the following needed substitutions which can be derived from the diagram.

$$\sin \theta = \frac{\text{opposite side}}{\text{hypotenuse}} = \frac{y}{r}$$

Pythagorean Identity $x^2 + y^2 = r^2$

Solving for $r: \sqrt{x^2 + y^2} = r$

● PROBLEM 28-4

Convert the equation $r = \tan \theta + \cot \theta$ to an equation in Cartesian coordinates.

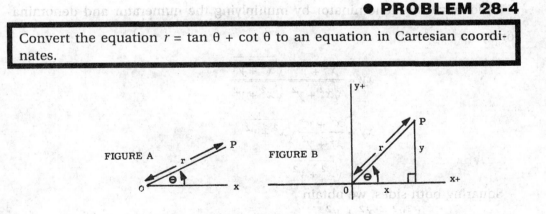

FIGURE A   FIGURE B

SOLUTION:

The given equation is expressed in polar coordinates (r, θ) where r is the radius vector, OP, and θ is the angle that r makes with the polar axis, OX. O is the fixed point called the pole. See figure A.

Since $\tan \theta \neq -\cot \theta$, then $r \neq 0$, and the graph of $r = \tan \theta + \cot \theta$ does not pass through the pole. If r were equal to zero, then the curve would pass through $(0, 0)$. Therefore, in the transformation of this equation to Cartesian coordinates, we must remember that $(x, y) \neq (0, 0)$. Now we must convert all expressions of r and θ into rectangular coordinates (x, y). If P is designated by the coordinates (x, y) in rectangular coordinates and by (r, θ) in polar coordinates, then the following relationships hold true: (See figure B.)

$$\tan \theta = \frac{\text{opposite side}}{\text{adjacent side}} = \frac{y}{x}$$

$$\cot \theta = \frac{\text{adjacent side}}{\text{opposite side}} = \frac{x}{y}$$

By the Pythagorean Identity $x^2 + y^2 = r^2$

Solve for r: $r = \sqrt{x^2 + y^2}$

Substitute these values for r, $\tan \theta$, and $\cot \theta$.

$$\sqrt{x^2 + y^2} = \frac{y}{x} + \frac{x}{y}$$

$$xy\sqrt{x^2 + y^2} = x^2 + y^2$$

Divide by $\sqrt{x^2 + y^2}$

$$xy = \frac{x^2 + y^2}{\sqrt{x^2 + y^2}}$$

Rationalize the denominator by multiplying the numerator and denominator by $\sqrt{x^2 + y^2}$

$$xy = \frac{x^2 + y^2}{\sqrt{x^2 + y^2}} \frac{\sqrt{x^2 + y^2}}{\sqrt{x^2 + y^2}}$$

$$xy = \frac{x^2 + y^2}{x^2 + y^2} \sqrt{x^2 + y^2}$$

$$xy = \sqrt{x^2 + y^2}$$

Squaring both sides, we obtain
$$x^2 y^2 = x^2 + y^2$$
where $x \neq 0$ and $y \neq 0$.

Find the parametric equations for $x^3 + y^3 - 4xy = 0$. (Hint: Substitute $x = ty$.)

SOLUTION:

Substituting $x = ty$, where t is the parameter, one has

$$(ty)^3 + y^3 - 4(ty)y$$
$$= t^3y^3 + y^3 - 4ty^2$$
$$= (t^3 + 1)y^3 + 4ty^2 = 0$$

Dividing by $y^2 \neq 0$,

$$(t^3 + 1)y + 4t = 0$$

$$y = -\frac{4t}{t^3 + 1}.$$

Then

$$x = ty = -\frac{4t^2}{t^3 + 1}$$

The parametric equations for the given equations are

$$\begin{cases} x = -\dfrac{4t^2}{t^3 + 1} \\ y = -\dfrac{4t}{t^3 + 1} \end{cases}$$

CHAPTER 29

FUNCTION

● PROBLEM 29-1

Let the domain of $M = \{(x, y): y = x\}$ be the set of real numbers. Is M a function?

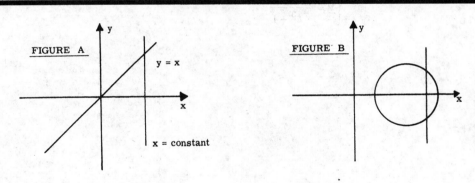

FIGURE A — $y = x$, $x = \text{constant}$

FIGURE B

SOLUTION:

The range is also the set of real numbers since $y = \{y \mid y = x\}$. The graph of $y = x$ is the graph of a line ($y = mx + b$, where $m = 1$ and $b = 0$). See figure A. If for every value of x in the domain, there corresponds only one y value then y is said to be a function of x. Since each element in the domain of M has exactly one element for its image, M is a function. Also notice that a vertical line ($x = \text{constant}$) crosses the graph $y = x$ only once. Whenever this is true the graph defines a function. Consult figure B.

The vertical line ($x = \text{constant}$) crosses the graph of the circle twice; i.e., for each x, y is not unique, therefore the graph does not define a function.

Sketch the graph of the following functions:

(a) $f(x) = \begin{cases} x & x \leq 4 \\ \dfrac{1}{2}x - 2 & x > 4 \end{cases}$

(b) $f(x) = |4x + 9|$

(c) $f(x) = \dfrac{|x|}{x + 1} \qquad x \neq -1$

SOLUTION:

(a)

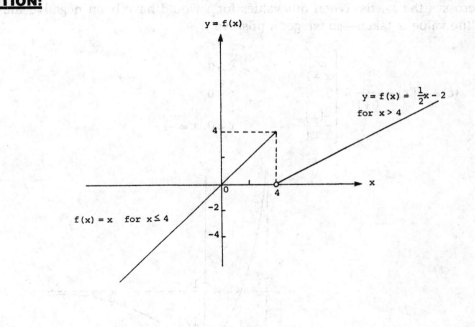

$$y = f(x)$$

$$y = f(x) = \tfrac{1}{2}x - 2 \text{ for } x > 4$$

$$f(x) = x \text{ for } x \leq 4$$

(b) $f(x) = |4x + 9| = \begin{cases} 4x + 9 & x > -\dfrac{9}{4} \\ 0 & x = -\dfrac{9}{4} \\ -(4x + 9) & x < -\dfrac{9}{4} \end{cases}$

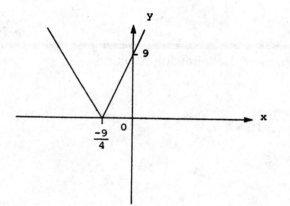

In this case we are graphing the equation of a straight line. However, because the equation is found under the absolute value signs, our line never crosses the x-axis. When our values for y would have been negative the absolute value is taken—so we get a positive y.

(c) $f(x) = \dfrac{|x|}{x+1} = \begin{cases} \dfrac{x}{x+1} & x > 0 \\ 0 & x = 0 \\ \dfrac{-(x)}{x+1} & x < 0,\ x \neq -1 \end{cases}$

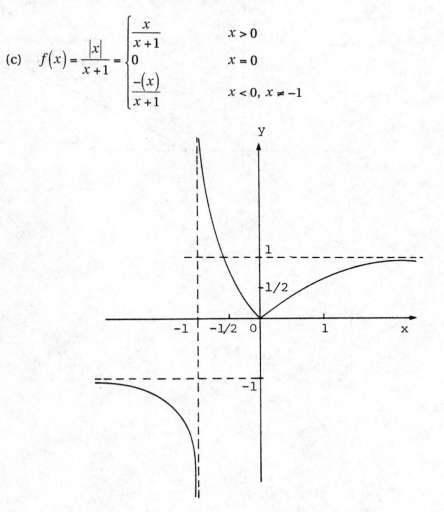

238

Draw a graph of the step function

$$y = \begin{cases} 2 & -2 \le x < -1 \\ 1 & -1 \le x < 0 \\ 0 & 0 \le x < 1 \\ 1 & 1 \le x < 2 \\ 2 & 2 \le x \le 3 \end{cases}$$

SOLUTION:

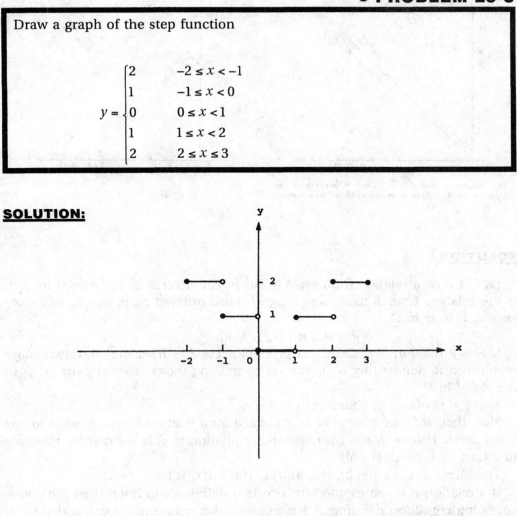

Given the relation $R = \{(9, 8), (10, 9), (11, 10)\}$ in the set $S \times S$, where $S = \{8, 9, 10, 11\}$.
(a) Find the inverse of R, and the complementary relation to R.
(b) Find the domains and the ranges of R and R^{-1}.
(c) Sketch R, R^{-1}, and R'.

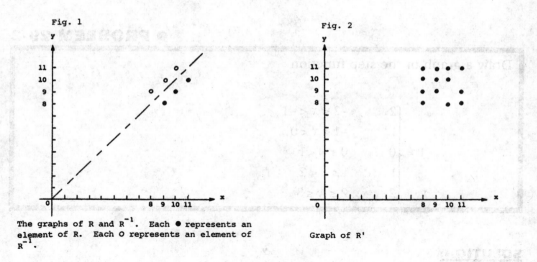

Fig. 1

The graphs of R and R^{-1}. Each ● represents an element of R. Each O represents an element of R^{-1}.

Fig. 2

Graph of R'

SOLUTION:

(a) Let R be a relation from set A to set B. The inverse of R, denoted by R^{-1}, is the relation from B to A consisting of those ordered pairs which, when reversed, belong to R.

$$R^{-1} = \{(x, y) \mid (x, y) \in R\}.$$

If R is a relation in a Cartesian-product set $A \times A$, then the complementary relation to R, denoted by R', is the set containing those ordered pairs (x, y) of $A \times A$ not in R.

$R' = \{(x, y) \mid (x, y) \notin R$ and $(x, y) \in A \times A\}$.

Note that R^{-1}, the inverse of R, is defined for a relation from any set A to any other set B. However, the complementary relation to R is defined for relations in a Cartesian-product only.

The given R is $R = \{(9, 8), (10, 9), (11, 10)\} = \{(x, y) \mid x = y + 1\}$

If a relation R is represented by a certain defining condition then the corresponding condition defining R^{-1} is obtained by replacing x for y and y for x. Hence

$R^{-1} = \{(x, y) \mid y = x + 1\} = \{(8, 9), (9, 10), (10, 11)\}$

$R' = \{(8, 8), (8, 9), (8, 10), (8, 11), (9, 9), (9, 10), (9, 11), (10, 10), (10, 11),$
$(10, 8), (11, 8), (11, 9), (11, 11)\}$

$= \{(x, y) \mid (x, y) \in S \times S$ and $(x, y) \notin R\}$

(b) The domain of a relation R is the set of all first elements of the ordered pairs which belong to R, and the range of R is the set of second elements. The domain of the given R is $\{9, 10, 11\}$ and the range of R is $\{8, 9, 10\}$. For R^{-1}, the domain is $\{8, 9, 10\}$ and the range is $\{9, 10, 11\}$. It is seen that as a result of the process of interchanging the components of the ordered pairs, the domain of R is the range of R^{-1} and the range of R is the domain of R^{-1}.

(c) The process of obtaining R^{-1} yields mirror images of the original points and creates correspondingly a set of ordered pairs which are the inverse relation. This is clearly observed from Figure 1.

Given the function f defined by the equation

$$y = f(x) = \frac{3x + 4}{5} \tag{1}$$

where the domain (and the range) of f is the set R of all real numbers.

(a) Find the equation $x = g(y) = f^{-1}(x)$ that defines f^{-1}.

(b) Show that $f^{-1}(f(x)) = x$.

(c) Show that $f(f^{-1}(x)) = y$.

SOLUTION:

(a) The definition of a function f is a set of ordered pairs (x, y) where,

    (1) x is an element of a set X,

    (2) y is an element of a set Y, and

    (3) no two pairs in f have the same first element.

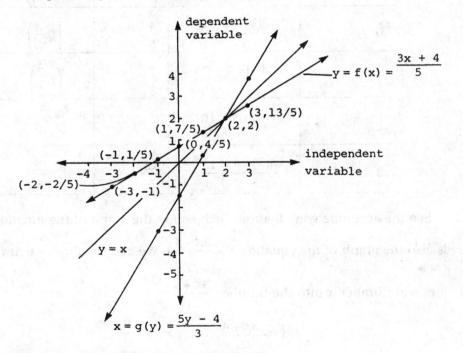

By definition, f is the infinite set of ordered pairs

$$\left\{ \left(x, \frac{3x + 4}{5} \right) \middle| x \in R \right\},$$

which includes $\left(0, \dfrac{4}{5}\right)$, $(2, 2)$, $(7, 5)$, $(12, 8)$, $(-3, -1)$, etc. Furthermore, no two ordered pairs have the same first element. That is, for each element of X a unique value of Y is assigned. For example, if $x = 0$ we obtain only one y value, $\dfrac{4}{5}$.

We construct the following table to calculate the x and corresponding y values. Note that x is the independent variable and y is the dependent variable.

x	$\dfrac{3x+4}{5} =$	y	(x, y)
-3	$\dfrac{3(-3)+4}{5} = \dfrac{-5}{5}$	-1	$(-3, -1)$
-2	$\dfrac{3(-2)+4}{5} = \dfrac{-2}{5}$	$\dfrac{-2}{5}$	$\left(-2, \dfrac{-2}{5}\right)$
-1	$\dfrac{3(-1)+4}{5} = \dfrac{1}{5}$	$\dfrac{1}{5}$	$\left(-1, \dfrac{1}{5}\right)$
0	$\dfrac{3(0)+4}{5} = \dfrac{4}{5}$	$\dfrac{4}{5}$	$\left(0, \dfrac{4}{5}\right)$
1	$\dfrac{3(1)+4}{5} = \dfrac{7}{5}$	$\dfrac{7}{5}$	$\left(1, \dfrac{7}{5}\right)$
2	$\dfrac{3(2)+4}{5} = \dfrac{10}{5}$	2	$(2, 2)$
3	$\dfrac{3(3)+4}{5} = \dfrac{13}{5}$	$\dfrac{13}{5}$	$\left(3, \dfrac{13}{5}\right)$

See the accompanying figure, which shows the graph of the function f (which is also the graph of the equation $y = \dfrac{3x+4}{5}$). We can say that f carries (or maps) any real number x into the number $\dfrac{3x+4}{5}$:

$$f : x \to \dfrac{3x+4}{5}.$$

Now to find the inverse function, we must find a function which takes each element of the original set Y and relates it to a unique value of X. There cannot be two values of X for a given value of Y in order for the inverse function to exist. That is, if this is true: (x_1, y) and (x_2, y), then there is no f^{-1}.

To find $x = g(y)$, we solve for x in terms of y.

Given:
$$y = \frac{3x + 4}{5}$$

Multiply both sides by 5,
$$5y = 3x + 4$$

Subtract 4 from both sides,
$$5y - 4 = 3x$$

Divide by 3 and solve for x,

$$x = \frac{5y - 4}{3} = f^{-1}(x) = g(y).$$

Choose y-values and find their corresponding x-values, as shown in the following table. Note that y is the independent variable and x is the dependent variable.

y	$g(y) = \dfrac{5y - 4}{3}$	x	(y, x)
-3	$\dfrac{5(-3) - 4}{3}$	$\dfrac{-19}{3} = -6\dfrac{1}{3}$	$\left(-3, -6\dfrac{1}{3}\right)$
-2	$\dfrac{5(-2) - 4}{3}$	$\dfrac{-14}{3} = -4\dfrac{2}{3}$	$\left(-2, -4\dfrac{2}{3}\right)$
-1	$\dfrac{5(-1) - 4}{3}$	$\dfrac{-9}{3} = -3$	$(-1, -3)$
0	$\dfrac{5(0) - 4}{3}$	$\dfrac{-4}{3} = -1\dfrac{1}{3}$	$\left(0, -1\dfrac{1}{3}\right)$
1	$\dfrac{5(1) - 4}{3}$	$\dfrac{1}{3}$	$\left(1, \dfrac{1}{3}\right)$
2	$\dfrac{5(2) - 4}{3}$	2	$(2, 2)$
3	$\dfrac{5(3) - 4}{3}$	$\dfrac{11}{3} = 3\dfrac{2}{3}$	$\left(3, 3\dfrac{2}{3}\right)$

See graph. Since there is only one value of y for each value of x, this equation defines the inverse function f^{-1}. The graph of f^{-1} is the image of the graph of f in the mirror $y = x$.

(b) Given $f(x) = \dfrac{3x + 4}{5} = y$. Then perform the operation of f^{-1} on $y = f(x)$

where $f^{-1}(x)\dfrac{5y - 4}{3}$. That is, substitute for y: $\dfrac{3x + 4}{5}$.

$$f^{-1}\big(f(x)\big)=f^{-1}\left(\frac{3x+4}{5}\right)=\frac{5\left(\dfrac{3x+4}{5}\right)-4}{3}=\frac{\dfrac{15x+20}{5}-4}{3}$$

$$=\frac{\dfrac{15x+20-20}{5}}{3}=\frac{3x}{3}=x,\text{ or}$$

$$f^{-1}\big(f(x)\big)=\frac{5f(x)-4}{3}=\frac{5\left(\dfrac{3x+4}{5}\right)-4}{3}=x.$$

(c) We now perform the operation of f on $f^{-1}(x)$. Substitute for $f^{-1}(x)$: $\dfrac{5y-4}{3}=x$. Note $f(x)=\dfrac{3x+4}{5}$

$$f\big(f^{-1}(x)\big)=f\left(\frac{5y-4}{3}\right)=\frac{3\left(\dfrac{5y-4}{3}\right)+4}{5}$$

$$=\frac{5y-4+4}{5}=\frac{5y}{5}=y=f(x)$$

Comment. Since $f=\left\{\left(x,\dfrac{3x+4}{5}\right)\right\}$, this function f may be thought of as a sequence of directions listing the operations that must be performed on x to get $\dfrac{3x+4}{5}$. These operations are, in order: take any number x, multiply it by 3, add 4, and then divide by 5. The inverse function

$$f^{-1}=\left\{\left(y,\frac{5y-4}{3}\right)\right\}$$

tells us to multiply by 5, subtract 4, and then divide by 3. This "undoes," in reverse order, the operations performed by f. The function f^{-1} could be called the **undoing function** because it undoes what the function f has done.

244

Investigate each of the following equations, determine the intercepts and symmetry, and draw the graph.

(a) $x^2 + y^2 = 9$

(b) $2x^2y - x^2 - y = 0$

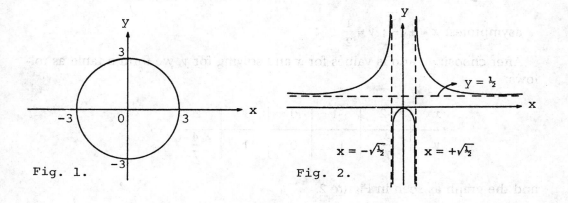

Fig. 1. Fig. 2.

SOLUTION:

(a) $x^2 + y^2 = 9$

intercepts: $x = 0$ $y = \pm 3$ (y-intercepts)
$y = 0$ $x = \pm 3$ (x-intercepts)

symmetry: The locus is symmetric with respect to the coordinate axes and the origin.

The locus exists for all values of x where $x \geq -3$ or $x \leq 3$, and all values of y where $y \geq -3$ or $y \leq 3$. The locus consists of one closed piece. Various values of x were chosen and the values of y calculated as in the table shown below. The graph was then drawn, as shown in Fig. 1.

x	−3	−2	−1	0	1	2	3
y	0	$\pm\sqrt{5}$	$\pm\sqrt{8}$	± 3	$\pm\sqrt{8}$	$\pm\sqrt{5}$	0

(b) $2x^2y - x^2 - y = 0$

intercepts: $x = 0$ $y = 0$ (y-intercept)
$y = 0$ $x = 0$ (x-intercept)

symmetry: The locus is symmetric with respect to the y-axis.

extent: $y = \dfrac{x}{2x^2 - 1}$, $x = \pm\sqrt{\dfrac{y}{2y - 1}}$

245

The locus exists for all $x \neq \pm \sqrt{\dfrac{1}{2}}$ (this comes from the inequality $2x^2 - 1 \neq 0$),

and for all y such that $\dfrac{y}{2y-1} \geq 0$. Find the value of y for which the numerator is

equal to zero, that is $y = 0$, and the value of y for which the denominator is

zero, $y = \dfrac{1}{2}$. Therefore, the locus exists for $y \leq 0$ and for $y > \dfrac{1}{2}$.

asymptotes: $x = \pm \sqrt{\dfrac{1}{2}}$; $y = \dfrac{1}{2}$

After choosing various values for x and solving for y, we form a table as follows:

x	−2	−1	0	1	2
y	$\dfrac{4}{7}$	1	0	1	$\dfrac{4}{7}$

and the graph as seen in Figure 2.

CHAPTER 30

LINEAR FUNCTIONS AND SYSTEMS OF LINEAR FUNCTIONS

● **PROBLEM 30-1**

(a) Find the zeros of the function f if $f(x) = 3x - 5$.

(b) Sketch the graph of the equation $y = 3x - 5$.

SOLUTION:

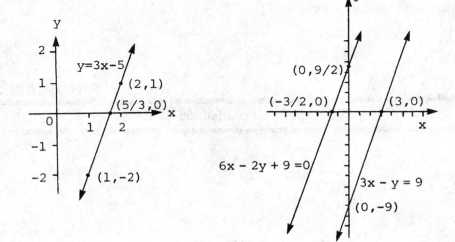

The equations are parallel. Thus, we must show that the two slopes are equal. In standard form the equation of a line is $y = mx + b$, where m is the slope.

Putting $3x - y = 9$ in standard form,

$$-y = 9 - 3x$$
$$y = -9 + 3x$$
$$y = 3x - 9$$

We find that the slope of the first line is 3. Putting $6x - 2y + 9 = 0$ in standard form,

$$-2y + 9 = -6x$$
$$-2y = -6x - 9$$
$$y = 3x + \frac{9}{2}$$

Therefore, the slope of this line is also 3. The slopes are equal, hence, the lines are parallel.

To graph these equations pick values of x and substitute them into the equation to determine the corresponding values of y. Thus, we obtain the following tables of values. Notice we need only **two** points to plot a line (two points determine a line).

$$6x - 2y + 9 = 0 \qquad\qquad 3x - y = 9$$

$$y = 3x + \frac{9}{2} \qquad\qquad y = 3x - 9$$

x	0	$-\dfrac{3}{2}$
y	$\dfrac{9}{2}$	0

x	0	3
y	-9	0

(See accompanying figure)

● **PROBLEM 30-2**

Construct the graph of the function defined by $y = 3x - 9$.

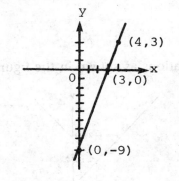

SOLUTION:

An equation of the form $y = mx + b$ is a linear equation; that is, the equation of a line.

A line can be determined by two points. Let us choose the intercepts. The x-intercept lies on the x-axis and the y-intercept is on the y-axis.

We find the intercepts by assigning 0 to x and solving for y and by assigning 0 to y and solving for x. It is helpful to have a third point. We find a third point by assigning 4 to x and solving for y. Thus, we get the following table of corresponding numbers:

x	$y = 3x - 9$	y
0	$y = 3(0) - 9 = 0 - 9 =$	-9
4	$y = 3(4) - 9 = 12 - 9 =$	3

Solving for x to get the x–intercept:
$$y = 3x - 9$$
$$y + 9 = 3x$$
$$x = \frac{y + 9}{3}$$

When $y = 0$, $x = \frac{9}{3} = 3$. The three points are $(0, -9)$, $(4, 3)$, and $(3, 0)$. Draw a line through them (see sketch).

● PROBLEM 30-3

Solve $\begin{cases} y = x + 4 \\ -x = y \end{cases}$ graphically.

SOLUTION:

First graph the two equations as shown in the figure.

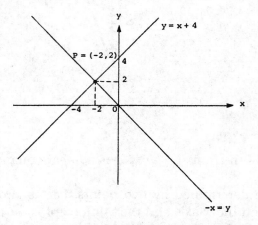

The solution of this system of equations is the intersection of the two lines. It's found graphically that the point of intersection is $P(-2, 2)$. Therefore, the solution of the given system of equations is $x = -2$, $y = 2$.

● **PROBLEM 30-4**

Determine the nature of the system of linear equations
$$x + 2y = 8$$
$$x - 2y = 2$$

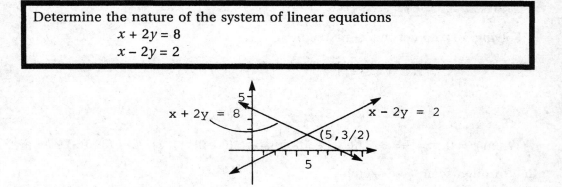

SOLUTION:

Add the two equations, eliminating the y-terms, to obtain a single equation in terms of x. Values of x satisfying this equation will yield solutions of the system.

$$
\begin{array}{rl}
x + 2y & = 8 \qquad\qquad (1) \\
+ \quad x - 2y & = 2 \qquad\qquad (2) \\
\hline
2x \qquad\ & = 10 \\
x \qquad\ & = 5
\end{array}
$$

250

Substituting $x = 5$ into equation (1) yields

$$y = \frac{(8-x)}{2} = \frac{(8-5)}{2} = \frac{3}{2}$$ or into equation (2) yields

$$y = \frac{(2-x)}{(-2)} = \frac{(2-5)}{(-2)} = \frac{3}{2}.$$ Thus, we have $x = 5$, $y = \frac{3}{2}$ as the only solution

of the system. Alternately, the figure indicates that the lines intersect in the

point $\left(5, \frac{3}{2}\right)$. The system is therefore consistent and independent. Substitution

of $x = 5$ and $y = \frac{3}{2}$ in both equations yields

$$5 + 2\left(\frac{3}{2}\right) = 8, \text{ or } 8 = 8$$

$$5 - 2\left(\frac{3}{2}\right) = 2, \text{ or } 2 = 2$$

so that $x = 5$, $y = \frac{3}{2}$ is a solution and the only solution of the system.

● PROBLEM 30-5

Determine the nature of the system of linear equations

$$2x + y = 6 \tag{1}$$
$$4x + 2y = 8 \tag{2}$$

SOLUTION:

These linear equations may be written in the standard form $y = mx + b$:

$$y = -2x + 6 \tag{3}$$
$$\text{and} \quad y = -2x + 4 \tag{4}$$

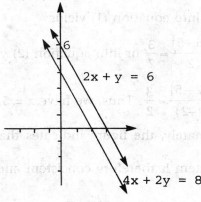

$$2x + y = 6$$
$$4x + 2y = 8$$

Observe that the slope of each line is $m = -2$, but the y-intercepts are different, that is, $b = 6$ for equation (3) and $b = 4$ for equation (4). The lines are therefore parallel and distinct. The graph above also indicates that the lines are parallel. The system is therefore inconsistent, and there is no solution.

● **PROBLEM 30-6**

Find the point of intersection of the graphs of the equations:

$$\begin{cases} x + y = 3 \\ 3x - 2y = 14 \end{cases}$$

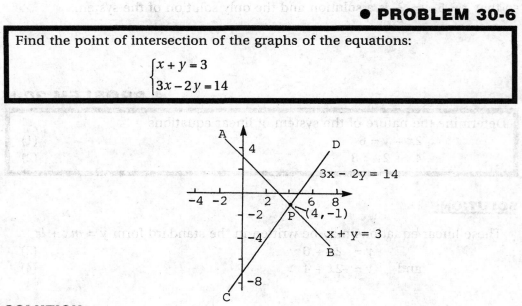

$$3x - 2y = 14$$
$$P \ (4, -1)$$
$$x + y = 3$$

SOLUTION:

To solve these linear equations, solve for y in terms of x. The equations will be in the form $y = mx + b$, where m is the slope and b is the intercept on the y-axis.

$$x + y = 3 \qquad \text{subtract } x \text{ from both sides}$$
$$y = 3 - x$$

$$3x - 2y = 14 \quad \text{subtract } 3x \text{ from both sides}$$
$$-2y = 14 - 3x \quad \text{divide by } -2.$$

$$y = -7 + \frac{3}{2}x$$

The graphs of the linear functions, $y = 3 - x$ and $y = -7 + \frac{3}{2}x$, can be determined by plotting only two points. For example, for $y = 3 - x$, let $x = 0$, then $y = 3$. Let $x = 1$, then $y = 2$. The two points on this first line are $(0, 3)$ and $(1, 2)$. For $y = -7 + \frac{3}{2}x$, let $x = 0$, then $y = -7$. Let $x = 1$, then $y = -5\frac{1}{2}$. The two points on this second line are $(0, -7)$ and $\left(1, -5\frac{1}{2}\right)$. To find the point of intersection P of

$$x + y = 3$$
and $$3x - 2y = 14,$$

solve them algebraically. Multiply the first equation by 2. Add these two equations to eliminate the variable y.

$$
\begin{array}{rl}
2x + 2y = & 6 \\
3x - 2y = & 14 \\
\hline
5x \quad\quad = & 20
\end{array}
$$

Solve for x to obtain $x = 4$. Substitute this into $y = 3 - x$ to get $y = 3 - 4 = -1$. P is $(4, 1)$. AB is the graph of the first equation, and CD is the graph of the second equation. The point of intersection P of the two graphs is the only point on both lines. The coordinates of P satisfy both equations and represent the desired solution of the problem. From the graph, P seems to be the point $(4, -1)$. These coordinates satisfy both equations, and hence are the exact coordinates of the point of intersection of the two lines.

To show that $(4, -1)$ satisfies both equations, substitute this point into both equations.

$$
\begin{array}{ll}
x + y = 3 & 3x - 2y = 14 \\
4 + (-1) = 3 & 3(4) - 2(-1) = 14 \\
4 - 1 = 3 & 12 + 2 = 14 \\
3 = 3 & 14 = 14
\end{array}
$$

CHAPTER 31

QUADRATIC EQUATIONS AND SYSTEMS OF QUADRATIC EQUATIONS

Graph the function $3x^2 + 5x - 7$.

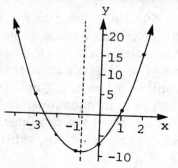

SOLUTION:

Let $y = 3x^2 + 5x - 7$. Substitute values for x and then find the corresponding values of y. This is done in the following table.

x	$y = 3x^2 + 5x - 7$
−4	21
−3	5
−2	−5
−1	−9
0	−7
1	1
2	15

These points are plotted and joined by a smooth curve in the figure.

Determine how the graph of $f(x) = ax^2 + bx + c$ is affected by
  (a) the sign and magnitude of a
  (b) the sign and magnitude of b
  (c) the sign and magnitude of c

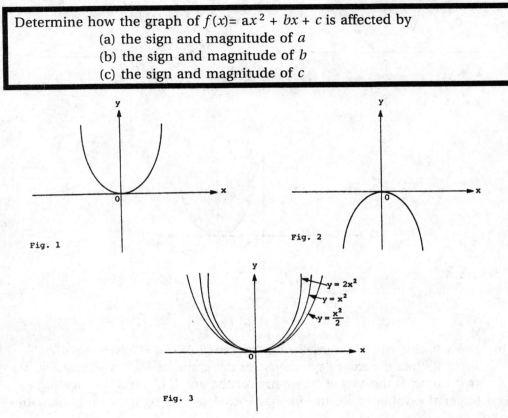

Fig. 1

Fig. 2

Fig. 3

SOLUTION:

(a) If $a > 0$, then the graph which is a parabola opens up (see Fig. 1).
   If $a < 0$, then the graph opens down (see Fig. 2).
   If $a = 0$, then we do not have a quadratic, but a linear function. As the value of a increases from $\frac{1}{2}$ to 1 to 2 etc., the graph stretches higher and becomes narrower (see Fig. 3).

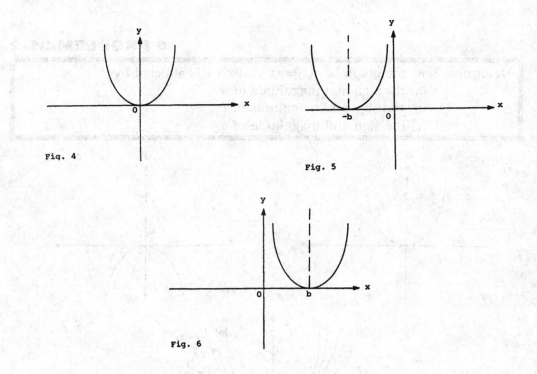

Fig. 4

Fig. 5

Fig. 6

(b) If $b = 0$, the axis of symmetry for the function is $x = 0$ (see Fig. 4).

If $b > 0$, then the axis of symmetry for the graph of f is $x = -b$ (see Fig. 5).

If $b < 0$, then the axis of symmetry for the graph of f is $x = b$ (see Fig. 6).

The larger the value of $|b|$ the further to the left or right of the y-axis the parabola is

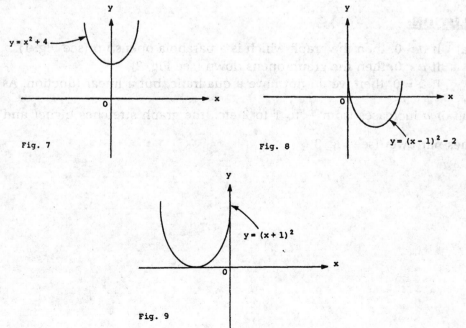

$y = x^2 + 4$

Fig. 7

$y = (x - 1)^2 - 2$

Fig. 8

$y = (x + 1)^2$

Fig. 9

256

(c) When written in the quadratic form

$$y = a(x - h)^2 + K \qquad \text{where} \quad a \to ax^2$$
$$b \to ahx$$
$$c \to ah^2 + K$$

If the value of $K > 0$ then the parabola is moved up K units (see Fig. 7).
If $K < 0$ then the parabola is moved down K units (see Fig. 8).
If $K = 0$ the parabola lies on $y = 0$ (see Fig. 9).

● PROBLEM 31-3

What is the minimum value of the expression $2x^2 - 20x + 17$?

SOLUTION:

Consider the function $y = 2x^2 - 20x + 17$. This function is defined by a second degree equation. The coefficient of its x^2 term is positive. Hence, the curve is a parabola opening upward. Thus, the minimum point of this curve occurs at the vertex. The x-coordinate is equal to

$$-\frac{\text{coefficient of } x \text{ term}}{2 \cdot \text{coefficient of } x^2 \text{ term}} = -\frac{b}{2a} = -\frac{(-20)}{2(2)} = \frac{20}{4} = 5.$$

For $x = 5$, $y = 2(5)^2 - 20(5) + 17 = -33$. Therefore, the minimum value of the expression $2x^2 - 20x + 17$ for any value of x is -33. This minimum value is assumed only when $x = 5$.

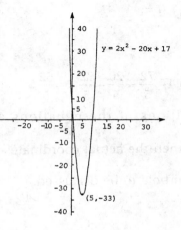

257

Solve for x and y: $\begin{cases} 9x^2 - 16y^2 = 144 & (1) \\ x - 2y = 4 & (2) \end{cases}$

SOLUTION:

Algebraic Solution

We solve equation (2) for x,

$$x = 4 + 2y \qquad (3)$$

and substitute this expression for x in equation (1). This gives

$$9(4 + 2y)^2 - 16y^2 = 144$$
$$9(16 + 16y + 4y^2) - 16y^2 = 144$$

Dividing both sides by 4, $\qquad 9(4 + 4y + y^2) - 4y^2 = 36$

Distributing, $\qquad 36 + 36y + 9y^2 - 4y^2 = 36$

Combining terms, $\qquad 36 + 36y + 5y^2 = 36$

Subtracting 36 from both sides, $\qquad 5y^2 + 36y = 0$

Factoring, $\qquad y(5y + 36) = 0$

Whenever the product of two numbers $ab = 0$, either $a = 0$ or $b = 0$; thus either

$$y = 0 \qquad \text{or} \qquad 5y + 36 = 0$$
$$5y = -36$$
$$y = \frac{-36}{5}$$

Thus, $y = 0, -\dfrac{36}{5}$.

Placing these values in linear equation (3):

when $y = 0$,

$$x = 4 + 2(0) = 4 + 0 = 4$$

when $y = -\dfrac{36}{5}$,

$$x = 4 + 2\left(-\frac{36}{5}\right) = 4 - \frac{72}{5} = \frac{20}{5} - \frac{72}{5} = -\frac{52}{5}$$

Thus, the two solutions of the equations are seen to be $(4, 0)$ and $\left(-\dfrac{52}{5}, -\dfrac{36}{5}\right)$ which are then the actual coordinates of the points of intersection of the line and the hyperbola to be discussed.

$$x = 4 + 2y$$

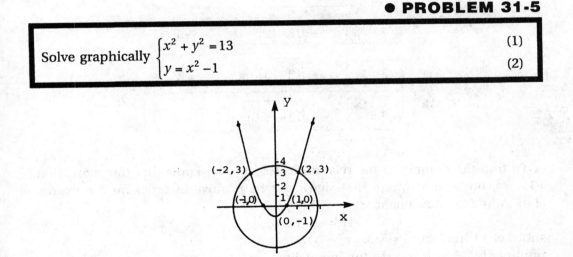

Geometric Solution

Construct the graph of each equation and note where the two graphs intersect. The graph of the first equation cuts the x-axis at $x = \pm 4$, and y is imaginary for any value of x between -4 and 4. The graph consists of the two curved branches in the diagram, and is a hyperbola.

The graph of the second equation is a straight line through the points $(4, 0)$ and $(0, -2)$. This line intersects the hyperbola at the points P and Q, whose coordinates are approximately $(4, 0)$ and $(-10, -7)$.

● PROBLEM 31-5

Solve graphically $\begin{cases} x^2 + y^2 = 13 & (1) \\ y = x^2 - 1 & (2) \end{cases}$

SOLUTION:

First, we must find the x and y intercepts. Set $y = 0$ to find the x-intercept or where the curve crosses the x-axis. Set $x = 0$ to find the y-intercept or where the curve crosses the y-axis. In equation (1), set $x = 0$, and find $y = \pm\sqrt{13} = \pm 3.6$. Then set $y = 0$, and find $x = \pm\sqrt{13}$. To get additional points, we solve for y.

259

$$x^2 + y^2 = 13$$
$$y^2 = 13 - x^2$$
$$y = \pm\sqrt{13 - x^2}$$

Then, set up a table. Choose various x values and calculate the corresponding y values (See graph).

x	$\pm\sqrt{13 - x^2} =$	y
−3.6	$\pm\sqrt{13 - (-3.6)^2}$	≈ 0
−3	$\pm\sqrt{13 - (-3)^2}$	± 2
−2	$\pm\sqrt{13 - (-2)^2}$	± 3
−1	$\pm\sqrt{13 - (-1)^2}$	± 3.5
0	$\pm\sqrt{13 - (0)^2}$	± 3.6
1	$\pm\sqrt{13 - (1)^2}$	± 3.5
2	$\pm\sqrt{13 - (2)^2}$	± 3
3	$\pm\sqrt{13 - (3)^2}$	± 2
3.6	$\pm\sqrt{13 - (3.6)^2}$	≈ 0

To find the domain of the relation, $\pm\sqrt{13 - x^2}$, we know that the expression, $13 - x^2$, under the square root sign must be positive in order for the expression to be real, not imaginary.

$$(13 - x^2) \geq 0$$

subtract 13 from both sides, $x^2 \geq -13$
multiply by −1 and reverse the inequality sign,

$$x^2 \leq 13$$

Take the square root of both sides.

$$|x| \leq \sqrt{13}$$

Another way to express $|b| \leq a$ is $-a \leq b \leq +a$. Thus,

$$-\sqrt{13} \leq x \leq +\sqrt{13}$$

Thus, for the relation $y = \pm\sqrt{13 - x^2}$, the domain is $\left\{ x \mid -\sqrt{13} \leq x \leq \sqrt{13} \right\}$. The curve is a circle. The general equation of a circle is $(x - h)^2 + (y - k)^2 = r^2$, where (h, k) is the center and r is the radius. In this case $(0, 0)$ or the origin is the center and r^2 is 13. Therefore, the radius $= +\sqrt{13}$.

In equation (2), y is a quadratic function of x; hence, the graph is a parabola. Set up a similar table for the quadratic function, $y = x^2 - 1$

x	$x^2 - 1 =$	y
-3	$(-3)^2 - 1$	8
-2	$(-2)^2 - 1$	3
-1	$(-1)^2 - 1$	0
0	$(0)^2 - 1$	-1
1	$(1)^2 - 1$	0
2	$(2)^2 - 1$	3
3	$(3)^2 - 1$	8

From the graphs we read the real solutions $(2, 3)$ and $(-2, 3)$. These are points of intersection for both curves.

To find the solutions algebraically substitute equation (2) into (1).

$$x^2 + y^2 = 13 \qquad\qquad (1)$$
$$y = x^2 - 1 \qquad\qquad (2)$$
$$x^2 + (x^2 - 1) = 13$$
$$x^2 + x^4 - 2x^2 + 1 = 13$$
$$x^4 - x^2 = 12$$
$$x^4 - x^2 - 12 = 0$$

Substitute z for x^2, i.e., $z = x^2$, to obtain a quadratic equation in z.

$$(x^2)^2 - (x^2) - 12 = 0$$
$$z^2 - z - 12 = 0$$
$$(z - 4)(z + 3) = 0$$

$$z - 4 = 0 \qquad\qquad z + 3 = 0$$
$$z = 4 \qquad\qquad z = -3$$

Therefore $\qquad x^2 = 4 \qquad\qquad x^2 = -3$

$$x = \pm 2 \qquad\qquad x \pm\sqrt{-3} = \pm\sqrt{3}i$$

Find the corresponding y-values by substituting into $y = x^2 - 1$.

$x = 2$	$x = -2$	$x = i\sqrt{3}$	$x = -i\sqrt{3}$
$y = (2)^2 - 1$	$y = (-2)^2 - 1$	$y = \left(i\sqrt{3}\right)^2 - 1$	$y = \left(-i\sqrt{3}\right)^2 - 1$
$= 3$	$= 3$	$y = i^2(3) - 1$	$= 3(i)^2 - 1$
		$= (-1)(3) - 1$	$= 3(-1) - 1$
		$= -4$	$= -4$

The algebraic solution gives $(2, 3)$, $(-2, 3)$, $\left(i\sqrt{3}, -4\right)$, and $\left(-i\sqrt{3}, -4\right)$. Notice that the imaginary solutions do not appear on the graph.

Solve $xy = 3$
         $x^2 + y^2 = 10$

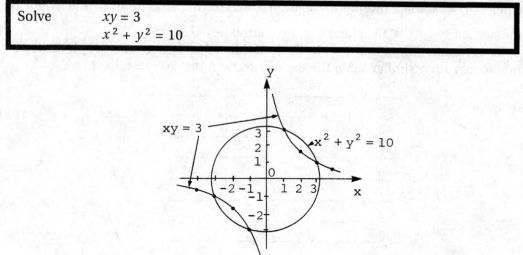

SOLUTION:

We solve the first equation for y to obtain $y = \dfrac{3}{x}$ and substitute in the second equation to obtain

$$x^2 + \left(\frac{3}{x}\right)^2 = 10$$

Squaring: $x^2 + \dfrac{9}{x^2} = 10$

Multiplying both sides by x^2: $x^2\left(x^2 + \dfrac{9}{x^2}\right) = x^2(10)$

Distributing: $x^4 + 9 = 10x^2$

Subtracting $10x^2$ from both sides: $x^4 - 10x^2 + 9 = 0$

Factoring: $(x^2 - 1)(x^2 - 9) = 0$

Thus,
$$x^2 - 1 = 0 \quad \text{or} \quad x^2 - 9 = 0$$
$$x^2 = 1 \qquad\qquad x^2 = 9$$
$$x = \pm 1 \qquad\qquad x = \pm 3$$

Therefore, $x = 1, -1, 3,$ or -3.

Since $y = \dfrac{3}{x}$, substituting these values in turn in this equation, we obtain the corresponding values for y:

$$x = 1 \qquad x = -1 \qquad x = 3 \qquad x = -3$$
$$y = 3 \qquad y = -3 \qquad y = 1 \qquad y = -1$$

To consider this system graphically, we notice that the second equation is the equation of a circle with radius $\sqrt{10}$, whereas the graph of the first equation is a hyperbola obtained from the following table. Also, the points $(1, 3)$ $(-1, -3)$, $(3, 1)$, $(-3, -1)$ belong to both the circle and the hyperbola, and the two graphs intersect at these points.

x	-5	-4	-3	-2	-1	1	2	3	4	5
y	$-\dfrac{3}{5}$	$-\dfrac{3}{4}$	-1	$-\dfrac{3}{2}$	-3	3	$\dfrac{3}{2}$	1	$\dfrac{3}{4}$	$\dfrac{3}{5}$

Plotting these points, and the circle with radius $\sqrt{10}$ (approximately equal to 3.16) we have the accompanying diagram.

CHAPTER 32

EQUATIONS OF DEGREE GREATER THAN TWO

Graph the function $y = x^3 - 9x$.

SOLUTION:

Choosing values of x in the interval $-4 \leq x \leq 4$, we have for $y = x^3 - 9x$,

x	-4	-3	-2	-1	0	1	2	3	4
y	-28	0	10	8	0	-8	-10	0	28

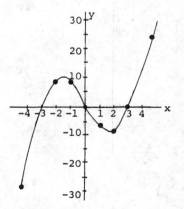

Notice that for each ordered pair (x, y) listed in the table there exists a pair $(-x, -y)$ which also satisfies the equation, indicating symmetry with respect to the origin. To prove that this is true for all points on the curve, we substitute $(-x, -y)$ for (x, y) in the given equation and show that the equation is un-

changed. Thus
$$-y = (-x)^3 - 9(-x) = -x^3 + 9x$$
or, multiplying each member by -1,
$$y = x^3 - 9x$$
which is the original equation.

The curve is illustrated in the figure. The domain and range of the function have no restrictions in the set of real numbers. The x-intercepts are found from
$$y = 0 = x^3 - 9x$$
$$0 = x(x^2 - 9)$$
$$0 = x(x - 3)(x + 3)$$

$x = 0$	$x - 3 = 0$	$x + 3 = 0$
	$x = 3$	$x = -3$

The curve has three x-intercepts at $x = -3$, $x = 0$, $x = 3$. This agrees with the fact that a cubic equation has three roots. The curve has a single y-intercept at $y = 0$ since for $x = 0$, $y = 0^3 - 9(0) = 0$.

● PROBLEM 32-2

Approximate the real roots of the equation
$$x^4 + 2x^3 - 5x^2 - 4x + 6 = 0.$$

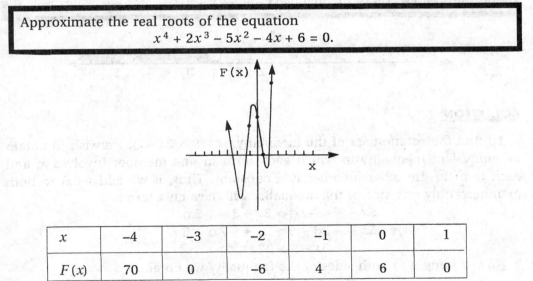

x	-4	-3	-2	-1	0	1
$F(x)$	70	0	-6	4	6	0

SOLUTION:

To find the real roots of the given equation, let us sketch the graph of the related polynomial function defined by $F(x) = x^4 + 2x^3 - 5x^2 - 4x + 6$. (See Figure)

When $F(x) = 0$, x is a root of the equation. From the table, two real roots are $x = -3$ and $x = 1$. Reducing $F(x)$ by dividing by $(x + 3)(x - 1)$ and solving, we find that $-\sqrt{2}$ and $+\sqrt{2}$ are also roots.

265

CHAPTER 33

INEQUALITIES

Find the solution set of inequality $5x - 9 > 2x + 3$.

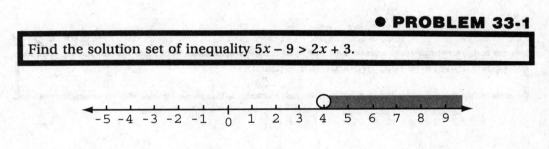

SOLUTION:

To find the solution set of the inequality $5x - 9 > 2x + 3$, we wish to obtain an equivalent inequality in which each term in one member involves x, and each term in the other member is a constant. Thus, if we add $(-2x)$ to both members, only one side of the inequality will have an x term:

$$5x - 9 + (-2x) > 2x + 3 + (-2x)$$
$$5x + (-2x) - 9 > 2x + (-2x) + 3$$
$$3x - 9 > 3$$

Now, adding 9 to both sides of the inequality we obtain,

$$3x - 9 + 9 > 3 + 9$$
$$3x > 12$$

Dividing both sides by 3, we arrive at $x > 4$.

Solve the inequality $\dfrac{4}{x-2} < 2$.

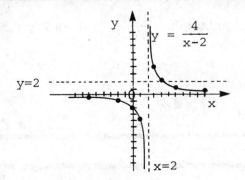

SOLUTION:

The inequality is meaningless for $x = 2$ because when $x = 2$ the denominator of the left member is 0, making the fraction undefined.

If $x > 2$, $x - 2$ is positive (since $x > 2$ is equivalent to $x - 2 > 0$), and multiplication of the given inequality by $x - 2$ yields

$$4 < 2(x - 2)$$
$$4 < 2x - 4$$
$$8 < 2x$$
$$4 < x$$
$$x > 4$$

Thus, the solution is the intersection of $x > 2$ and $x > 4$, $x > 2 \cap x > 4$, which is $\{x \mid x > 4\}$.

If $x < 2$, $x - 2$ is negative (since $x < 2$ is equivalent to $x - 2 < 0$), and multiplication by $x - 2$ yields

$$4 > 2(x - 2)$$

because multiplication by a negative number reverses an inequality.

Distributing, $\qquad\qquad 4 > 2x - 4$

Adding 4 to both sides, $\qquad 8 > 2x$

Dividing both sides by 2, $\quad 4 > x$, or $x < 4$

Thus the solution is the intersection of $x < 2$ and $x < 4$, $x < 2 \cap x < 4$, which is $\{x \mid x < 2\}$. Hence

$$\frac{4}{x-2} < 2$$

if $x < 2$ or if $x > 4$.

A graphical solution of the problem (see diagram) can be obtained by sketching the equilateral hyperbola $y = \dfrac{4}{(x-2)}$ and the line $y = 2$. The hyperbola may be sketched from its vertical asymptote $x = 2$, its horizontal asymptote $y = 0$, its intercepts $x = 0$, $y = -2$, and a few other points obtained by substitution and symmetry. It is then possible to observe the values of x for which the hyperbola is below the line, namely,

$$x < 2 \text{ and } x > 4.$$

The same diagram also shows that  $\left[\dfrac{4}{(x-2)}\right] > 2$ for $2 < x < 4$.

Solve $2x - 3y \geq 6$.

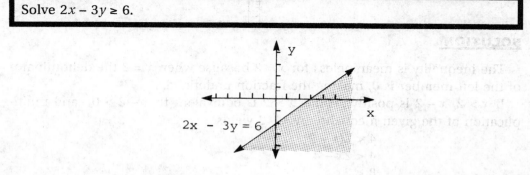

2x − 3y = 6

SOLUTION:

The statement $2x - 3y \geq 6$ means $2x - 3y$ is greater than or equal to 6. Symbolically, we have $2x - 3y > 6$ or $2x - 3y = 6$. Consider the corresponding equality and graph $2x - 3y = 6$. To find the x-intercept, set $y = 0$.

$$2x - 3y = 6$$
$$2x - 3(0) = 6$$
$$2x = 6$$
$$x = 3$$

{3, 0} is the x-intercept.

To find the y-intercept, set $x = 0$

$$2x - 3y = 6$$
$$2(0) - 3y = 6$$
$$-3y = 6$$
$$y = -2$$

{0, −2} is the y-intercept.

A line is determined by two points. Therefore, draw a straight line through the two intercepts {3, 0} and {0, −2}. Since the inequality is mixed, a solid line is drawn through the intercepts. This line represents the part of the statement $2x - 3y = 6$.

268

We must now determine the region for which the inequality $2x - 3y > 6$ holds.

Choose two points to decide on which side of the line the region $2x - 3y > 6$ lies. We shall try the points $(0, 0)$ and $(5, 1)$.

For $(0, 0)$

$$2x - 3y > 6$$
$$2(0) - 3(0) > 6$$
$$0 - 0 > 6$$
$$0 > 6$$

False

For $(5, 1)$

$$2x - 3y > 6$$
$$2(5) - 3(1) > 6$$
$$10 - 3 > 6$$
$$7 > 6$$

True

The inequality, $2x - 3y > 6$, holds true for the point $(5, 1)$. We shade this region of the xy-plane. That is, the area lying below the line $2x - 3y = 6$ and containing $(5, 1)$.

Therefore, the solution contains the solid line, $2x - 3y = 6$ and the part of the plane below this line for which the statement $2x - 3y > 6$ holds.

● **PROBLEM 33-4**

Solve the following system graphically.

$$y - x > -3$$
$$y - 2x < 2$$
$$x + y - 3 < 0$$

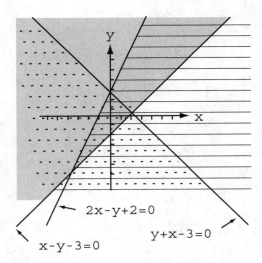

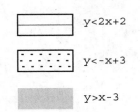

y<2x+2

y<-x+3

y>x-3

2x-y+2=0

y+x-3=0

x-y-3=0

SOLUTION:

We may rewrite the system

$$y > x - 3$$
$$y < 2x + 2$$
$$y < -x + 3$$

Graph the linear equation, $y = mx + b$, for each inequality as a straight dotted line. Thus, we graph

$$y = x - 3$$
$$y = 2x + 2$$
$$y = -x + 3$$

To determine in what region of the $x - y$ plane the inequality holds, select points on both sides of the corresponding dotted line and substitute them into the variable statement. Shade in the side of the line whose point makes the inequality a true statement.

The graphs of the variable sentences are represented in the accompanying figure by diagonal, horizontal, and vertical shading, respectively.

The triple-shaded triangular region is the set of all points whose coordinate pairs satisfy all three conditions as defined by the three inequalities in the system.

CHAPTER 34

LOGARITHMS, EXPONENTIALS, AND EXPONENTS

● **PROBLEM 34-1**

Construct the graph of $y = \log_2 x$.

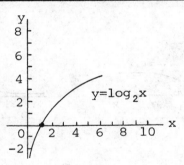

$$y = \log_2 x$$

SOLUTION:

The equations $u = \log_b v$ and $v = b^u$ are equivalent. Therefore, the relation $y = \log_2 x$ is equivalent to $x = 2^y$. Hence, we assume values of y and compute the corresponding values of x, creating the following table:

x:	$\dfrac{1}{8}$	$\dfrac{1}{4}$	$\dfrac{1}{2}$	1	2	4	8
y:	−3	−2	−1	0	1	2	3

For example, if $y = -3$, then $x = 2^y = 2^{-3} = \dfrac{1}{2^3} = \dfrac{1}{8}$.

The points corresponding to these values are plotted on the coordinate system in the figure. The smooth curve joining these points is the desired graph of $y = \log_2 x$. It should be noted that the graph lies entirely to the right of the y-axis. The graph of $y = \log_b x$ for any $b > 1$ will be similar to that in the figure. Some of the properties of this function which can be noted from the graph are

    I. $\log_b x$ is not defined for negative values of x or zero.

    II. $\log_b 1 = 0$.

    III. If $x > 1$, then $\log_b x > 0$.

    IV. If $0 < x < 1$, then $\log_b x < 0$.

● **PROBLEM 34-2**

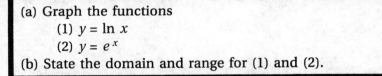

(a) Graph the functions

    (1) $y = \ln x$

    (2) $y = e^x$

(b) State the domain and range for (1) and (2).

SOLUTION:

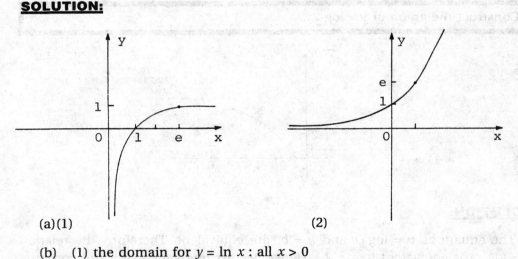

  (a)(1)   (2)

  (b) (1) the domain for $y = \ln x$: all $x > 0$

          the range for $y = \ln x$: all real numbers

      (2) the domain for $y = e^x$: all real numbers

          the range for $y = e^x$: all $y > 0$

Construct the graph of $y = 3^x$.

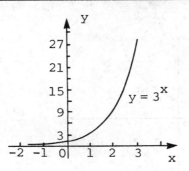

SOLUTION:

Assume values of x and compute the corresponding values of y by substituting into $y = 3^x$ obtaining the following table of values:

x:	−3	−2	−1	0	1	2	3
y:	$\dfrac{1}{27}$	$\dfrac{1}{9}$	$\dfrac{1}{3}$	1	3	9	27

The points corresponding to these pairs of values are plotted on the coordinate system of the figure and these points are joined by a smooth curve, which is the desired graph of the function. Note that the values of y are all positive. Furthermore, if $x < 0$, then y increases to a small extent as x does. If $x > 0$, y increases at a more rapid rate.

● PROBLEM 34-4

Draw the graph of each of the following equations:
   (a) $y = 2^x$
   (b) $y = \left(\dfrac{1}{2}\right)^x$

SOLUTION:

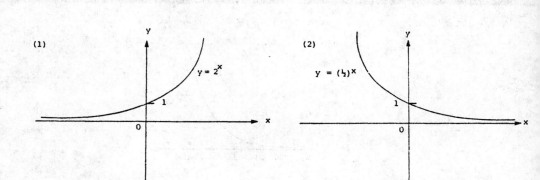

(1)

$y = 2^x$

1

0

(2)

$y = (\tfrac{1}{2})^x$

1

0

CHAPTER 35

TRIGONOMETRIC, INVERSE TRIGONOMETRIC, AND HYPERBOLIC FUNCTIONS

Graph   (a) $y = \sin x$
         (b) $y = 4 \sin x$
         (c) $y = \sin 4x$

         (d) $y = \sin\left(x + \dfrac{\pi}{4}\right)$

         (e) $y = A \sin(Bx + C) + D$
where A, B, C, D are real constants.

SOLUTION:

(a)

$y = \sin x$ is a periodic function with period $T = 2\pi$. Its amplitude is

$$\frac{1}{2}\left[\left(y_{max}\right)-\left(y_{min}\right)\right]=\frac{1}{2}\left[1-(-1)\right]=1.$$

The graph is symmetrical with respect to the origin.

(b) The graph of $y = 4 \sin x$ is the same as $y = \sin x$ except that the amplitude is

$$\frac{1}{2}\left[\left(y_{max}\right)-\left(y_{min}\right)\right]=\frac{1}{2}\left[4-(-4)\right]=4.$$

(c) $y = \sin 4x$ has an amplitude 1, but a period of

$$T = \frac{2\pi}{4} = \frac{\pi}{2}.$$

(d) $y = \sin\left(x + \frac{\pi}{4}\right)$ has period $T = 2\pi$, amplitude 1, and phase shift of $\frac{\pi}{4}$ ($\frac{\pi}{4}$ is also called the phase angle).

Note that the graph of $y = \sin\left(x + \frac{\pi}{4}\right)$ can be obtained by simply shifting the graph of $y = \sin x$ by $\dfrac{\pi}{4}$ to the left of the origin.

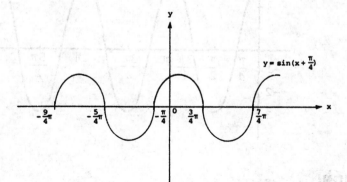

(e) For $y = A \sin(Bx + C) + D$, the constant $|A|$ is the amplitude of the function, the constant B decides the period of the function, $T = \dfrac{2\pi}{|B|}$. C is the phase angle, and D will shift the graph of $y = A \sin(Bx + C)$ up (or down) along the y-axis by D units for positive (or negative) D.

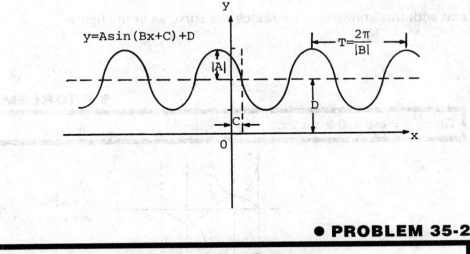

● **PROBLEM 35-2**

Sketch three periods of the graph $y = 3 \cos 2x$.

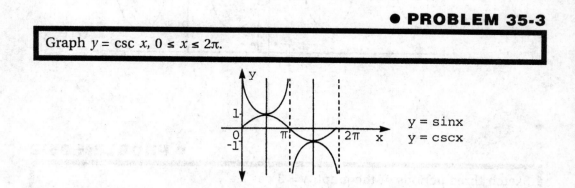

SOLUTION:

The coefficient of the function is 3, which means that the maximum and minimum values are 3 and –3, respectively. The period of the cosine function is the coefficient of x multiplied by $\frac{\pi}{2}$ radians. Therefore, the period of the cosine function given in this problem is

$$2\left(\frac{\pi}{2} \text{ radians}\right) = \pi \text{ radians}$$

and with this knowledge, we sketch the curve as in the figure.

● PROBLEM 35-3

Graph $y = \csc x$, $0 \le x \le 2\pi$.

$y = \sin x$

$y = \csc x$

SOLUTION:

To plot points for the function cosecant of x, first find the y-values of the reciprocal function, the sine of the angle x.

278

x	0		$\dfrac{\pi}{2}$	π		$\dfrac{3\pi}{2}$	2π
$\sin x$	0		1	0		−1	0
$\csc x$	not defined		1	not defined		−1	not defined

Since the sine and cosecant are reciprocals, we state the following conclusions based on properties of real numbers.

(1) For $0 \le x \le \dfrac{\pi}{2}$, $0 \le \sin x \le 1$ and $\csc x \ge 1$.

In fact, as $\sin x$ increases, $\csc x$ decreases. For example:

$\sin 0° = \sin 0 = 0$ $\qquad\qquad\qquad$ $\csc 0 = \text{undefined}$

$\sin 30° = \sin \dfrac{\pi}{6} = \dfrac{1}{2} = .5000$ $\qquad$ $\csc \dfrac{\pi}{6} = 2$

$\sin 45° = \sin \dfrac{\pi}{4} = \dfrac{1}{\sqrt{2}} = \dfrac{\sqrt{2}}{2} \approx \dfrac{1.414}{2} = .7070$ $\qquad$ $\csc \dfrac{\pi}{4} = \sqrt{2} \approx 1.414$

$\sin 90° = \sin \dfrac{\pi}{2} = 1.000$ $\qquad\qquad$ $\csc \dfrac{\pi}{2} = 1$

(2) For $\dfrac{\pi}{2} \le x \le \pi$, $\sin x$ decreases from 1 to 0. Hence, $\csc x$ will increase from 1 to very large values. We can observe this from specific examples:

$\sin \dfrac{\pi}{2} = 1$ $\qquad\qquad\qquad\qquad$ $\csc \dfrac{\pi}{2} = 1$

$\sin \dfrac{2}{3}\pi = \dfrac{\sqrt{3}}{2} \approx .87$ $\qquad\qquad$ $\csc \dfrac{2}{3}\pi \approx 1.15$

$\sin \dfrac{3}{4}\pi \approx .707$ $\qquad\qquad\quad$ $\csc \dfrac{3}{4}\pi \approx 1.4$

$\sin \dfrac{5}{6}\pi = .500$ $\qquad\qquad\quad$ $\csc \dfrac{5}{6}\pi = 2$

$\sin \pi = 0$ $\qquad\qquad\qquad\quad$ $\csc \pi = \text{undefined}$

(3) For $\pi \le x \le \dfrac{3\pi}{2}$, $\sin x$ decreases from 0 to −1. Hence, $\csc x$ will be increasing and will increase from very large negative values to −1.

(4) For $\dfrac{3\pi}{2} \le x \le 2\pi$, $-1 \le \sin x \le 0$, and the graph will be increasing.

Hence, $\csc x$ will decrease from −1 to very large negative values. The student can verify conclusions (3) and (4) in a similar manner to that used for (1) and (2), that is, choosing specific angles between $\dfrac{\pi}{2}$ and $\dfrac{3\pi}{2}$, and then between $\dfrac{3\pi}{2}$ and 2π.

The graphs of both functions are shown in the accompanying figure. Note that the range of the sine function is $-1 \leq \sin x \leq 1$, but the range of the cosecant function is $\csc x \geq 1$ or $\csc x \leq -1$.

● PROBLEM 35-4

Graph   (a) $y = \cot x$
            (b) $y = \sec x$
            (c) $y = \csc x$

SOLUTION:

(a) $y = \cot x = \dfrac{\cos x}{\sin x} = \dfrac{1}{\tan x}$

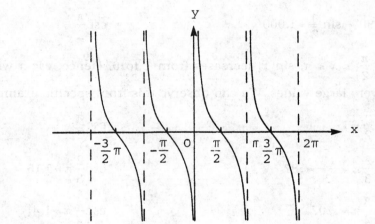

(b) $y = \sec x = \dfrac{1}{\cos x}$, $x \neq 2k\pi + \dfrac{\pi}{2}$, $k = 0,\ \pm1,\ \pm2,\ldots.$

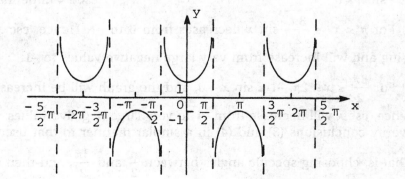

(c) $y = \csc x = \dfrac{1}{\sin x}, \ x \neq 2k\pi, \ k = 0, \ \pm 1, \ \pm 2, \ldots.$

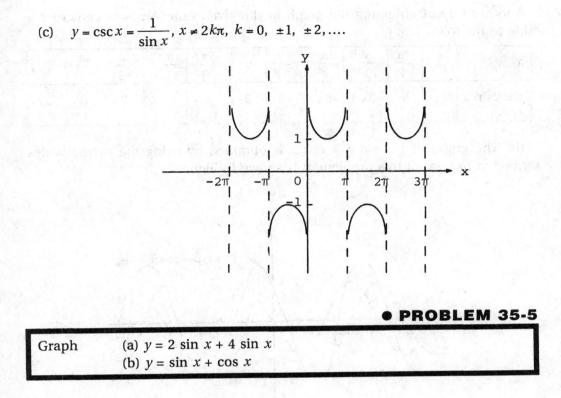

● **PROBLEM 35-5**

Graph   (a) $y = 2 \sin x + 4 \sin x$
         (b) $y = \sin x + \cos x$

SOLUTION:

(a) To obtain the graph of $y = 2 \sin x + 4 \sin x$ we first draw the graphs of $y_1 = 2 \sin x$ and $y_2 + 4 \sin x$ as shown in Figure 1. Next, draw the graph of $y = y_1 + y_2$ by adding corresponding ordinates as illustrated in Figure 1. For instance, at $x = a_1$, the ordinate of y is $a_1 d_1$, which is the algebraic sum of the ordinates $a_1 b_1$ of y_1 and $a_1 c_1$ of y_2.

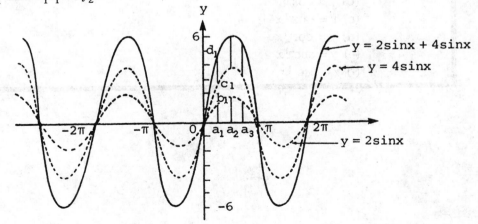

Another way of obtaining the graph of the given function is to construct a table as the following:

x	....	$-\dfrac{\pi}{2}$	$-\dfrac{\pi}{3}$	$-\dfrac{\pi}{4}$	$-\dfrac{\pi}{6}$	0	$\dfrac{\pi}{6}$	$\dfrac{\pi}{4}$	$\dfrac{\pi}{3}$	$\dfrac{\pi}{2}$	....
$y = 2\sin x$ $+ 4\sin x$	....	-6	$-3\sqrt{3}$	$-3\sqrt{2}$	-3	0	3	$3\sqrt{2}$	$3\sqrt{3}$	6	....

(b) The graph of $y = \sin x + \cos x$ is obtained by using the methods described in part (a) of this problem; it is shown in Figure 2.

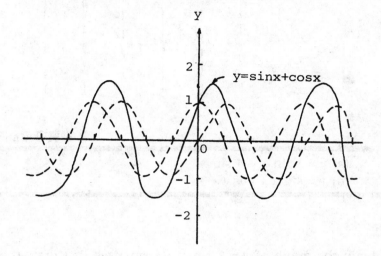

● **PROBLEM 35-6**

Graph   (a) $y = \sin^{-1} x$
           (b) $y = \cos^{-1} x$
           (c) $y = \tan^{-1} x$
           (d) $y = \cot^{-1} x$
           (e) $y = \sec^{-1} x$
           (f) $y = \csc^{-1} x$

SOLUTION:

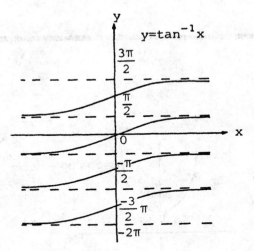

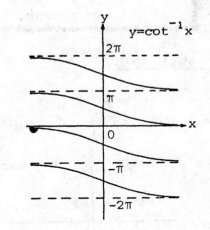

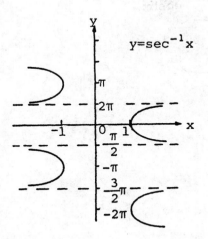

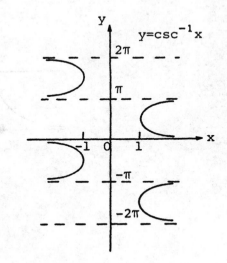

Graph   (a) $y = \sinh x$
         (b) $y = \cosh x$
         (c) $y = \tanh x$

SOLUTION:

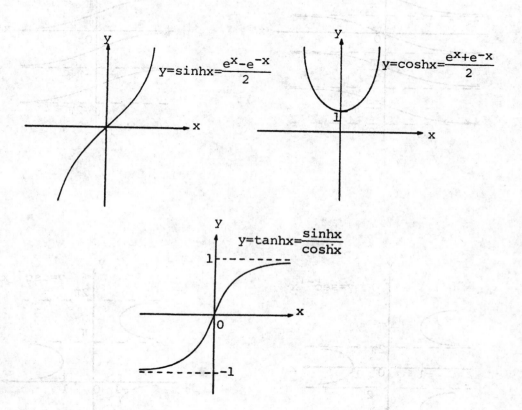

CHAPTER 36

CIRCLES, PARABOLAS, ELLIPSES, AND HYPERBOLAS

● **PROBLEM 36-1**

Graph the equation $2x^2 + 2y^2 - 13 = 0$.

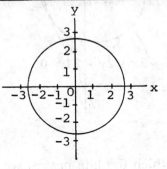

SOLUTION:

In order to verify that this is the equation of a circle, we put the equation in the standard form: add 13 to both sides of the given equation.

$$2x^2 + 2y^2 - 13 + 13 = 0 + 13$$
$$2x^2 + 2y^2 = 13$$

Divide both sides of this equation by 2.

$$\frac{2x^2 + 2y^2}{2} = \frac{13}{2}$$

or

$$x^2 + y^2 = \frac{13}{2}, \text{ which is the standard form for}$$

the equation of a circle with its center at the origin (0, 0) and

$$\text{radius} = r = \sqrt{\frac{13}{2}} = \frac{\sqrt{13}}{\sqrt{2}} = \frac{\sqrt{13}}{\sqrt{2}} \frac{\sqrt{2}}{\sqrt{2}} = \frac{\sqrt{26}}{2}.$$

Therefore, the radius of the circle is approximately $\frac{5.1}{2}$ or 2.55. The graph is represented in the figure.

● **PROBLEM 36-2**

Find the equation of the line drawn from the point (8, 6) tangent to the circle $x^2 + y^2 + 2x + 2y - 24 = 0$.

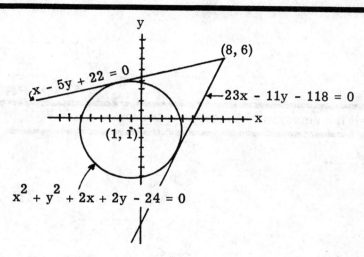

SOLUTION:

Given a point through which the line passes, we can fully describe the line only after we have found its slope. According to the point-slope form of a linear equation, the equations of the lines passing through (8, 6) are given by $y - 6 = m(x - 8)$, where m is the slope. When m is the slope of the tangent, the equation, $y - 6 = m(x - 8)$, is the equation of the tangent. The equation can be rewritten as $y = mx - 8m + 6$.

To find the unique intersection point of the line and the circle, the tangency point, we can substitute $y = mx - 8m + 6$ into the equation for the circle and solve for x. Since the line is a tangent line, there can only be one value for x. This last fact will assist us in determining the slope of the line. Hence,

$$x^2 + (mx - 8m + 6)^2 + 2x + 2(mx - 8m + 6) - 24 = 0$$
$$x^2 + (m^2x^2 - 16m^2x + 12mx + 64m^2 - 96m + 36) + 2x +$$
$$(2mx - 16m + 12) - 24 = 0 \text{ which reduces to,}$$
$$(m^2 + 1)x^2 - (16m^2 - 14m - 2)x + (64m^2 - 112m + 24) = 0$$

286

By the quadratic formula,

$$x = \frac{-\left[-\left(16m^2 - 14m - 2\right)\right] \pm \sqrt{\left[-\left(16m^2 - 14m - 2\right)\right]^2 - 4\left(m^2 + 1\right)\left(64m^2 - 112m + 24\right)}}{2\left(m^2 + 1\right)}$$

Since x is a coordinate of a tangency point, it can only take on one value. Hence, the discriminant must equal zero. By setting the discriminant equal to zero we can solve for m and, thereby, determine fully the equation of the tangent line.

$$[-(16m^2 - 14m - 2)^2 - 4(m^2 + 1)(64m^2 - 112m + 24) = 0$$
$$(256m^4 - 448m^3 + 132m^2 + 56m + 4) - (256m^4 - 448m^3$$
$$+ 352m^2 - 448m + 96) = 0$$
$$- 220m^2 + 504m - 92 = 0$$
$$- 4(55m^2 - 126m + 23) = 0$$

By factoring we only need to solve $(5m - 1)(11m - 23) = 0$.

Hence, $m = \dfrac{1}{5}$ or $m = \dfrac{23}{11}$. By substituting back into our equation for the tangent line, $y - 6 = m(x - 8)$, we find that there are two tangent lines that can be drawn to the circle from the point (8, 6), a point external to the circle.

$$y - 6 = \frac{1}{5}(x - 8) \quad \text{and} \quad y - 6 = \frac{23}{11}(x - 8)$$
$$5y - 30 = x - 8 \qquad 11y - 66 = 23x - 184$$

Hence, $x - 5y + 22 = 0$ and $23x - 11y - 118 = 0$ are the equations of the tangent lines required in this problem. The figure shows the circle and its tangents.

● **PROBLEM 36-3**

Draw the graphs of $f(x) = x^2$, $g(x) = 3x^2$, and also $h(x) = \dfrac{1}{2}x^2$ on one set of coordinate axes.

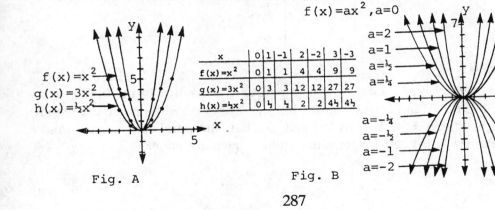

x	0	1	-1	2	-2	3	-3
$f(x) = x^2$	0	1	1	4	4	9	9
$g(x) = 3x^2$	0	3	3	12	12	27	27
$h(x) = \frac{1}{2}x^2$	0	½	½	2	2	4½	4½

Fig. A   Fig. B

287

SOLUTION:

We construct a composite table showing the values of each function corresponding to selected values for x.

In the example, we graphed three instances of the function $f(x) = ax^2$, $a > 0$. For different values of a, how do the graphs compare? (Fig. 1a). Assigning a given value to a has very little effect upon the main characteristics of the graph. The coefficient a serves as a "stretching factor" relative to the y-axis. As a increases, the two branches of the curve approach the y-axis. The curve becomes "thinner." As a decreases, the curve becomes "flatter" and aproaches the x-axis.

The graph of $f(x) = ax$, $a \neq 0$, is called a parabola. (Fig. 1b). The point $(0, 0)$ is the vertex, or turning point, of the curve; the y-axis is the axis of symmetry. The value of a determines the shape of the curve. For $a > 0$ the parabola opens upward and for $a < 0$ the parabola opens downward.

● PROBLEM 36-4

Discuss the graph of the parabola $(x - a)^2 = 4p(y - b)$, and find its axis, focus, directrix, vertex, and latus rectum.

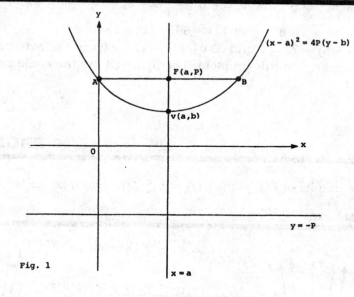

Fig. 1

SOLUTION:

The graph of $(x - a)^2 = 4p(y - b)$ is a parabola, as shown in the figure. It is concave up if $p > 0$, and concave down if $p < 0$. Note that when $p = 0$, the graph is a straight line, $x = a$. Also as $|p|$ gets smaller, the parabola becomes narrower, whereas as $|p|$ gets bigger, the parabola becomes wider.

The vertex of the parabola is $V(a, b)$, its axis is $x = a$, the focus is $F(a, p)$, the directrix is $y = -p$, and the latus rectum is the segment AB (as shown in Fig. 1), which is a part of the line $y = p$.

● PROBLEM 36-5

Discuss the graph of $\dfrac{x^2}{25} + \dfrac{y^2}{9} = 1$.

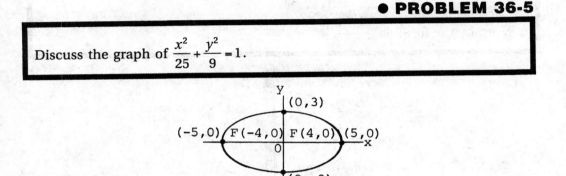

SOLUTION:

Since this is an equation of the form $\dfrac{x^2}{a^2} + \dfrac{y^2}{b^2} = 1$, with $a = 5$ and $b = 3$, it represents an ellipse. The simplest way to sketch the curve is to find its intercepts.

If we set $x = 0$, then

$$y = \sqrt{\left(1 - \frac{x^2}{25}\right)9} = \sqrt{\left(1 - \frac{0^2}{25}\right)9} = \pm 3$$

so that the y-intercepts are at $(0, 3)$ and $(0, -3)$. Similarly, the x-intercepts are found for $y = 0$:

$$x = \sqrt{\left(1 - \frac{y^2}{9}\right)25} = \sqrt{\left(1 - \frac{0^2}{9}\right)25} = \pm 5$$

to be at $(5, 0)$ and $(-5, 0)$ (see figure). To locate the foci we note that

$$c^2 = a^2 - b^2 = 5^2 - 3^2$$
$$c^2 = 25 - 9 = 16$$
$$c = \pm 4$$

The foci lie on the major axis of the ellipse. In this case it is the x-axis since $a = 5$ is greater than $b = 3$. Therefore, the foci are $(\pm c, 0)$, that is, at $(-4, 0)$ and $(4, 0)$. Therefore, the foci are at $(-4, 0)$ and $(4, 0)$. The sum of the distances from any point on the curve to the foci is $2a = 2(5) = 10$.

The latus rectum of an ellipse is the chord through either focus perpendicular to the major axis. Show that the length of the latus recta of ellipse

$$\frac{x^2}{a^2} + \frac{y^2}{b^2} = 1$$

is given by the formula $\dfrac{\left(2b^2\right)}{a}$.

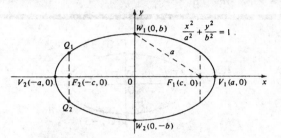

SOLUTION:

In the accompanying figure, ellipse $\dfrac{x^2}{a^2} + \dfrac{y^2}{b^2} = 1$, has foci $(-c, 0)$ and $(c, 0)$ and

the latus rectum $\overline{Q_1Q_2}$. We are asked to show $Q_1Q_2 = \dfrac{2b^2}{a}$. To find the length

of Q_1Q_2, we first find the coordinates of Q_1 and Q_2. To find $Q_1(x_1, y_1)$ note that both foci lie on the x-axis. Since the major axis is the line determined by the foci, the major axis is the x-axis. Further, since the latus recta are perpendicular to the major axis, this implies that the latus rectum Q_1Q_2 is a vertical line. Since every point on a vertical line has the same x-coordinate, then $Q_1(x_1, y_1)$ and $Q_2(x_2, y_2)$ must have the same x as $F_2(-c, 0)$. Thus, $x_1 = x_2 = -c$. To complete locating Q_1 and Q_2, we now find their y-coordinates. Note that Q_1 is a point on the ellipse and thus (x_1, y_1) must satisfy the equation

$$\frac{x^2}{a^2} + \frac{y^2}{b^2} = 1.$$

Discuss the graph of $\dfrac{x^2}{9} - \dfrac{y^2}{9} = 1.$

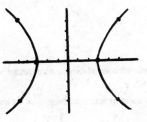

SOLUTION:

$\dfrac{x^2}{9} - \dfrac{y^2}{9} = 1$ is an equation of the form $\dfrac{x^2}{a^2} + \dfrac{y^2}{b^2} = 1$ with $a = 3$ and $b = 3$.

Therefore, the graph is a hyperbola. The x-intercepts are found by setting $y = 0$:

$$\frac{x^2}{9} - \frac{0^2}{9} = 1$$

$$x^2 = 9$$

$$x = \pm 3$$

Thus, the x-intercepts are at $(-3, 0)$ and $(3, 0)$. There are no y-intercepts since for $x = 0$ there are no real values of y satisfying the equation, i.e., no real value of y satisfies

$$\frac{0^2}{9} - \frac{y^2}{9} = 1$$

$$y^2 = -9, \; y = \sqrt{-9}.$$

Solving the original equation for y:

$$y = \sqrt{\left(1 - \frac{x^2}{9}\right)(-9)} \quad \text{or} \quad y = \sqrt{x^2 - 9}$$

shows that there will be no permissible values of x in the interval $-3 < x < 3$. Such values of x do not yield real values for y. For $x = 5$ and $x = -5$ use the equation for y to obtain the ordered pairs $(5, 4)$, $(5, -4)$, $(-5, 4)$, and $(-5, -4)$ as indicated in the figure. The foci of the hyperbola are located at $(\pm c, 0)$, where

$$c^2 = a^2 + b^2$$

$$c^2 = 3^2 + 3^2 = 9 + 9 = 18$$

$$c = \pm \sqrt{18} = \pm 3\sqrt{2}$$

Therefore, the foci are at $\left(-3\sqrt{2}, \, 0\right)$ and $\left(3\sqrt{2}, \, 0\right)$.

Graph the equation $xy = -4$.

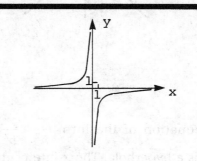

SOLUTION:

The graph of the equation, $xy = c$, is a hyperbola for all non-zero real values of c. In this case, $c = -4$ and thus the particular equation is $xy = -4$. Since the product is negative, the values of x and y must have different signs. If x is positive, then y is negative and so part of the graph lies in quadrant IV. On the other hand, if x is negative, then y is positive and the other part of the hyperbola is located in quadrant II. If we solve for y, then $y = \dfrac{-4}{x}$ and $x \neq 0$. Then the graph never touches the y-axis. Thus, the line $x = 0$ is an asymptote of the graph. On the other hand, solving for x, we have $x = \dfrac{-4}{y}$ and $y \neq 0$. Thus the graph never crosses the x-axis and the line $y = 0$ is an asymptote. We now prepare a table of values by selecting values for x and finding the corresponding values for y. See table and graph.

x	$\dfrac{-4}{x} =$	y
-3	$\dfrac{-4}{-3}$	$\dfrac{4}{3} = 1\dfrac{1}{3}$
-2	$\dfrac{-4}{-2}$	2
-1	$\dfrac{-4}{-1}$	4
1	$\dfrac{-4}{1}$	-4
2	$\dfrac{-4}{2}$	-2
3	$\dfrac{-4}{3}$	$\dfrac{-4}{3} = -1\dfrac{1}{3}$

Find the equation for the set of points the difference of whose distances from (5, 0) and (–5, 0) is 6 units.

$$\frac{x^2}{9} - \frac{y^2}{16} = 1$$

SOLUTION:

We find the desired equation by choosing an arbitrary point (x, y) and computing the difference of its distance from (5, 0) and (–5, 0). Applying the distance formula for the distance between two points (a_1, b_1) and (a_2, b_2),

$d = \sqrt{(a_1 - a_2)^2 + (b_1 - b_2)^2}$. From (x, y) to (5, 0) is d_1 from (x, y) to (–5, 0) is d_2.

$$d_1 = \sqrt{(x - 5)^2 + y^2} \; ; \; d_2 = \sqrt{(x + 5)^2 + y^2} \; ;$$

We are told that the difference of these distances, $d_2 - d_1$, is 6.

Hence, $\sqrt{(x + 5)^2 + y^2} - \sqrt{(x - 5)^2 + y^2} = 6.$

$$\sqrt{(x + 5)^2 + y^2} = 6 + \sqrt{(x - 5)^2 + y^2}$$

Squaring both sides:

$$\left(\sqrt{(x + 5)^2 + y^2} \right)^2 = \left(6 + \sqrt{(x - 5)^2 + y^2} \right)^2$$

$$\left(\sqrt{(x + 5)^2 + y^2} \right)^2 = 36 + 12\sqrt{(x - 5)^2 + y^2} + \left(\sqrt{(x - 5)^2 + y^2} \right)^2$$

Since $\left(\sqrt{a} \right)^2 = \sqrt{a}\sqrt{a} = \sqrt{a \cdot a} = \sqrt{a^2} = a$,

$$\left(\sqrt{(x + 5)^2 + y^2} \right)^2 = (x + 5)^2 + y^2 \text{ and } \left(\sqrt{(x - 5)^2 + y^2} \right)^2 = (x - 5)^2 + y^2.$$

Thus we obtain,

$$(x - 5)^2 + y^2 = 36 + 12\sqrt{(x - 5)^2 + y^2} + (x - 5)^2 + y^2$$

$$x^2 + 10x + 25 + y^2 = 36 + 12\sqrt{(x-5)^2 + y^2} + x^2 - 10x + 25 + y^2$$

Adding $-\left(x^2 + 25 + y^2\right)$ to both sides,

$$x^2 + 10x + 25 + y^2 - \left(x^2 + 25 + y^2\right) = 36 + 12\sqrt{(x-5)^2 + y^2} + x^2$$
$$-10x + 25 + y^2 - \left(x^2 + 25 + y^2\right)$$

$$10x = 36 + 12\sqrt{(x-5)^2 + y^2} - 10x$$

Adding $-36 + 10x$ to both sides,

$$10x - 36 + 10x = 36 + 12\sqrt{(x-5)^2 + y^2} - 10x - 36 + 10x$$

$$20x - 36 = 12\sqrt{(x-5)^2 + y^2}$$

Dividing both sides by 4,

$$5x - 9 = 3\sqrt{(x-5)^2 + y^2}$$

Squaring both sides,

$$(5x-9)^2 = \left(3\sqrt{(x-5)^2 + y^2}\right)^2$$

$$(5x-9)(5x-9) = 3^2\left(\sqrt{(x-5)^2 + y^2}\right)^2$$

$$25x^2 - 90x + 81 = 9[(x-5)^2 + y^2]$$
$$25x^2 - 90x + 81 = 9(x^2 - 10x + 25 + y^2)$$
$$25x^2 - 90x + 81 = 9x^2 - 90x + 225 + 9y^2$$

Adding $-(9x^2 - 90x + 9y^2)$ to both sides,
$$25x^2 - 90x + 81 - (9x^2 - 90x + 9y^2) = 9x^2 - 90x + 225 + 9y^2$$
$$- (9x^2 - 90x + 9y^2)$$
$$25x^2 - 9x^2 - 9y^2 + 81 = 225$$
$$16x^2 - 9y^2 + 81 = 225$$

Adding -81 to both sides,
$$16x^2 - 9y^2 = 144.$$

Dividing both sides by 144,

$$\frac{16x^2}{144} - \frac{9y^2}{144} = \frac{144}{144} \text{ or}$$

$$\frac{x^2}{9} - \frac{y^2}{16} = 1$$

which is the standard form for the equation of a hyperbola.

From the form of the equation we can determine its graph. When the center is at the origin and its vertices are at $(a, 0)$ and $(-a, 0)$, the equation of the hyperbola is $\dfrac{x^2}{a^2} - \dfrac{y^2}{b^2} = 1$.

In this case, the vertices are $(3, 0)$ and $(-3, 0)$ since $a^2 = 9$ and $a = \pm 3$ (see figure).

However, when the vertices lie on the y-axis, the equation of the hyperbola is $\dfrac{y^2}{a^2} - \dfrac{x^2}{b^2} = 1$.

The vertices would then be $(0, a)$ and $(0, -a)$.

CHAPTER 37

POLAR COORDINATES AND PARAMETRIC EQUATIONS

Draw the graph of $\rho = 2 \cos \theta$.

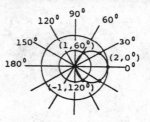

SOLUTION:

We assign values to θ and find the corresponding values of ρ, giving the following table:

θ	$\cos \theta$	$\rho = 2 \cos \theta$
0°	1	2
30°	.87	1.74
60°	.5	1
90°	0	0
120°	−.5	−1
150°	−.87	−1.74
180°	−1	−2
Values from 180° to 360° give the same points. (Check this.)		

We then plot the points (ρ, θ) and draw a smooth curve through them. We get the graph of the figure. The equation which defines the path of P may involve only one of the variables (ρ, θ). In that case the variable which is not mentioned may have any and all values.

Given the figure below, is it possible to add points to the graph so that the final figure will have (a) symmetry about the polar axis, (b) symmetry about the 90°-axis, (c) symmetry about the pole? If so, add these points.

SOLUTION:

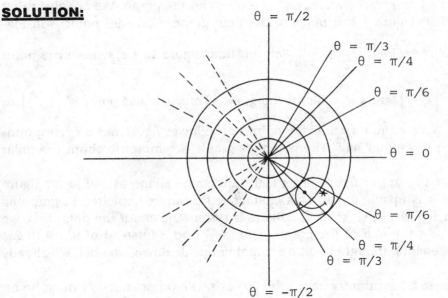

Fig. 1

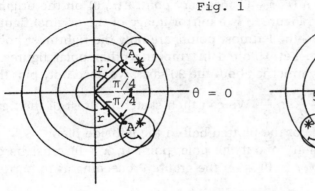

Fig. 2   Fig. 3

297

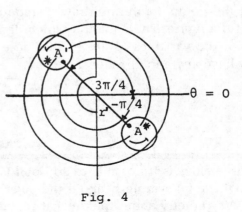

Fig. 4

(a) For there to be symmetry about the polar axis, point $(r, -\theta)$ must be on the completed graph whenever (r, θ) is a point on the graph. We are given that every point in Figure 1 is a point of the final graph. Consider point A in Figure 2, with coordinates $\left(r', -\frac{\pi}{4}\right)$. For the final figure to be symmetric, point $\left(r', -\frac{\pi}{4}\right)$ or $\left(r', \frac{\pi}{4}\right)$ must also be on the graph. Thus, we add point A' $\left(r', \frac{\pi}{4}\right)$ to the graph. We continue until every point in the lower figure has a corresponding point in the upper half. The complete graph is symmetric about the polar axis.

Note that the upper figure has exactly the same shape as the lower figure except that it is upside down. This characteristic can be exploited in graphing other polar figures. If we know the figure is symmetric about the polar axis, we need only plot the half of the graph—from $\theta = 0$ to π (instead of $\theta = 0$ to 2π) and then sketching the other half by "flipping upside down" the half we already have.

For there to be symmetry about the 90°-axis, the point $(r, \pi - \theta)$ must be on the completed graph whenever (r, θ) is a point on the graph. Proceeding as in part (a), we add a point A'$(r', \pi - \theta)$ for every point A(r', θ) on the original figure. The result (shown in Figure 3) is a mirror image of the original figure (notice the position of eyes)—the leftmost points are now the rightmost points.

This characteristic can be exploited in graphing other polar figures. If we know that the figure is symmetric about the 90°-axis, we need only plot the half of the graph—from $\theta = -\frac{\pi}{2}$ to $\frac{\pi}{2}$. We can then sketch the rest of the figure by drawing the mirror image of the plotted half in the left side plane.

For there to be symmetry about the pole, point $(r, \pi + \theta)$ must be on the completed graph whenever (r, θ) is on the graph. Proceeding as in part (a), we

298

add a point A'$(r', \pi + \theta)$ for every A(r', θ) on the original figure. The result is a figure that can be obtained from the original figure by (1) drawing the mirror image of the original in the left plane, and (2) "flipping upside down" the mirror image about the polar axis.

In exploiting the pole symmetry for graphing other polar figures, the two–step flip may be rather hard to see. The better way is to graph any half of the graph $(-\dfrac{3\pi}{4} \le \theta \le \dfrac{\pi}{4}$, for example) and, for each point, locate the point directly opposite the points in the graph (the point such that the pole is the midpoint of the point and the graphed point).

With polar-axis symmetry, we need only graph $0 \le \theta \le \pi$. With 90°-axis symmetry, we need only graph $-\dfrac{\pi}{2} \le \theta \le \dfrac{\pi}{2}$. If a figure has both 90°-axis and polar axis, note that if we plot $0 \le \theta \le \dfrac{\pi}{2}$, by the polar-axis symmetry, we also know $-\dfrac{\pi}{2} \le \theta < 0$. Thus, we know $-\dfrac{\pi}{2} \le \theta \le \dfrac{\pi}{2}$. Because of the 90°-axis symmetry, we know $\dfrac{\pi}{2} \le \theta \le \dfrac{3\pi}{2}$. Therefore, given 90°-axis and polar-axis symmetry, we need only graph $0 \le \theta \le \dfrac{\pi}{2}$ to plot the whole graph.

Similarly, given all three types of symmetry, it can be shown that we need only plot $0 \le \theta \le \dfrac{\pi}{4}$.

● PROBLEM 37-3

Graph $r^2 = 4 \cos 2\theta$.

SOLUTION:

Before blindly plotting points, let us examine the equation for simplifying factors such as symmetries.

(1) Polar-Axis Symmetry. A figure is symmetric about the polar axis, if for every point (r, θ) on the graph $(r, -\theta)$ is also a point of the graph. Suppose (r_0, θ_0) is on the graph. Thus, $r_0{}^2 = 4 \cos 2\theta_0$. Since $\cos x = \cos (-x)$, it must be true that $r_0{}^2 = 4 \cos (2\theta_0) = 4 \cos (-2\theta_0) = 4 \cos 2 (-\theta_0)$. Thus, if (r_0, θ_0) is a point on the graph, then $(r_0, -\theta_0)$ is also on the graph. The figure $r^2 = 4 \cos 2\theta$ is symmetric about the polar axis.

299

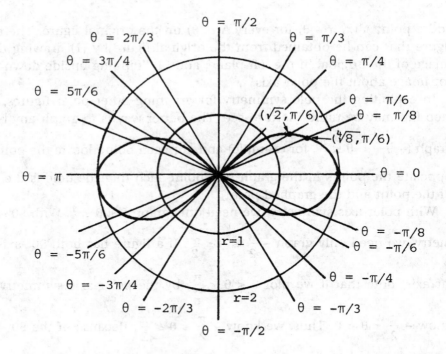

$\theta = \pi/2$

$\theta = 2\pi/3$ $\theta = \pi/3$

$\theta = 3\pi/4$ $\theta = \pi/4$

$\theta = 5\pi/6$ $\theta = \pi/6$

$\theta = \pi/8$

$(\sqrt{2}, \pi/6)$

$(\sqrt[4]{8}, \pi/6)$

$\theta = \pi$ $\theta = 0$

$\theta = -\pi/8$

$r = 1$ $\theta = -\pi/6$

$\theta = -5\pi/6$

$\theta = -3\pi/4$ $\theta = -\pi/4$

$r = 2$

$\theta = -2\pi/3$ $\theta = -\pi/3$

$\theta = -\pi/2$

(2) **Symmetry about the 90°-axis.** A figure is symmetric about the 90°-axis if, for every point (r, θ) on the graph, $(r, \pi - \theta)$ is also a point on the graph. Suppose (r_0, θ_0) is a point on the graph. Then we must show $r_0^2 = 4 \cos 2(\pi - \theta_0)$ is also a point on the graph. Working backwards, we use the identity $\cos 2\psi = 2 \cos^2 \psi - 1$ to show that $r_0^2 = 4 \cos 2(\pi - \theta_0)$ is true if and only if $r_0^2 = 4(2 \cos^2 (\pi - \theta_0) - 1)$. Since $\cos (\pi - \theta) = -\cos \theta$, $r_0^2 = 4(2 \cos^2 (\pi - \theta_0) - 1)$ is true if and only if $r_0^2 = 4(2 (-\cos \theta_0)^2 - 1) = 4(2 \cos^2 \theta_0 - 1) = 4 \cos 2\theta_0$. But, we know that, since (r_0, θ_0) is a point on the graph, it must be true that $r_0^2 = 4 \cos 2\theta_0$. Thus, $r_0^2 = 4 \cos 2(\pi - \theta_0)$. Therefore, every other equation must also be true. Thus, $(r, \pi - \theta)$ is a point on the graph if (r, θ) is on the graph. The figure is thus symmetric about the 90°-axis.

(3) **Symmetry with respect to the pole.** A figure is symmetric about the pole if, for every point (r, θ) on the graph, $(r, \pi + \theta)$ is also a point on the graph. Working backward as above, we obtain $r_0^2 = 4 \cos 2(\pi + \theta_0) = 4(2 \cos^2 (\pi + \theta_0) - 1) = 4(2 [-\cos \theta_0]^2 - 1) = 4(2 \cos^2 \theta_0 - 1) = 4 \cos 2\theta_0$. Since (r_0, θ_0) is given to be on the graph, then $r_0^2 = 4 \cos 2\theta_0$ is a true statement; and, thus, for every point (r_0, θ_0) on the graph, the point $(r_0, \theta_0 + \pi)$ is also on the graph. The figure is symmetric about the pole.

We now have three symmetries, and thus, we need only consider values of θ between 0 and $\frac{\pi}{4}$. Two other important results are

(1) **The curve is bounded.** Note $\cos x \leq 1$. Therefore, $4 \cos^2 2\theta \leq 4$. Since $r^2 = 4 \cos^2 2\theta$, it must be true that $r \leq 2$. Since there is an upper limit to r, the curve is bounded.

300

(2) To find the intercepts with the polar axis, either $r = 0$, or $\theta = 0$, or $\theta = \pi$. If $r = 0$, then $0^2 = 4 \cos 2\theta$ or $\cos 2\theta = 0$. Since only $\cos \pm \dfrac{\pi}{2}$ has a cosine of 0, 2θ

$= \pm \dfrac{\pi}{2}$, or $\theta = \pm \dfrac{\pi}{4}$. Thus, $\left(0, \dfrac{\pi}{4}\right)$, and $\left(0, -\dfrac{\pi}{4}\right)$ are intercepts with the polar axis.

If $\theta = 0$, then $r^2 = 4 \cos 0 = 4$ or $r = \pm 2$ and $(2, 0)$ and $(-2, 0)$ are points on the graph. Solving for r with $\theta = \pi$ yields the same points. Thus, the axis intercepts are $(\pm 2, 0)$ and $\left(0, \pm \dfrac{\pi}{4}\right)$.

Using the above information (the symmetries and the intercepts), and with the points calculated below, we obtain the accompanying graph.

For convenience of calculations, it is best to express r in terms of θ. Thus, if $r^2 = 4 \cos 2\theta$, then $r = 2\sqrt{\cos 2\theta}$. For $\theta = \dfrac{\pi}{8}$,

$$r = 2\sqrt{\cos \dfrac{\pi}{4}} = 2\sqrt{\dfrac{\sqrt{2}}{2}} = \sqrt{4 \cdot \dfrac{\sqrt{2}}{2}} = \sqrt{\dfrac{2}{\sqrt{2}}} = \sqrt{\sqrt{8}} = \sqrt[4]{8}.$$

Thus, $\left(\sqrt[4]{8}, \dfrac{\pi}{8}\right)$ is a point on the graph for $\theta = \dfrac{\pi}{6}, r = 2\sqrt{\cos \dfrac{\pi}{3}} = 2\sqrt{\dfrac{1}{2}} = \sqrt{2}$.

Thus, $\left(\sqrt{2}, \dfrac{\pi}{6}\right)$ is a point on the graph.

● PROBLEM 37-4

Graph the parametric equations

(a) $\begin{cases} x = 2t \\ y = t + 4 \end{cases}$ (b) $\begin{cases} x = \cos \theta \\ y = \sin \theta \end{cases}$ (c) $\begin{cases} x = 4t \\ y = \dfrac{2}{t} \end{cases}$

SOLUTION:

(a) One of the methods for graphing these kinds of equations is to change them to regular equations without parameters. For instance, t in

$$\begin{cases} x = 2t \\ y = t + 4 \end{cases} \qquad\qquad \text{(1)} \\ \text{(2)}$$

is eliminated as the following:

From equation (1) $t = \dfrac{x}{2}$.

Substituting in equation (2), $y = \dfrac{x}{2} + 4$, $x - 2y + 8 = 0$

which is a straight line whose graph is easily constructed by choosing two points on the line, as shown in Fig. 1.

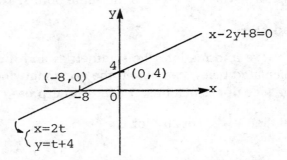

Note that another method for graphing would be using the table as shown below.

t	-2	-1	0	1	2
x	-4	-2	0	2	4
y	2	3	4	5	6

$$\begin{cases} x = 2t \\ y = t + 4 \end{cases}$$

(b) $\begin{cases} x = \cos\theta \\ y = \sin\theta \end{cases}$
                                                       (3)
(4)

Squaring equations (3) and (4) and adding them together, one obtains

$$\begin{cases} x^2 = \cos^2\theta \\ y^2 = \sin^2\theta \end{cases}, \quad x^2 + y^2 = \cos^2\theta + \sin^2\theta = 1$$

Hence, the graph is a circle of radius 1, with center 0 (0, 0).

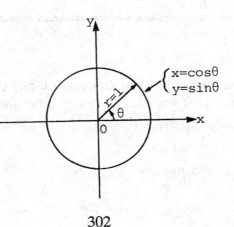

302

(c) $\begin{cases} x = 4t \\ y = \dfrac{2}{t} \end{cases}$ (5)
(6)

From equation (6), $t = \dfrac{2}{y}$. Substituting in equation (5), $x = \dfrac{8}{y}$, $xy - 8 = 0$. The graph is shown in Fig. 3.

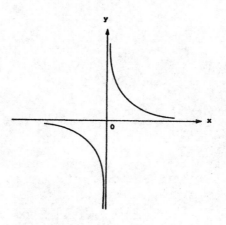

SECTION 4

CALCULUS

CHAPTER 38

LIMITS

● **PROBLEM 38-1**

Find $\lim\limits_{x \to 2}\left(\dfrac{x^2 - 5}{x + 3}\right)$

SOLUTION:

For the numerator only

$$\lim_{x \to 2}\left(x^2 - 5\right) = 4 - 5 = -1$$

For the denominator only

$$\lim_{x \to 2}\left(x + 3\right) = 5$$

Therefore, $\qquad \lim\limits_{x \to 2}\left(\dfrac{x^2 - 5}{x + 3}\right) = -\dfrac{1}{5}$

Using the method of simple substitution, we find that $\lim\limits_{x \to -3} f(x) = \infty$. There is no limit.

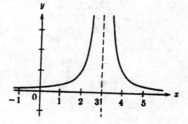

Find

(a) $\lim\limits_{x \to 3^+} \dfrac{x^2 + x + 2}{x^2 - 2x - 3}$ (b) $\lim\limits_{x \to 3^-} \dfrac{x^2 + x + 2}{x^2 - 2x - 3}$ (c) $\lim\limits_{x \to 3} \dfrac{x^2 + x + 2}{x^2 - 2x - 3}$

SOLUTION:

(a) $\lim\limits_{x \to 3^+} \dfrac{x^2 + x + 2}{x^2 - 2x - 3} = \lim\limits_{x \to 3^+} \dfrac{x^2 + x + 2}{(x-3)(x+1)}$

The limit of the numerator is 14. To find the limit of the denominator,

$$\lim_{x \to 3^+} (x-3)(x+1) = \lim_{x \to 3^+} (x-3) \bullet \lim_{x \to 3^+} (x+1) = 0 \bullet 4 = 0$$

Thus, the limit of the denominator is 0, as the denominator is approaching 0 through positive values. Consequently,

$$\lim_{x \to 3^+} \frac{x^2 + x + 2}{x^2 - 2x - 3} = +\infty$$

(b) $\lim\limits_{x \to 3^-} \dfrac{x^2 + x + 2}{x^2 - 2x - 3} = \lim\limits_{x \to 3^-} \dfrac{x^2 + x + 2}{(x-3)(x+1)}$

As in part (a), the limit of the numerator is 14 here also. To find the limit of the denominator,

$$\lim_{x \to 3^-} (x-3)(x+1) = \lim_{x \to 3^-} (x-3) \bullet \lim_{x \to 3^-} (x+1) = 0 \bullet 4 = 0$$

In this case, the limit of the denominator is again zero, but since the denominator is approaching zero through negative values,

$$\lim_{x \to 3^-} \frac{x^2 + x + 2}{x^2 - 2x - 3} = -\infty$$

(c) $\lim\limits_{x \to 3} \dfrac{x^2 + x + 2}{x^2 - 2x - 3} = |\infty|$

Find

(a) $\lim\limits_{x \to 2} \dfrac{x^3 - 6x^2 + 3x + 10}{x^2 + x - 6}$ (b) $\lim\limits_{x \to 0^+} \dfrac{\ln(x)}{\sin(x)}$

SOLUTION:

(a) By L'Hopital's Rule, the limit becomes

$$\lim_{x \to 2} \frac{\frac{d}{dx}\left(x^3 - 6x^2 + 3x + 10\right)}{\frac{d}{dx}\left(x^2 + x - 6\right)} = \lim_{x \to 2} \frac{3x^2 - 12x + 3}{2x + 1} = \frac{12 - 24 + 3}{5} = \frac{-9}{5}$$

(b) By L'Hopital's Rule, the limit becomes

$$\lim_{x \to 0^+} \frac{\frac{d}{dx}\left[\ln(x)\right]}{\frac{d}{dx}\left[\sin(x)\right]} = \lim_{x \to 0^+} \frac{\frac{1}{x}}{\cos(x)} = \frac{\frac{1}{0}}{1} = \infty$$

CHAPTER 39

CONTINUITY

Investigate the continuity of the expression
$$y = \frac{x^2 - 9}{x - 3} \text{ at } x = 2.$$

SOLUTION:

For a function to be continuous at a point, in this case, 2, it must satisfy three conditions: (1) $f(2)$ is defined, (2) $\lim\limits_{x \to 2} f(x)$ exists, (3) $\lim\limits_{x \to 2} f(x) = f(2)$.

For $x = 2$, $y = f(x) = f(2) = \dfrac{(2)^2 - 9}{2 - 3} = 5$.

Also, $\lim\limits_{x \to 2} \dfrac{x^2 - 9}{x - 3} = 5$.

Therefore, the function is continuous at $x = 2$.

Determine whether the function $y = \dfrac{1}{x - 2}$ is continuous at (a) $x = 0$, (b) $x = 1$, and (c) $x = 2$.

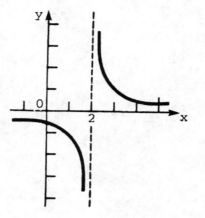

SOLUTION:

(a) $\lim\limits_{x\to 0} \dfrac{1}{x-2} = \lim\limits_{x\to 0} \dfrac{1}{0-2} = -\dfrac{1}{2}$

$f(0) = -\dfrac{1}{2}$

Therefore, $\lim\limits_{x\to 0} \dfrac{1}{x-2} = f(0) = -\dfrac{1}{2}$,

and the function is continuous at $x = 0$, because the limit exists at $x = 0$ and $= f(0)$.

(b) $\lim\limits_{x\to 1} \dfrac{1}{x-2} = -1$

$f(1) = -1$

The function is continuous at $x = 1$, because the limit exists at $x = 1$ and $= f(1)$.

(c) $\lim\limits_{x\to 2} \dfrac{1}{x-2} = \lim\limits_{x\to 2} \dfrac{1}{0} = \pm\infty$.

The limit does not exist at $x = 2$ because the function is not defined at this point, i.e., if we approach from the left the function approaches $-\infty$, from the right, it goes to $+\infty$.

● **PROBLEM 39-3**

If $h(x) = \sqrt{4 - x^2}$, prove that $h(x)$ is continuous in the closed interval $[-2, 2]$.

308

SOLUTION:

To prove continuity we employ the following definition: A function defined in the closed interval (a, b) is said to be continuous in (a, b) if and only if it is continuous in the open interval (a, b), as well as continuous from the right at a and continuous from the left at b. The function h is continuous in the open interval $(-2, 2)$. We must now show that the function is continuous from the right at -2 and from the left at 2. Therefore, we must show that $f(-2)$ is defined and $\lim\limits_{x \to -2^+} f(x)$ exists and that these are equal. Also, we must show that $f(2) = \lim\limits_{x \to 2^-} f(x)$. We have

$$\lim_{x \to -2^+} \sqrt{4 - x^2} = 0 = h(-2), \text{ and}$$

$$\lim_{x \to 2^-} \sqrt{4 - x^2} = 0 = h(2).$$

Thus, h is continuous in the closed interval $[-2, 2]$.

CHAPTER 40

DELTA (Δ) FUNCTION AND DERIVATIVE

● **PROBLEM 40-1**

Find the slope of each of the following curves at the given point, using the Δ-method.

   (a) $y = 3x^2 - 2x + 4$ at (1, 5)

   (b) $y = x^3 - 3x + 5$ at (−2, 3)

SOLUTION:

The slope of a given curve at a specified point is the derivative, in this case $\frac{\Delta y}{\Delta x}$, evaluated at that point.

(a) From the Δ-method we know that:

$$\frac{\Delta y}{\Delta x} = \frac{f(x + \Delta x) - f(x)}{\Delta x}.$$

For the curve $y = 3x^2 - 2x + 4$, we find:

$$\frac{\Delta y}{\Delta x} = \frac{3(x + \Delta x)^2 - 2(x + \Delta x) + 4 - (3x^2 - 2x + 4)}{\Delta x}$$

$$= \frac{3x^2 + 6x\Delta x + 3(\Delta x)^2 - 2x - 2\Delta x + 4 - 3x^2 + 2x - 4}{\Delta x}$$

$$= \frac{6x\Delta x + 3(\Delta x)^2 - 2\Delta x}{\Delta x}$$

$$= 6x + 3\Delta x - 2$$

$$\lim_{\Delta x \to 0} \frac{\Delta y}{\Delta x} = \lim_{\Delta x \to 0} 6x + 3\Delta x - 2 = 6x - 2$$

At $(1, 5)$ $\frac{\Delta y}{\Delta x} = 4$ is the required slope.

(b) Again using the Δ-method, $\frac{\Delta y}{\Delta x}$ for the curve: $y = x^3 - 3x + 5$, can be found as follows:

$$\frac{\Delta y}{\Delta x} = \frac{f(x + \Delta x) - f(x)}{\Delta x}.$$

$$\frac{\Delta y}{\Delta x} = \frac{(x + \Delta x)^3 - 3(x + \Delta x) + 5 - \left(x^3 - 3x + 5\right)}{\Delta x}$$

$$= \frac{x^3 + 3x^2\Delta x + 3x(\Delta x)^2 + (\Delta x)^3 - 3x - 3\Delta x + 5 - x^3 + 3x - 5}{\Delta x}$$

$$= \frac{3x^2\Delta x + 3x(\Delta x)^2 + (\Delta x)^3 - 3\Delta x}{\Delta x}$$

$$= 3x^2 + 3x\Delta x + (\Delta x)^2 - 3$$

$$\lim_{\Delta x \to 0} \frac{\Delta y}{\Delta x} = \lim_{\Delta x \to 0} 3x^2 + 3x\Delta x + (\Delta x)^2 - 3 = 3x^2 - 3$$

At $(-2, 3)$ $\frac{\Delta y}{\Delta x} = 9$ is the required slope.

● **PROBLEM 40-2**

Find the derivative of the function: $y = 2x^2 + 3x$, by the delta process.

SOLUTION:

By definition,

$$y'(x) = \lim_{\Delta x \to 0} \frac{f(x + \Delta x) - f(x)}{\Delta x}.$$

Since
$$f(x) = 2x^2 + 3x,$$
$$f(x + \Delta x) = 2(x + \Delta x)^2 + 3(x + \Delta x).$$

Substituting, we obtain

$$y'(x) = f'(x) = \lim_{\Delta x \to 0} \frac{2(x + \Delta x)^2 + 3(x + \Delta x) - (2x^2 + 3x)}{\Delta x}.$$

Simplifying, we have

$$f'(x) = \lim_{\Delta x \to 0} \frac{4x\Delta x + 2(\Delta x)^2 + 3\Delta x}{\Delta x}$$

$$= \lim_{\Delta x \to 0} 4x\Delta x + 2\Delta x + 3.$$

Now, as $\Delta x \to 0$ the term: $2\Delta x$, drops out and we have
   $f'(x) = 4x + 3$.

● PROBLEM 40-3

Find the derivative $f(x) = \dfrac{2}{(3x + 1)}$, using the Δ-method.

SOLUTION:

By definition,

$$\frac{dy}{dx} = f'(x) = \lim_{\Delta x \to 0} \frac{f(x + \Delta x) - f(x)}{\Delta x}.$$

Since

$$f(x) = \frac{2}{(3x + 1)},$$

$$f(x + \Delta x) = \frac{2}{3(x + \Delta x) + 1}.$$

Substituting, we obtain

$$f'(x) = \lim_{\Delta x \to 0} \frac{\dfrac{2}{[3(x + \Delta x) + 1]} - \dfrac{2}{(3x + 1)}}{\Delta x}$$

At this point we cannot substitute 0 for Δx because we would obtain a 0 in the denominator. Multiplying out and obtaining a common denominator we have

$$\lim_{\Delta x \to 0} \frac{6x + 2 - 6x - 6\Delta x - 2}{(3x + 3\Delta x + 1)(3x + 1)\Delta x}$$

$$= \frac{-6\Delta x}{(3x + 3\Delta x + 1)(3x + 1)(\Delta x)}$$

$$= \lim_{\Delta x \to 0} \frac{-6}{(3x + 3\Delta x + 1)(3x + 1)}$$

We can now substitute 0 for Δx, and we obtain

$$-\frac{6}{(3x + 1)^2} = f'(x).$$

● **PROBLEM 40-4**

Given $f(x) = x^{\frac{2}{3}}$, find $f'(x)$ using the Δ-method.

SOLUTION:

By definition,

$$\frac{dy}{dx} = f'(x) = \lim_{\Delta x \to 0} \frac{f(x + \Delta x) - f(x)}{\Delta x}$$

$$f(x) = x^{\frac{2}{3}}.$$

Therefore, $f(x + \Delta x) = (x + \Delta x)^{\frac{2}{3}}.$

Substituting, we have

$$\lim_{\Delta x \to 0} \frac{(x + \Delta x)^{\frac{2}{3}} - x^{\frac{2}{3}}}{\Delta x}.$$

We wish to rewrite this in a form in which Δx can approach the limit, 0. Direct substitution at this point would leave a 0 in the denominator. Since multiplication by 1 does not change the value, we multiply

$$\frac{(x + \Delta x)^{\frac{2}{3}} - x^{\frac{2}{3}}}{\Delta x}$$

by

$$\frac{(x + \Delta x)^{\frac{4}{3}} + (x + \Delta x)^{\frac{2}{3}} x^{\frac{2}{3}} + x^{\frac{4}{3}}}{(x + \Delta x)^{\frac{4}{3}} + (x + \Delta x)^{\frac{2}{3}} x^{\frac{2}{3}} + x^{\frac{4}{3}}},$$

which is equal to 1. Doing this we have,

$$f'(x) = \lim_{\Delta x \to 0} \frac{\left[(x+\Delta x)^{\frac{2}{3}} - x^{\frac{2}{3}}\right]\left[(x+\Delta x)^{\frac{4}{3}} + (x+\Delta x)^{\frac{2}{3}}x^{\frac{2}{3}} + x^{\frac{4}{3}}\right]}{\Delta x \left[(x+\Delta x)^{\frac{4}{3}} + (x+\Delta x)^{\frac{2}{3}}x^{\frac{2}{3}} + x^{\frac{4}{3}}\right]}$$

$$= \lim_{\Delta x \to 0} \frac{(x+\Delta x)^2 - x^2}{\Delta x \left[(x+\Delta x)^{\frac{4}{3}} + (x+\Delta x)^{\frac{2}{3}}x^{\frac{2}{3}} + x^{\frac{4}{3}}\right]}$$

from which $\qquad y' = -\dfrac{4x}{9y}.$

Evaluating this derivative at the point (1, 2), we have

$$y' = -\frac{4}{18} = -\frac{2}{9}.$$

Thus the slope of the desired tangent line is $-\dfrac{2}{9}$.

The equation of a straight line at a given point can be expressed in the form $y - y_1 = m(x - x_1)$. Here $x_1 = 1$ and $y_1 = 2$ and the slope $m = -\dfrac{2}{9}$. Substituting, we obtain

$$y - 2 = -\frac{2}{9}(x-1)$$

$$9y - 18 = -2x + 2$$

$2x + 9y - 20 = 0$, which is the equation of the tangent line. The slope could also have been found by solving the equation of the curve for y, and then differentiating.

● PROBLEM 40-5

Find the equations of the tangent line and the normal to the curve: $y = x^2 - x + 3$, at the point (2, 5).

SOLUTION:

Since the equation of a straight line passing through a given point can be expressed in the form: $y - y_1 = m(x - x_1)$, this is appropriate for finding the equations of the tangent and normal. Here $x_1 = 2$ and $y_1 = 5$. The slope, m, of the tangent line is found by taking the derivative, $\frac{dy}{dx}$, of the curve: $y = x^2 - x + 3$.

$$\frac{dy}{dx} = 2x - 1.$$

At $(2, 5)$, $\frac{dy}{dx} = 2(2) - 1 = 3$; therefore, the slope, m, of the tangent line is 3. Substituting x_1, y_1 and m into the equation $y - y_1 = m(x - x_1)$ we obtain
$$y - 5 = 3(x - 2),$$
as the equation of the tangent line, or
$$3x - y - 1 - 0.$$

Since the slope of the normal is given by: $m' = -\frac{1}{m}$, and since $m = 3$, the slope of the normal is $-\frac{1}{3}$. Substituting $x_1 = 2$, $y_1 = 5$ and the slope of the normal, $m' = -\frac{1}{3}$, into the equation $y - y_1 = m'(x - x_1)$, we obtain

$$y - 5 = -\frac{1}{3}(x - 2), \text{ or}$$
$$x + 3y - 17 = 0.$$
This is the equation of the normal.

● **PROBLEM 40-6**

Find the sixth derivative of $y = x^6$.

SOLUTION:

First derivative $\quad = 6x^{6-1} = 6x^5$
Second derivative $\ = 5 \times 6x^{5-1} = 30x^4$
Third derivative $\quad = 4 \times 30x^{4-1} = 120x^3$
Fourth derivative $\ = 3 \times 120x^{3-1} = 360x^2$
Fifth derivative $\quad = 2 \times 360x^{2-1} = 720x^1 = 720x$

Sixth derivative $= 1 \times 720x^{1-1} = 720x^0 = 720$

The seventh derivative is seen to be zero, and therefore the function $y = x^6$ has seven derivatives.

Find the derivative of $f(x) = (x^2 + 1)(1 - 3x)$.

SOLUTION:

Using the theorem for differentiating a product of terms, i.e., $d(uv) = udv + vdu$

$f'(x) = (x^2 + 1)(-3) + (1 - 3x)2x = -9x^2 + 2x - 3.$

Find the derivative of $f(x) = \dfrac{x^2 + 1}{1 - 3x}$.

SOLUTION:

Using the theorem for differentiating a quotient of terms, i.e.:

$$\frac{d}{dx}\left(\frac{u}{v}\right) = \frac{v\dfrac{du}{dx} - u\dfrac{dv}{dx}}{v^2},$$

$$f'(x) = \frac{(1-3x)(2x) - (x^2+1)(-3)}{(1-3x)^2}$$

$$= \frac{-3x^2 + 2x + 3}{(1-3x)^2}$$

CHAPTER 41

APPLICATIONS OF THE DERIVATIVE

Where are the maxima and minima of $y = 3x^3 + 4x + 7$?

SOLUTION:

$$y = 3x^3 + 4x + 7, \text{ then } \frac{dy}{dx} = 9x^2 + 4 = 0, \ x^2 = -\frac{4}{9},$$

$$x = \pm\sqrt{-\frac{4}{9}} = \pm\frac{2i}{3}.$$

This is an imaginary quantity. Since these are not real roots, in this example y has neither a maximum nor a minimum.

Determine the critical points of $f(x) = 3x^4 - 4x^3$ and sketch the graph.

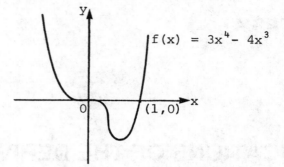

$f(x) = 3x^4 - 4x^3$

(1,0)

SOLUTION:

To determine the critical points we find $f'(x)$, set it equal to 0, and solve for x. These are the abscissas of the critical points. Differentiating, we have $f'(x) = 12x^3 - 12x^2 = 12x^2(x - 1)$. Therefore, $x = 0, 1$ are the critical values. We now examine $f'(x)$ when $x < 0$, when $1 > x > 0$, and when $x > 1$ to determine whether there is a maximum, minimum or neither at each critical point. We find that, when $x < 0$, $f'(x)$ is negative. When $1 > x > 0$, $f'(x)$ is also negative, and when $x > 1$, $f'(x)$ is positive. Because $f'(x)$ changes sign from – to + at $x = 1$, this is a minimum. At $x = 0$ there is no change in sign, $f'(x)$ is negative when $x < 0$ and when $0 < x < 1$, therefore this is neither a maximum nor a minimum. Because $f'(0) = 0$, f has a horizontal tangent at $x = 0$, as shown in the figure. Such a point is known as a point of inflection.

Additional insight can be obtained by taking the second derivative:

$$f''(x) = \frac{d}{dx}\left[f'(x)\right] = \frac{d}{dx}\left(12x^2 - 12x^2\right)$$

$$= 36x^2 - 24x$$

$$= + \text{ at } x = 1, \text{ a minimum}$$

but $\qquad\qquad = 0 \text{ at } x = 0.$

A maximum, on the other hand, would yield a negative second derivative.

● **PROBLEM 41-3**

What rectangle of maximum area can be inscribed in a circle of radius r?

SOLUTION:

Let $x =$ one side of the rectangle. The other side is obtained by the square root of the diagonal squared minus the square of the one side.

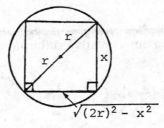

$$\sqrt{(2r)^2 - x^2}$$

The diagonal is equal to $2r$. The other side =

$$\sqrt{(2r)^2 - x^2} = \sqrt{4r^2 - x^2} \text{ . (See diagram.)}$$

$$A = x\sqrt{4r^2 - x^2} = \text{area of rectangle.}$$

To obtain a maximum value we find $A' = \dfrac{dA}{dx}$ and set it equal to 0. Solving for x we obtain a critical value. We have

$$\frac{dA}{dx} = x \bullet \frac{d}{dx}\left(\sqrt{4r^2 - x^2}\right) + \sqrt{4r^2 - x^2} \bullet 1 = 0$$

for a maximum or minimum.

$$x \bullet \frac{1}{2}\left(4r^2 - x^2\right)^{-\frac{1}{2}} \bullet (-2x) + \sqrt{4r^2 - x^2} = 0$$

or

$$-\frac{x^2}{\left(4r^2 - x^2\right)^{\frac{1}{2}}} + \left(4r^2 - x^2\right)^{\frac{1}{2}} = 0$$

which reduces to

$$\frac{-x^2 + 4r^2 - x^2}{\left(4r^2 - x^2\right)^{\frac{1}{2}}} = 0$$

$$\frac{4r^2 - 2x^2}{\left(4r^2 - x^2\right)^{\frac{1}{2}}} = 0$$

Now, the denominator $\sqrt{4r^2 - x^2}$ cannot be 0 because this is the value of a side of the rectangle. Therefore the numerator,

$$4r^2 - 2x^2 = 0 \text{ and}$$

$$x^2 = 2r^2 \text{ or}$$

$$x = r\sqrt{2} = \text{one side and}$$

$$\left(4r^2 - x^2\right)^{\frac{1}{2}} = \left(4r^2 - r^2 \bullet 2\right)^{\frac{1}{2}} = \left(2r^2\right)^{\frac{1}{2}} = r\sqrt{2}$$

= other side. The figure is a square.

Determine the relative maxima, relative minima, and points of inflection of the function

$$f(x) = \frac{1}{4}x^4 - \frac{3}{2}x^2.$$

Sketch the graph.

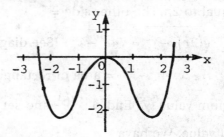

SOLUTION:

The derivatives are

$$f'(x) = x^3 - 3x \text{ and } f''(x) = 3x^2 - 3.$$

The critical points are solutions of $x^3 - 3x = 0$. We obtain $x = 0$, $\sqrt{3}$, $-\sqrt{3}$. The Second Derivative Test tells us that

$x = 0$ is a relative maximum;

$x = \sqrt{3}$, $-\sqrt{3}$ are relative minima.

The possible points of inflection are solutions of $3x^2 - 3 = 0$; that is $x = +1$, -1. Since $f''(x)$ is negative for $-1 < x < 1$ and positive for $|x| > 1$, both $x = 1$ and $x = -1$ are points of inflection. We construct the table

x	-2	$-\sqrt{3}$	-1	0	1	$\sqrt{3}$	2
f	-2	$-\frac{9}{4}$	$-\frac{5}{4}$	0	$-\frac{5}{4}$	$-\frac{9}{4}$	-2
f'	$-$	0	$+$	0	$-$	0	$+$
f''	$+$	$+$	0	$-$	0	$+$	$+$

The graph is symmetrical with respect to the y-axis.

CHAPTER 42

THE INTEGRAL

Integrate $\int \frac{2x}{x+1}dx$.

SOLUTION:

To integrate the given expression we manipulate the integrand to obtain the form $\int \frac{du}{u}$. This can be done as follows:

$$\int \frac{2x}{x+1}dx = 2\int \frac{x}{x+1}dx$$

$$= 2\int \left(\frac{x+1}{x+1} - \frac{1}{x+1} \right)dx$$

$$= 2\int \left(1 - \frac{1}{x+1} \right)dx$$

$$= 2\int dx - 2\int \frac{dx}{x+1}$$

Now, applying the formula $\int \frac{du}{u} = \ln u$, we obtain

$$\int \frac{2x}{x+1}dx = 2x - 2\ln(x+1) + C.$$

Integrate the expression $\int \sqrt{3x+4}\,dx$.

SOLUTION:

$\int \sqrt{3x+4}\,dx = \int (3x+4)^{\frac{1}{2}}\,dx$. In integrating this function, we use the formula $\int u^n\,du = \dfrac{u^{n+1}}{n+1} + C$, with $u = (3x+4)$, $du = 3dx$, and $n = \dfrac{1}{2}$. We obtain

$$\int (3x+4)^{\frac{1}{2}}\,dx = \frac{1}{3}\int (3x+4)^{\frac{1}{2}}\,3dx$$

$$= \frac{1}{3}\left[\frac{(3x+4)^{\frac{3}{2}}}{\frac{3}{2}}\right] + C$$

$$= \frac{2}{9}(3x+4)^{\frac{3}{2}} + C$$

Integrate the expression $\int x^2 e^{x^3}\,dx$.

SOLUTION:

To integrate this expression, we wish to consider the formula: $\int e^u\,du = e^u + C$. In this case we have $u = x^3$. Then $du = 3x^2\,dx$. Applying the formula, we obtain

$$\int x^2 e^{x^3}\,dx = \frac{1}{3}\int e^{x^3}(3x^2\,dx) = \frac{1}{3}e^{x^3} + C.$$

Find the finite area above the x-axis and under the curve
$$y = x^3 - 9x^2 + 23x - 15.$$

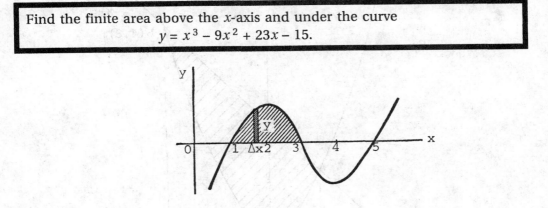

SOLUTION:

A sketch of the curve helps to determine the limits of the integral which give us the required area. From the diagram, the limits are the intersections of the curve and the x-axis, giving the limits: $x = 1$, $x = 3$, $x = 5$. But we are only concerned with the area above the x-axis and under the curve, therefore the limits we use are: $x = 1$ and $x = 3$. Now set up the integral. The area is equal to the integral of the upper function of x, $y = x^3 - 9x^2 + 23x - 15$, minus the lower function of x, $y = 0$ (the x-axis). Therefore, we write

$$A = \int_1^3 \left(x^3 - 9x^2 + 23x - 15\right) - (0)dx$$

$$= \int_1^3 \left(x^3 - 9x^2 + 23x - 15\right)dx$$

$$= \frac{x^4}{4} - 3x^3 + \frac{23x^2}{2} - 15x \Big]_1^3$$

$$= \left(\frac{81}{4} - 81 + \frac{207}{2} - 45\right) - \left(\frac{1}{4} - 3 + \frac{23}{2} - 15\right)$$

$$= 4$$

Find the area bounded by the parabola $2y = x^2$, and the line $y = x + 4$.

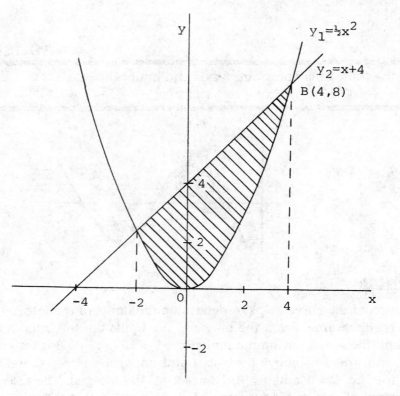

SOLUTION:

The limits of the integral which give the required area are the points of intersection of the two functions. To find the points of intersection, we set the two functions equal and solve for x.

$$\frac{x^2}{2} = x + 4 \qquad x^2 = 2x + 8 \qquad x^2 - 2x - 8 = 0$$

$$(x - 4)(x + 2) = 0$$
$$x = 4 \qquad x = -2$$

The line $y = x + 4$, is above the parabola $y = \dfrac{x^2}{2}$.

Therefore, the area can be found by taking the integral of the upper function minus the lower function, or the line minus the parabola, from $x = -2$ to $x = 4$. Solving, we obtain

$$A = \int_{-2}^{4} \left[(x + 4) - \frac{x^2}{2} \right] dx$$

$$= \left[\frac{x^2}{2} + 4x - \frac{x^3}{6} \right]_{-2}^{4}$$

$$= \frac{40}{3} + \frac{14}{3} = 18$$

INDEX

Numbers on this page refer to PROBLEM NUMBERS, not page numbers.

Absolute value, 1-6
  of equations, 4-2, 4-3
Alternating series, 14-5
  test, 14-7
Angles:
  coterminal with, 16-2, 16-3
  primary, 16-3
  relating radians to degrees, 16-1
Antilog:
  characteristic of, 15-5, 15-6
  mantissa of, 15-5, 15-6
  to evaluate a product, 15-8

Banach's fixed point theorem, 14-6

Circles:
  area of a sector of, 16-4
  equation from points, 26-3
  equation from radius and center of, 26-1
  equation from radius, center, and tangent lines, 26-4
  points of intersection of two, 26-5
  graphical solution for line tangent to, 36-2
  graphing of, 29-6, 36-1
  intercepts of, 29-6
  intersection with a hyperbola, 31-6
  length of an arc of, 16-5, 16-6
  radius and center from equation, 26-2
  symmetry in, 29-6
Common difference, 14-2, 14-3
Common ratio, 14-5
Comparison test, 14-12

Completing the square, 11-6
Continuity:
  at a point, 39-1, 39-2
  over an interval, 39-3
Derivative:
  by delta method, 40-1, 40-2, 40-3, 40-4
  of a product, 40-7
  of a quotient, 40-8
  n-1 method, 40-6
  to find normal lines to a curve, 40-5
  to find tangent lines to a curve, 40-5
Distance formula:
  applications, 24-7
  between two points, 24-6, 24-8
  definition, 24-5
  for a hyperbola, 36-9
Dividing equations, 4-9
Division of a segment, 24-4

Ellipse:
  area of, 26-12
  equation of, 26-10, 26-11
  graphing of, 36-5, 36-6
  latus rectum of, 36-6
Equations in fractional form:
  involving quadratics, 11-3
  multiplication of, 5-9
  simplifying of, 4-4, 4-5, 4-6, 5-8
  solutions to, 9-6, 9-7
  with unlike denominators, 5-7
Equation of a line:
  equidistant from two other lines, 25-8
  general form, 25-4
  intercept form, 25-4

passing through two points, 25-6
point-slope form, 25-4
slope-intercept form, 25-4
two-point form, 25-4
Equations of fourth degree:
  roots of, 12-6
  roots solved for graphically, 32-2
  solution by quadratic formula, 12-5
Equations of third degree:
  coefficients of, 12-1
  graphing of, 32-1
  roots of, 12-3
  solutions of, 12-2
Exponent:
  fractional, 6-9
  operations with, 6-4, 6-5
  properties of, 6-3, 6-6
  properties of negative, 6-1, 6-7
  zero as, 6-2
Exponential form, 6-8
Exponential functions:
  base of, 15-10
  evaluated using logarithms, 15-7
  graphing of, 34-2, 34-3, 34-4
  solved using logarithms, 15-11
Factoring:
  polynomials, 5-2
  highest common factor, 5-1
  formula for a^2-b^2, 5-3
  formula for a^3+b^3, 5-4
  formula for a^4-b^4, 5-5
Family of lines, 25-9
Field properties:
  additive, 1-3
  distributive, 1-3
Fractions:
  least common denominator, 3-6
  simplifying, 3-5, 3-6, 3-7
Functions:
  complement of, 29-4
  composition of, 8-12
  critical points of, 41-2
  degree of, 8-6, 8-7
  domain of, 8-1, 8-4

extent of, 29-6
graphing the absolute value of, 29-2
graphing the complement of, 29-4
graphing the domain of, 29-1
graphing the inverse of, 29-4
graphing the range of, 29-1
inverse of, 8-11, 15-14, 29-5
maxima of, 41-1
minima of, 41-1
range of, 8-1, 8-2, 8-3, 8-4, 8-5
relative maxima, 41-4
relative minima, 41-4
symmetry in, 29-6
value at a point, 8-2
zeroes of, 8-8, 8-9

Geometric series, 14-14

Hyperbola:
  center of, 26-13
  eccentricity of, 26-13
  equation from foci and a point,
    26-16
  equation from vertices and
    eccentricity of, 26-14
  equation of conjugate of, 26-15
  foci of, 26-13
  graphing of, 36-7, 36-8, 36-9
  intersection with a circle, 31-6
  vertices of, 26-13
Hyperbolic functions, 23-1
  equations involving, 23-2
  graphing of, 35-7
Inequalities:
  as an identity, 13-3
  compound statement of, 13-2
  conditional, 13-3
  graphical solution of a system of,
    33-3
  inconsistent, 13-3
  intersection of, 13-6
  involving absolute values, 13-8

involving equations in fractional form, 13-11

involving equations of third degree, 13-12

involving quadratic equations, 13-10, 13-11

properties of reciprocal, 13-7

solved graphically, 33-1, 33-2

solution set of, 13-4

union of, 13-5

Integration:

    area between two curves, 42-5

    area under a curve, 42-4

    by rearranging integrand, 42-1

    $n+1$ method, 42-2

    of an exponential function, 42-3

Intercepts:

    x, 25-3

    y, 25-3

Intervals, 13-1

    largest value over an, 13-9

Inverse hyperbolic functions, 23-1

    definition, 23-3

Inverse trigonometric functions:

    arc cosine, 21-2, 21-3

    arc tangent, 21-1, 21-3

    equations involving, 21-6

    graphing of, 35-6

Law of proportions, 7-3

Least common multiple, 5-6

L'Hopital's rule, 14-15, 38-3

Limits, 38-1, 38-2, 38-3

Linear functions:

    definition of, 9-1

    graphing of, 29-2, 30-1

    inverse of, 8-10

    involving radicals, 9-8, 9-9

    rearrangement of, 9-5

    solution of, 9-2, 9-3, 9-4

    zeroes of, 30-1

Logarithms:

    as an exponent, 15-1

    change of bases of, 15-2

colog, 15-9

equations involving, 15-12

found by interpolation, 15-7

graphing of, 34-1

of an exponent, 15-3

of a product, 15-3

of a quotient, 15-3

of a radical, 15-3

solved by use of known values, 15-4

to evaluate a product, 15-8

Maximizing area, 41-3

Mean value theorem, 14-16

Midpoint, 24-3

Multiplying equations, 4-8

    FOIL method, 4-7

Natural logarithms:

    functions of, 15-14

    graphing of, 34-2

    properties of, 15-13

Non-linear function, 9-1

Numbers:

    complex, 1-4

    even, 1-4

    integers, 1-4, 1-5

    irrational, 1-4

    natural, 1-4

    odd, 1-4

    prime, 1-4

    rational, 1-4, 1-5

    real, 1-4, 1-5

    zero, 1-4

Number line postulate, 1-2

Number line spacing, 1-1

Order of operations, 3-1, 3-2, 3-3, 3-4, 4-1

p-series, 14-14
Parabola:
  axis of, 36-4
  directrix of, 26-8, 36-4
  equation of, 26-6
  equation of tangent line to, 26-7,
    26-9
  focus of, 26-8
  graphing of, 36-3, 36-4
  latus rectum of, 36-4
  vertex of, 36-4
Parallel lines, 25-5, 25-7
Parametric equations, 28-5
  graphing of, 37-4
Perpendicular lines, 25-7
Point of division formula, 24-2
Point of inflection, 41-4
Polar coordinates:
  graphing equations in, 37-3
  symmetry graphs of equations in,
    37-2
  transformation to, 28-1
  transformation to Cartesian
    coordinates, 28-3, 28-4
  transformation to rectangular
    coordinates, 28-2
Power series:
  absolute convergence of, 14-18
  conditional convergence of, 14-18
  interval of convergence, 14-18
  radius of convergence, 14-18
  ratio test, 14-18
  root test, 14-18
Progressions:
  arithmetic, 14-1, 14-2
  geometric, 14-5, 14-7
  harmonic, 14-9, 14-10
  sum of arithmetic, 14-4
  sum of geometric, 14-7
Projection, 24-1
Proportionals, 7-3

Quadratic equations:
  graphing of, 31-1, 31-2
  in factored form, 11-1
  involving fractional exponents, 11-5
  involving radicals, 11-4
  minimum value of, 31-3
  roots of, 11-8
  with equal roots, 11-9
Quadratic formula, 11-7
  the discriminant, 11-10

Ratio:
  of numbers, 7-1
  of variables, 7-2
Repeating decimal, 1-7, 1-8
  rationalized by geometric
    progression, 14-8

Scientific notation, 1-9
Sequence:
  based on a general term, 14-6
  limit of, 14-16
  sum of arithmetic, 14-4
Series:
  absolute convergence of, 14-17
  conditional convergence of, 14-17
  convergence of, 14-12, 14-13
  numerical value of, 14-11
  ratio test, 14-13, 14-17
  sum of arithmetic, 14-13
Sets:
  cell, 2-2
  complement of, 2-3, 2-4
  conjunction, 13-6
  disjoint and exhaustive, 2-2
  disjunction, 13-5
  empty, 2-2
  subset, 2-1
  universal, 2-3
Set operations:
  intersection, 2-6
  laws of, 2-5

subtraction, 2-7
union, 2-6
Slope:
    at a point, 40-1
    of a line, 24-9, 25-1, 25-2, 25-3
Solving triangles, 20-1, 20-2, 20-3
Step function, 29-3
Systems involving quadratic
    equations, 11-11, 11-12, 11-13
    solved graphically, 31-4, 31-5
Systems involving equations of fourth
    degree, 12-7
Systems of equations of third degree,
    12-4
Systems of linear equations:
    applications, 10-6, 10-7, 10-8, 10-9
    solved graphically, 30-3, 30-4, 30-5,
      30-6,
    with three unknowns, 10-4, 10-5
    with two unknowns, 10-1, 10-2,
      10-3

Transformation of coordinates:
    for rotation of axes, 27-3, 27-4
    to a new origin, 27-2
    to complete the square, 27-1
Triangles:
    area of, 24-9
    interior angles of, 24-9
    isosceles, 24-7
    oblique, 20-1
    right, 16-7

Trigonometric equations, 22-1, 22-2,
    22-3, 22-4, 22-5, 22-6
Trigonometric formulas:
    for cosine, 19-1
    for cotangent, 19-1
    for difference of sines, 19-3
    for products of sines and cosines,
      19-2
    for sine, 19-1
    for $\sin^2(x)$, 19-3
    for sum of cosines, 19-4
    for sum of sines, 19-4, 19-7
    for tangent, 19-1
    for $\tan(u + v)$, 19-8
    for $\tan^2(x)$, 19-3
    law of cosines, 20-2
    applications, 17-5
    as defined on a triangle, 17-6
    found by interpolation, 18-1, 18-2,
      18-3, 18-4
    graphing of, 35-1, 35-2, 35-3, 35-4
    graphing the sum of, 35-5
    interrelationship between, 17-4
    of inverse trigonometric functions,
      21-4, 21-5
    sign of, 17-1
    value at a point, 17-2, 17-3
Trigonometric identities, 19-5, 19-6,
    19-9, 19-10, 19-11
    for triangles, 20-4

"Varies inversely," 7-4, 7-5

The ESSENTIALS®
of MATH & SCIENCE

Each book in the ESSENTIALS series offers all essential information of the field it covers. It summarizes what every textbook in the particular field must include, and is designed to help students in preparing for exams and doing homework. The ESSENTIALS are excellent supplements to any class text.

The ESSENTIALS are complete and concise with quick access to needed information. They serve as a handy reference source at all times. The ESSENTIALS are prepared with REA's customary concern for high professional quality and student needs.

Available in the following titles:

Advanced Calculus
Algebra & Trigonometry I & II
Anatomy & Physiology
Astronomy
Automatic Control Systems /
    Robotics
Biochemistry
Biology I & II
Biology of the Universe
Boolean Algebra
Calculus I, II & III
Chemistry
Complex Variables I & II
Computer Science I & II
Data Structures I & II
Differential Equations

Electric Circuits
Electromagnetics I & II
Electronic Communications II
Electronics I & II
Fluid Mechanics / Dynamics I
Genetics: Unlocking the
    Mysteries of Life
Geometry I & II
Group Theory I & II
Heat Transfer II
LaPlace Transforms
Linear Algebra
Math for Computer Applications
Math for Engineers II
Mechanics I, II & III
Microbiology

Modern Algebra
Numerical Analysis I & II
Organic Chemistry I & II
Physical Chemistry II
Physics I & II
Pre-Calculus
Probability
Real Variables
Set Theory
Statistics I & II
Strength of Materials &
    Mechanics of Solids II
Thermodynamics II
Topology
Transport Phenomena I & II

If you would like more information about any of these books,
complete the coupon below and return it to us or visit your local bookstore.

MAXnotes®

REA's Literature Study Guides

MAXnotes® are student-friendly. They offer a fresh look at masterpieces of literature, presented in a lively and interesting fashion. **MAXnotes**® offer the essentials of what you should know about the work, including outlines, explanations and discussions of the plot, character lists, analyses, and historical context. **MAXnotes**® are designed to help you think independently about literary works by raising various issues and thought-provoking ideas and questions. Written by literary experts who currently teach the subject, **MAXnotes**® enhance your understanding and enjoyment of the work.

Available **MAXnotes**® include the following:

Absalom, Absalom!	Hard Times	On the Road
The Aeneid of Virgil	Heart of Darkness	Othello
Animal Farm	Henry IV, Part I	Paradise
Antony and Cleopatra	Henry V	Paradise Lost
As I Lay Dying	The House on Mango Street	A Passage to India
As You Like It	I Know Why the Caged	Plato's Republic
The Autobiography of	Bird Sings	Portrait of a Lady
Malcolm X	The Iliad	A Portrait of the Artist
The Awakening	Invisible Man	as a Young Man
Beloved	Jane Eyre	Pride and Prejudice
Beowulf	Jazz	A Raisin in the Sun
Billy Budd	The Joy Luck Club	Richard II
The Bluest Eye, A Novel	Jude the Obscure	Romeo and Juliet
Brave New World	Julius Caesar	The Scarlet Letter
The Canterbury Tales	King Lear	Sir Gawain and the
The Catcher in the Rye	Leaves of Grass	Green Knight
The Color Purple	Les Misérables	Slaughterhouse-Five
The Crucible	Lord of the Flies	Song of Solomon
Death in Venice	Macbeth	The Sound and the Fury
Death of a Salesman	The Merchant of Venice	The Stranger
Dickens Dictionary	Metamorphoses of Ovid	Sula
The Divine Comedy I: Inferno	Metamorphosis	The Sun Also Rises
Dubliners	Middlemarch	A Tale of Two Cities
The Edible Woman	A Midsummer Night's Dream	The Taming of the Shrew
Emma	Moll Flanders	Tar Baby
Euripides' Medea & Electra	Mrs. Dalloway	The Tempest
Frankenstein	Much Ado About Nothing	Tess of the D'Urbervilles
Gone with the Wind	Mules and Men	Their Eyes Were Watching God
The Grapes of Wrath	My Antonia	Things Fall Apart
Great Expectations	Native Son	To Kill a Mockingbird
The Great Gatsby	1984	To the Lighthouse
Gulliver's Travels	The Odyssey	Twelfth Night
Handmaid's Tale	Oedipus Trilogy	Uncle Tom's Cabin
Hamlet	Of Mice and Men	Waiting for Godot
		Guide to Literary Terms

*If you would like more information about any of these books,
complete the coupon below and return it to us or visit your local bookstore.*

Research & Education Association
61 Ethel Road W., Piscataway, NJ 08854
Phone: (732) 819-8880   **website: www.rea.com**

Please send me more information about your MAXnotes® books.

Name _____

Address _____

City _____ State _____ Zip _____

REA's Test Preps
The Best in Test Preparation

- REA "Test Preps" are **far more** comprehensive than any other test preparation series
- Each book contains up to **eight** full-length practice tests based on the most recent exams
- **Every** type of question likely to be given on the exams is included
- Answers are accompanied by **full** and **detailed** explanations

REA publishes over 70 Test Preparation volumes in several series. They include:

Advanced Placement Exams (APs)
Art History
Biology
Calculus AB & BC
Chemistry
Economics
English Language & Composition
English Literature & Composition
European History
French Language
Government & Politics
Latin
Physics B & C
Psychology
Spanish Language
Statistics
United States History
World History

College-Level Examination Program (CLEP)
Analyzing and Interpreting Literature
College Algebra
Freshman College Composition
General Examinations
General Examinations Review
History of the United States I
History of the United States II
Introduction to Educational Psychology
Human Growth and Development
Introductory Psychology
Introductory Sociology
Precalculus
Principles of Management
Principles of Marketing
Spanish
Western Civilization I
Western Civilization II

SAT Subject Tests
Biology E/M
Chemistry
French
German
Literature
Mathematics Level 1, 2
Physics
Spanish
United States History

Graduate Record Exams (GREs)
Biology
Chemistry
Computer Science
General
Literature in English
Mathematics
Physics
Psychology

ACT - ACT Assessment
ASVAB - Armed Services Vocational Aptitude Battery
CBEST - California Basic Educational Skills Test
CDL - Commercial Driver License Exam
CLAST - College Level Academic Skills Test
COOP & HSPT - Catholic High School Admission Tests
ELM - California State University Entry Level Mathematics Exam
FE (EIT) - Fundamentals of Engineering Exams - For Both AM & PM Exams

FTCE - Florida Teacher Certification Examinations
GED - (U.S. Edition)
GMAT - Graduate Management Admission Test
LSAT - Law School Admission Test
MAT - Miller Analogies Test
MCAT - Medical College Admission Test
MTEL - Massachusetts Tests for Educator Licensure
NJ HSPA - New Jersey High School Proficiency Assessment
NYSTCE - New York State Teacher Certification Examinations
PRAXIS PLT - Principles of Learning & Teaching Tests
PRAXIS PPST - Pre-Professional Skills Tests
PSAT/NMSQT
SAT
TExES - Texas Examinations of Educator Standards
THEA - Texas Higher Education Assessment
TOEFL - Test of English as a Foreign Language
TOEIC - Test of English for International Communication
USMLE Steps 1,2,3 - U.S. Medical Licensing Exams

Research & Education Association
61 Ethel Road W., Piscataway, NJ 08854
Phone: (732) 819-8880   **website: www.rea.com**

Please send me more information about your Test Prep books.

Name _____

Address _____

City _____ State _____ Zip _____